Dirty Whites **and** Dark Secrets

*Revisiting New England: The New Regionalism*

SERIES EDITORS

Siobhan Senier
University of New Hampshire

Adam Sweeting
Boston University

Darren Ranco
Dartmouth College

David H. Watters
University of New Hampshire

This series presents fresh discussions of the distinctiveness of New England culture. The editors seek manuscripts examining the history of New England regionalism; the way its culture came to represent American national culture; the interaction between that "official" New England culture and the people who lived in the region; and local, subregional, or even biographical subjects as microcosms that explicitly open up and consider larger issues. The series welcomes new theoretical and historical perspectives and is designed to cross disciplinary boundaries and appeal to a wide audience.

For a complete list of books available in this series, please visit www.upne.com

Sally Hirsh-Dickinson, *Dirty Whites and Dark Secrets: Sex and Race in* Peyton Place

Benjamin L. Hartley, *Evangelicals at a Crossroads: Revivalism and Social Reform in Boston, 1860–1910*

Ronald J. Zboray and Mary Saracino Zboray, *Voices without Votes: Women and Politics in Antebellum New England*

James W. Baker, *Thanksgiving: The Biography of an American Holiday*

Monica Chiu, editor, *Asian Americans in New England: Culture and Community*

Aífe Murray, *Maid as Muse: How Servants Changed Emily Dickinson's Life and Language*

Scott Molloy, *Irish Titan, Irish Toilers: Joseph Banigan and Nineteenth-Century New England Labor*

Joseph A. Conforti, editor, *Creating Portland: History and Place in Northern New England*

Deborah Pickman Clifford and Nicholas R. Clifford, *"The Troubled Roar of the Waters": Vermont in Flood and Recovery, 1927–1931*

JerriAnne Boggis, Eve Allegra Raimon, and Barbara A. White, editors, *Harriet Wilson's New England: Race, Writing, and Region*

Kimberly A. Jarvis, *Franconia Notch and the Women Who Saved It*

Christopher Johnson, *This Grand and Magnificent Place: The Wilderness Heritage of the White Mountains*

William Brown and Joanne Pope Melish, editors, *The Life of William J. Brown of Providence, R.I.*

Denis R. Caron, *A Century in Captivity: The Life and Trials of Prince Mortimer, a Connecticut Slave*

David L. Richards, *Poland Spring: A Tale of the Gilded Age, 1860–1900*

Paul M. Searls, *Two Vermonts: Geography and Identity, 1865–1910*

Judith Bookbinder, *Boston Modern: Figurative Expressionism as Alternative Modernism*

Donna M. Cassidy, *Marsden Hartley: Race, Region, and Nation*

Sally Hirsh-Dickinson

# *Dirty Whites* and **dark secrets**

## Sex and Race in *Peyton Place*

University of New Hampshire Press
*Durham, New Hampshire*

University of New Hampshire Press
An imprint of University Press of New England
www.upne.com
© 2011 University of New Hampshire
All rights reserved
Manufactured in the United States of America
Designed by Katherine B. Kimball
Typeset in Sabon by Integrated Publishing Solutions

University Press of New England is a member of the Green Press Initiative. The paper used
in this book meets their minimum requirement for recycled paper.

For permission to reproduce any of the material in this book, contact Permissions,
University Press of New England, One Court Street, Suite 250, Lebanon NH 03766; or
visit www.upne.com

5 4 3 2 1

Library of Congress Cataloging-in-Publication Data
Hirsh-Dickinson, Sally.
Dirty whites and dark secrets : sex and race in Peyton Place / Sally Hirsh-Dickinson.
    p. cm. — (Revisiting New England: The new regionalism)
Includes bibliographical references and index.
ISBN 978-1-61168-041-6 (cloth : alk. paper) — ISBN 978-1-61168-042-3 (pbk. : alk.
paper) — ISBN 978-1-61168-215-1 (e-book)
1. Metalious, Grace. Peyton Place.   2. Sex in literature.   3. Race in literature.   4. New
England—In literature.   I. Title.
PS3525.E77P434 2011
813'.54—dc23     2011027300

*To my family*

# Contents

# Acknowledgments

From the beginning, this seemed to be the least likely of projects to ever see the light of day. It certainly would not have done so had it not been for the extraordinary and singular network that formed to support me and see me through. Sarah Sherman at the University of New Hampshire provided me with much professional and practical guidance during the many years it took to get this work off the ground. Brigitte Bailey, Monica Chiu, and Delia Konzett, also at the University of New Hampshire, and John Ernest at West Virginia University offered critical insights and lively discussion that helped to give my ideas shape and nuance. Siobhan Senier literally steered me to Richard Pult at a conference we were attending, and I thank her for her interest in my work and for acting as a motive force to get it in the pipeline. Richard Pult and Ann Brash at University Press of New England have fielded my queries and shepherded me through the publishing process with kindness and good humor. My work has benefited considerably from the care and expertise of Beth Gianfagna at Log House Editorial Services. Peter Mascuch introduced me to *Peyton Place* during my last semester of coursework and changed the direction of my life as a result. Jennifer Scanlon has been a gracious and enthusiastic supporter of this project and has worked to create opportunities to discuss new approaches to *Peyton Place*. Ardis Cameron and Emily Toth did the hard work of bringing Metalious into the academy, and for this I am in their debt. Without their efforts, this one surely would never have come to pass.

Rivier College's Department of English and Communications provided me with a Books and Materials Grant that saw me through to the finish. Sr. Therese Larochelle approved many a travel grant through which I was able to try out these ideas in public forums. More important than these, however, is the collegiality and kindness that I have received from my colleagues at the college: Tim Doherty, Marcoux Faiia, Paul Lizotte, Larry Maness, Virginia Ryan, Brad Stull, Sr. Lucille Thibodeau, and Liz Wright.

Liz was especially helpful in providing late-stage feedback that enabled me to see my ideas in a fresh light. Karin Lagro was always an interested listener, and Sharon Dean never failed to send kind words when news of the next step reached her. To Karen Pratt I owe deep thanks for administrative support and for the conversations that have brightened many a day in the trenches. Donna Page, Dan Speidel, and the staff at Regina Library have kept me steeped in scholarship. Holly Klump's warp-speed interlibrary loan volleys never ceased to amaze me.

While I was still in the midst of an early draft of this work, Colby-Sawyer College engaged me as a Visiting Instructor, and I have the following former colleagues, now friends, to thank for their support of my work: Pat Anderson, Donna Berghorn, David Elliot, Hester Fuller, Lynn Garrioch, Craig Greenman, Thomas Kealy, Melissa Meade, Ann Page Stecker, and Margaret Wiley. Landon Hall, Elizabeth Krajewski, and Carrie Thomas at the Susan Colgate Cleveland Library at Colby-Sawyer all acted as sounding boards for my ideas when I found myself in need of a stroll away from my workspace at the window.

My colleagues at New Hampshire Public Radio have been wonderfully supportive and have provided me with opportunities to literally broadcast my ideas to whomever wished to tune in. Karol Iwany has been a dream come true, caring for both my baby girl and then my baby boy while I labored over this baby. My appreciation goes also to Denise Daniel, Linda Douglas, Mary Kate Ryan, and Mary Stewart for allowing me to vet academic writing in a creative forum. Marcia and Phoebe Harrison; Sarah Duclos and Norman Sedgley; David and Paula Dickinson; and Jeff, Yangchen, Tenzin, Norbu, and Ngawang Dickinson often entertained my family while I was writing. Sarah gets special credit for commiserating with my husband about what it's like being married to an academic. Josephine Crisp shook a loving finger in my face and told me to finish already. Laura Smith was indispensable throughout this process, a simply wonderful reader and respondent who never failed to provide levity along with her valuable feedback. Dawn Dreyer and Marlana Patton, two wonderful women with whom I have shared decades of friendship, always reminded me of all that I do have, even when what I didn't have was a finished book.

My phenomenal mother-in-law, Donna Crisp Duclos, has always shown enormous generosity of time, spirit, space (for which we are eternally thankful), and faith that I would really get this volume written. My brother, Marc, kept me laughing, as well as current in my musical tastes, from beginning to end, as ever. My parents, Joanne and Richard Hirsh, never doubted that I would do this—the hard way. And so I did, with their love and support. My fabulous, fantastic daughter, Beatrice, has blossomed with this project and has tapped into grown-up reserves of patience during the writing of this book. For this, she deserves to have her efforts memorialized in print. She and her little brother, Oliver, have book-ended this project with their respective arrivals, and two more loveable book-ends there never were.

Finally, there is Spencer: my partner in marriage, parenthood, and playtime. It is entirely possible, as he well knows, that I would not have done this without him. I am immeasurably grateful to him for his heart, his humor, and his unyielding faith in my work and my ability to get it done at long last.

Dirty Whites **and** Dark Secrets

# Introduction

## More Than the Sum of Its Scandals: A "More Accurate Measure" of *Peyton Place*

In the years that I have been devoting my academic energies to exploring constructions of race in Grace Metalious's much-maligned 1956 best seller, *Peyton Place*, I have met with a fair measure of cynicism about my work. Upon first disclosing the subject of my scholarship to colleagues or introducing it into cocktail party conversation, the range of disbelieving responses runs from astonishment to amusement, often with a dash of puzzlement thrown in for good measure. "On what grounds is *Peyton Place* the stuff of academic inquiry?" "You're writing the *whole* book on *Peyton Place*?" "You know, some people in Gilmanton *still* don't like to talk about it." Although I have also encountered some people who are delighted by the idea that a novel of *Peyton Place*'s dubious character has infiltrated the ivory tower, for the most part, it remains a sensitive subject. On the ground in Gilmanton, New Hampshire, the town widely believed to have been the basis for Metalious's portrayal of the seamy side of small-town New England, there are still those who resist discussions of the novel and Metalious. Outside of Gilmanton, Metalious and *Peyton Place* remain bywords for scandal. The *Concord Monitor*, a New Hampshire daily, ran an editorial in the summer of 2007 comparing the content of a cluster of that season's local news stories—which included an Internet porn scandal involving a high school athletic director, witness-tampering charges against a local fire chief, and the embezzlement of hundreds of thousands of dollars from a school cafeteria—to the sort of tawdriness and bad behavior associated with Metalious's novel. In an attempt to counterbalance the season's more disturbing stories, the column presented vignettes affirming the selflessness and charitable endeavors of New Hampshire residents. "Metalious," concludes the *Monitor*, ". . . would have you believe that a community is the sum of its scandals. But in truth, the more accurate measure of a place is the often unsung good works of its dedicated volunteers" ("Amid Scandals," B4).

The *Concord Monitor*'s application of *Peyton Place* to a set of local scandals is typical. It reads the novel as an exposé and concludes that the accumulation and revelation of a community's secrets is the work's aim. While I understand how such readings arise, I believe that they misunderstand the nature of the critique the novel offers. I do not think that *Peyton Place* suggests that civic identity is born only out of those human frailties that become part of public discourse. I do think, however, that the novel takes its small town to task for the ways in which it deals with, or more frequently, does *not* deal with the abuses of power that often constitute scandalous behavior. The scandals listed by the *Monitor* are marked by abuses of power, privilege, position, and prominence. As an alternative to the newspaper's editorial opinion, I would suggest that "the more accurate measure of a place" is not necessarily the "good works" that balance out the bad. In addition to the more inspiring acts of human charity that seek to contribute to a community's betterment, a place may also be measured by how it deals with the dysfunction it knows is present. Does it acknowledge the dysfunction or enable it? How is justice enacted and who is protected? To take an example from the pages of the *Monitor*, which is the more damning and damaging to a community: a high school athletic director who is under investigation for possessing "innocent photos of a dozen or so female students and pornographic photos of women of similar appearance" ("Another Prominent Citizen," par. 2), or the school district officials who decide not to inform police of the matter because "they did not believe any laws had been broken" (Timmins, par. 9)?

Interestingly, the *Monitor* addressed this issue in a separate editorial just two days before it invoked the specter of Grace Metalious. Noting that the athletic director's "breach of trust can't be healed," the paper goes on to say that "the biggest damage from his actions was to the ability of all students and parents to trust teachers and administrators. That's what the district will have to struggle to repair" ("Another Prominent Citizen," par. 7). Had the editors at the *Monitor* referenced *Peyton Place* in the context of this insight, they would have hit upon a more accurate reading of the work the novel does, or, in their words, what "Metalious would have you believe." *Peyton Place*, contrary to the *Monitor*'s view, is not a catalogue of scandal for scandal's sake. Rather, the novel suggests that abuses of power, whether private or public, reveal the structure and machinery of power and privilege at work within a community, a society, and a nation.

*Peyton Place* will always remain, however begrudgingly to some, a "New Hampshire" novel and will, of course, retain its regional association with New England. Though it will continue to resonate on a local level because of its origins, the novel's national prominence, its extraordinary commercial success when it was first published in 1956, and its persistence in the American cultural vocabulary as a synonym for rampant impropriety indicate that the issues it speaks to are anything but localized. In its broadest sense, my work investigates the roots and nature of the scandal for which the novel is famous. Specifically, I argue that the outcry against the novel may have been sparked by its manner of conflating race and sexuality, and by the interrogation into dysfunctional whiteness brought about by such representations within the narrative. *Dirty Whites and Dark Secrets* seeks to foreground Metalious's critique of power and privilege by linking its consolidation, exercise, and excesses to the anxiety-ridden relationship between her New England town's white identity and its black history. The ideological whiteness that maintains Peyton Place's small-town New England identity at the same time produces the village's collective shame and silence about its black founding father. This racialized force not only produces such public prohibitions, but its deep structures give rise to the town's private perversions. It is this connection that my work seeks to investigate.

## More Than Just a Dirty Book

To return to those discussions I've had over the years about my work: once the initial amusement (whether cynical or subversive) has worn off about my professional dedication to *Peyton Place*, I am often asked, "Well, what about it?" When I state that I am looking at representations of race in the novel, there comes a long and perplexed pause that I often quickly fill in by explaining what many people forget or never knew in the first place: that the Peyton of the place is a black man. The novel was known in its time not for what it had to say about constructions of race, about racial injustice, about the history of racist practices in the United States. It was, of course, known for being a "dirty" book, a designation that obscured *Peyton Place*'s merits as a well-told story within a recognizable tradition. *Peyton Place* is, at first blush, a female *bildungsroman*, charting the lives of its three female protagonists over the course of nearly nine years (1936–44) in a small, New Hampshire mill town. Constance MacKenzie (née Standish) has built a life for herself after a youthful indiscretion safely beyond the town's borders with a New York family man, after whom her adolescent daughter Allison MacKenzie is named. His early death and a discreet attorney have allotted Constance enough money to establish a small boutique in town in order to support herself and her daughter. As a bulwark against "getting herself talked about," upon her return to Peyton Place, Constance passes herself off as a young widow, a viable fiction that, in effect, excuses her single motherhood. Despite her long-ago dalliance, Constance believes herself to be utterly disinterested in sex. This self-deception is exposed later in the novel; however, its mystique effectively revirginizes her and keeps her out of reach of any potential suitors.

While Constance is very practical and no-nonsense about her day-to-day life, Allison is a bookish daydreamer who is frustrated by her sense of difference from her mother and her peers. Constance is also recognized by the town as its most eligible and least accessible woman until a swarthy newcomer blows into town. Allison, however, is introduced as sensitive, brooding, and awkward, and remains so for the better part of the book. Selena Cross, an old-soul of a thirteen-year-old who lives on the tar-paper shack side of town, is the novel's third major point of interest. Where Allison ruminates on being different for her lack of nuclear family, Selena's differences are evident, her "honey-tan" skin remarkable for "never fad[ing] to sallowness in the long months of the harsh New England winter" (31). All three experience a coming of age within the action of the novel.

Allison's story is perhaps the most typical in its "adolescence to adulthood" trajectory. She begins as a moody, broody teenager who bickers with her mother, pines for her dead father, learns of her illegitimacy, escapes to New York City in search of authorial fame, and, like her mother before her, falls into the bed of a family man. When she returns home, wiser to the world, it is only with a broken heart and not a bastard love-child, and by novel's end, we are led to believe that she is ready to reconcile with her mother. Constance's transformation occurs through a belated and violent sexual reawakening with the new man in town. And whereas Allison and Constance seem to be drawn more for purposes of reader identification, it is Selena's story that provides the backbone of the novel.

Though a great deal transpires in *Peyton Place*, the events occur behind closed doors or are retold through the town's long memory of the past. The overt "action" of the novel revolves around Selena's killing of her incestuous stepfather, Lucas; the murder's discovery; and her trial. As the novel deals with Selena's situation and the scandal it causes for the community, the story is as much about the town as it is about Constance, Allison, and Selena. Metalious divulges the details in the lives of otherwise minor characters—the wife of the town drunk, the parents of Selena's high school sweetheart, the father-son dynasty that rules over the mill and its workers—and in so doing catalogues a long list of unpleasantness, bad behavior, and broken taboos. In the 372 pages of the novel there are instances or intimations of premarital sex, adultery, rape, incest, abortion, two oblique references to masturbation, female sexual desire and agency, suicide, homicide, religious hypocrisy, voyeurism, and a mother who regularly administers enemas to her teenage son. *Peyton Place* succeeded in making private spaces public, turning insides out, interrogating norms, and giving just about everyone in town something to hide.

One secret that Peyton Place seems collectively unanimous about repressing is the truth about the town's origins. The founding father of this homogeneously white town was a black man named Samuel Peyton, an escaped slave whose legacy looms over the town in the form of the castle he built when he came to settle in the woods of New Hampshire. The castle and the story behind it are mentioned, evaded, and elided five times before the tale is told in full by the town gossip to a newspaperman in town to cover Selena Cross's murder trial. Full disclosure is not offered until within fifty pages of the novel's end, at which time we learn, among other things, that Peyton made a small fortune overseas, married a white French woman, and returned to the States, where he intended to purchase property on Boston's Beacon Hill. Having been prevented from doing so on account of his race, Peyton was so disgusted by the hypocrisy of northern racism that he retreated into the wilds of New Hampshire and built himself a castle from which he vowed never to emerge. His rage at northern two-facedness is rumored to have led him to run arms to the South during the Civil War. It is in the wake of this history that the town comes into being.

Metalious's strategy of repeatedly mentioning and repressing the story until the end of the book suggests the considerable heft assigned to this particular secret. While on the face of it, the deferral of Peyton's tale seems to have been meant to add to the shock value of the novel—save for learning of Allison's adventures in New York, Peyton's is the last rattling of closeted skeletons in the book—closer examination suggests that it is part of a larger strategy at work throughout *Peyton Place*, one conscious and critical of the construction and maintenance of racial categories.

## Small-Town Dystopia

The term "Peyton Place" entered the popular lexicon shortly after the novel arrived on the nation's bookshelves and has remained a loaded reference ever since as shorthand for a den of iniquities masquerading as an upstanding community. The town Metalious sketches is, on its surface, a model northern New England town, complete with its requisite church spires and white clapboard buildings, school bells and scarlet-tipped trees. Located along the banks of the Connecticut River across from White River Junction, Vermont, Peyton Place is provincial enough that neither the Great Depression nor the Good War seems to have much impact on life in the town. The community is ethnically and racially homogeneous save for a scant few descendants of eastern and southern European immigrants. Its grade school classrooms democratize Peyton Place's social stratifications, at least from September to June. However, upon dismissing her eighth-grade class for the summer, Miss Elsie Thornton is weary at the thought that whatever parity she has been able to effect between the mill owner's son and the shack dweller's daughter is only temporary (8–9). Despite her wishes to the contrary and her best efforts, many of Peyton Place's children are predestined to remain limited by socioeconomic circumstance or unfairly blessed by birthright. Peyton Place wears its lines of demarcation frankly; it is a small burb like many others, with wealthy and underprivileged sides of town. On its swankiest avenue, Chestnut Street, live two mill owners, the town's most successful lawyer, a bank president, the chairman of the town's board of selectmen, the town doctor, and a newspaper editor—Peyton Place's heaviest hitters, its "backbone." "Between them," Metalious writes, "the men who lived on Chestnut Street provided jobs for Peyton Place. They took care of its aches and pains, straightened out its legal affairs, formed its thinking and spent its money. Between themselves, these men knew more about the town and its people than anyone else" (21). This concentration of power is inversely matched on the fringes of town by the disenfranchisement and dilapidation of Peyton Place's tar-paper shacks, inhabited by its mill hands and woodsmen. Though no point of pride for the middle and upper classes in town, the shacks are tolerated—and ignored whenever possible—as a necessary substrate to the overall economic well-being of the community. As long as the shack dweller paid his bills, he and his family would be left alone in charitable neglect:

> To be in debt was the one—and only—cardinal sin to men like Lucas Cross, and it was behind this fact that the small-town northern New Englander, of

more settled ways and habits, hid when confronted with the reality of the shack dwellers in his vicinity.

"They're all right," the New Englander was apt to say, especially to a tourist from the city. "They pay their bills and taxes and they mind their own business. They don't do any harm." (29)

The MacKenzies, Constance and Allison, live in a middle-class neighborhood characterized by single-family Cape Codders painted white with green trim. This surface sameness of the architecture, which prevents Allison from distinguishing her home from those surrounding it from her perch overlooking the town at Road's End, seems to mask what Allison feels are significant differences between herself and her peers, her family and others in town. In looking up the definition of the word *neighbor* in the dictionary, she finds that a neighbor is "one who dwelt in the same vicinity with one," and realizes by default that "a neighbor was not a friend" (12). This dystopic view of life in a small town, though mixed with a fair measure of appropriately adolescent angst, reveals the gradual dismantling of the idealized construction of New England and the small town in the American imaginary. Community, throughout much of *Peyton Place*, is less about tightly knit and warmly maintained affiliations and dearly held shared traditions than it is about happenstance of proximity.

## The Myth of New England

In her reputedly naughty portrayal of a New England town, Metalious violated one of America's sacrosanct institutions: the belief in New England as the bedrock of American morals and values. This faith in the region's inherent goodness did not arise organically out of its soil. New England's reputation as pristine moral compass for the nation was deliberately crafted and refined by entrepreneurs and artists alike. This did little to mitigate the shocked and disapproving responses of readers who felt that Metalious had gored a sacred cow. The vision of New England that Metalious so disturbed and unsettled with *Peyton Place*, though defended and held dear in the national psyche, had really only existed for just over a century. Despite pretensions to an inherent goodness and rightness of character and community in the region, the pure and wholesome New England of the American imagination was in effect a carefully cultivated ideal, inorganic and entrepreneurial. Prior to the development of tourism in the White Mountains in the 1830s, northern New England was still frontier country and was reputed to be "only half civilized, a place where

Southern New England's vaunted habits of literacy, piety, and order faded into frontier slovenliness and godlessness" (Brown, 42).

Once northern New England's frontier had been opened and safe and scenic passage through the Whites had been cleared, a burgeoning tourist industry developed, as artists and enterprising businessmen joined forces to create out of the rugged landscape of New Hampshire an experience imbued with the weight of history and the promise of American possibility. During the 1820s and 30s, America's literati and a few of its accomplished visual artists—among them Washington Irving, Catherine Sedgwick, Nathaniel Hawthorne, Ralph Waldo Emerson, Henry David Thoreau, and Thomas Cole—sought to create the American landscape. Sarah Josepha Hale issued the rallying cry to fellow writers, suggesting that the desolate wilderness might be helpfully transformed through the literary cultivation of "interesting associations" and appealing to and eliciting "the affections" (Brown, 46). It was a campaign to literally and figuratively draw meaning from the land—to manufacture or inspire affective responses to the scenery.

The idea worked. Before long, city folk would travel to rural New England to make contact with a kind of lost authenticity, obscured by the hectic pace and obligations of life in the metropolis. New England, to borrow Ardis Cameron's phrase, was perceived and experienced as a sort of "valuable corrective" to the intensity and ruthlessness of life in urban centers. Its pace was slower and deliberate, and its concerns were spiritually closer to the things that really mattered—putting food on the table, maintaining a roof over one's head, making the most of the land. It was also an escape for white city-dwellers from the teeming and dark-hued masses who were arriving in their midst from southern and eastern Europe. Peyton Place itself is neither remote nor rural. It boasts both industry and capitalism; in its mills and storefronts, both are alive and well. In effect, though, Metalious's version of northern New England revisits, and to some degree reinstates, its preindustrial reputation for "slovenliness and godlessness," exposing as artifice any pretense to purity and wholesomeness. The idea of purity is thoroughly disrupted through the tale of the town's ancestry—all of the current residents of Peyton Place are white; its founder, however, is black.

## The Revolt from the Village

Distrust of, and disillusionment with, the small town as America's moral compass are not unique to *Peyton Place*; Metalious was, in the 1950s, only the latest American author to dismantle the myth of good neighborliness and the moral superiority of the small town. In this respect, the novel has been linked to the "revolt from the village" tradition of early-twentieth-century midwestern writers. In her introduction to *Peyton Place*, Ardis Cameron suggests that Metalious's novel was more than just another such tale, a subcategory of American storytelling under the umbrella of which many early reviewers of the book categorized Metalious's work (xiii). It was the literature of the village rebels (as Anthony Channell Hilfer calls them in his book-length study of the genre) that *New York Times* reviewer Carlos Baker evoked in his review of *Peyton Place*, comparing Metalious to Sinclair Lewis as an ally in the attack "against the false fronts and bourgeois pretensions of allegedly respectable communities" (par. 3). This favorable comparison to Lewis's work invites an exploration of *Peyton Place* in the context of the small-town narrative, and the "revolt from the village" subgenre in particular. Like those authors whose works have been said to renounce of the myth of the small town, Metalious's work exhibits some ambivalence in this regard, despite the rigor with which it exposes the lie of the American village idyll. It does, after all, have something of a happy ending in which the three main female characters are effectively rehabilitated, as is the town itself. Cameron's point that in "turn[ing] the private into the political" *Peyton Place* was much more than another story of a small town gone bad is well taken, as scholars of the village revolt have reconsidered the usefulness of this designation because of its tendency to obscure the finer nuances of the stories so categorized. Like the works of other so-called village rebels, such as Edgar Lee Masters, Sherwood Anderson, and Sinclair Lewis, *Peyton Place* can be said to be both of the tradition and more than a generic example of a story that takes to task the myth of American small-town life. The revolt Metalious stages is not simply against the stifling limitations of life in a small town but against the racism structuring the heart of the American national imaginary.

Whether or not *Peyton Place* belongs to the revolt from the village tradition depends in part on whether one grants that such a tradition exists. The designation has been contested since very soon after it was first formalized by Carl Van Doren in a 1921 *Nation* article so titled. In it Van Doren discusses the themes of dullness, disillusionment, and despair common to several narratives of the small town by a number of midwestern writers, key among them Masters, Anderson, and Lewis, in the early decades of the twentieth century. He claims that prior to the 1915 publication of Masters's *Spoon River Anthology*, literary treatments of the American village were predominantly marked by "sentimental affection and un-wearied interest" in the "essential goodness and heroism which . . . lie beneath unexciting surfaces" (Van Doren, 407). With the advent of *Spoon River*, the characteristic peace, pleasantry, and equanimity that had pre-viously characterized existence in the nation's literary small towns was officially shattered. In 1919, Sherwood Anderson's *Winesburg, Ohio* re-vealed a community—an "ordinary annex of hell" according to Morris Dickstein (xi)—whose repressive, mundane consensus made grotesques of its citizens, their inner lives catalyzed, haunted, and distorted by the limits of acceptability. And in 1920, *Main Street*, Sinclair Lewis's satirical portrait of midwestern provincialism and mediocrity, rounded out the holy trinity of revolt from the village texts. *Main Street*'s publication be-came the culminating event in the village revolt, "a memorable episode in literary history" by Van Doren's proximate estimation in 1921. The novel alternately offended, intrigued, and entertained contemporary audiences; that its readership numbered in the "thousands and hundreds of thou-sands" signified that "complacency was not absolutely victorious and that the war was on" (Van Doren, 410).

Since Van Doren's declaration of war in the form of the village revolt, literary critics and some of the writers in question have resisted the coin-age, one that over time has accumulated pejorative connotations. Anthony Channell Hilfer, a proponent of the category, who calls it "an accepted rubric of historical criticism," observes that few writers were willing to admit that they were part of any such protest (3). In " 'The Revolt That Wasn't,' " Barry Gross asserts that Masters, Anderson, and Lewis in par-ticular were not in revolt against the American small town per se, but rather that they rebelled against "the *myth* of the village as the great good place, as simple and innocent, pure and virtuous, democratic and egali-tarian" (5). Masters himself disavowed any such rebellious intentions in *Spoon River*. In an interview with August Derleth, he objects to the "re-volt" designation, contending that critics missed some of the heart and hope in his work. "To say that I was in revolt against village life . . . is being just about as silly as you can get. . . . There never was anything to this revolt from the village business." Denying any deliberate rebellion, Masters speaks in behalf of his fellow chroniclers of small-town life, claim-ing, "We didn't do any such thing. Maybe Lewis was backing away from something that hurt him, but he wasn't rebelling against the American small town any more than I was" (qtd. in Gross, 5). Some recent critics have viewed the "revolt" designation as something of a pox, blighting any work unfortunate enough to be so categorized. The application of the label to *Winesburg, Ohio* was, according to Stephen Ennis, "an action from which the stories have never completely recovered" (qtd. in Tilley, 46). Also in defense of *Winesburg*, David D. Anderson shows particular pique about the revolt from the village classification, arguing that its continued use and application among scholars and critics demonstrates the poor judgment of "people who should know better" (1).

Even so, in his recent examination of literary regionalism's cosmopolitan influence, Tom Lutz admits the tradition into his analysis. His position nods to the narrowness for which the "revolt" label has been taken to task, but does so for reasons different than those pointed to by other critics. If the category is problematic, it is not because it hems in texts according to narrowness of theme, Lutz suggests, but rather because it has bracketed a particular era in American literature, the late 1910s and early 1920s. For Lutz, "something like a revolt from the village had always been part of literary regionalism, and something like regional pride and commitment continued to infuse the best 'revolt' literature" (106). The latter may result in part from the nostalgia with which the depictions were mixed, as these writers often wrote about the hometowns of their youth (Hilfer, 4). While Lutz's inclusiveness risks diluting the force of the thematic similarities that Van Doren recognized among those writers that inspired his initial coinage, the label persists and continues to elicit debate. Lutz's use of the term throughout his book—he devotes a full chapter to a look at the revolt from the village through his formulation of literary cosmopolitanism—maintains the designation's legitimacy within scholarly criticism.

My concern here is not to resolve this debate; rather, it is to answer Cameron's comment in her introduction that *Peyton Place* exceeds the boundaries of the village revolt designation, a remark that takes as a given the existence of such a body of literature because of the frequent references made to it in the early reviews of the book. The cultural disturbance caused by Metalious's novel recalls the reception of two of the big three village revolt titles, *Spoon River Anthology* and *Main Street*. Soon after it was published, *Spoon River* became the nation's best-selling volume of poetry to date, famous and infamous for what Van Doren calls "an almost incomparably abundant feast of scandal," owing largely to the poet's handling of sex, "an instinct which, secretive everywhere, has rarely ever been so much so as in the American villages of fiction" (407). Dubbing Masters "the Kinsey of his day" for indulging in and disclosing the sexual peccadilloes of the characters, May Swenson describes *Spoon River* in terms that could just as well be applied to *Peyton Place*: "Few of the ingredients of human corruption and vulnerability are missing from the depositions of these underground witnesses, and the *Anthology* remains fascinating if for nothing else than to untangle the lurid web of small town scandal provocatively placed before us" (xiii). Yet unlike *Spoon River*'s "underground witnesses," *Peyton Place*'s characters continue to live with their secrets and therefore must contrive strategies for their continued coexistence with their neighbors in the community.

Similarly, the American public's reception of *Main Street* prefigured that of *Peyton Place* some four decades later, becoming what Mark Schorer, in his biography of Lewis, describes as "the most sensational event in twentieth-century American publishing history" up to that time. *Main Street* debunked the myth of the American small town "as the best place after all, the real America, America at the roots, America at its kindest, its friendliest, its human best" (268, 271). Though it seemed to many at the time that Lewis approached American village life with scathing novelty, the only true innovation was his use of satire; clear-eyed depictions of the small town as "narrow and cruel" had been penned and published by American writers long before him, though sentimental portraits of village life predominated the literary village landscape (Schorer, "Introduction," 2). Setting the stage for *Main Street*'s reception were ongoing urban industrialization and the resultant drawing down of small-town populations. Two decades into the twentieth century, the demographic and economic shift to urban areas in the United States had sapped the small town of its vitality. As a result, its attitudes and mores seemed to many to be repressive and regressive. Furthermore, those who desired a broader horizon but were unable to move beyond the village boundaries became "corrupted in their discontent" (Schorer, *Sinclair Lewis . . . Life*, 271). This socioeconomic shift converged with the hagiographic status of the American small town that continued to persist in the national imaginary such that, despite earlier gimlet-eyed treatments of life in the nation's villages, Lewis's novel "broke in the literary atmosphere like an explosion, like something absolutely new and absolutely devastating" (Schorer, "Introduction," 2).[1]

In 1956, *Peyton Place* evoked, or perhaps it is more correct to say provoked, this same impression of devastating newness. Of course, the stage having been set by the village rebels before her, Metalious's exposé was not unique in its revelations about life in Small Town, U.S.A. Like Masters, Lewis, and other authors who critiqued village life, Metalious "show[s] an American world characterized by a startling and oppressive lack of emotional or mental freedom" (Hilfer, 32). Similarly, in taking as the novel's title the town in which it is set, *Peyton Place*, like other such works, signals the influence of the place on its people through its "emphasis on the effect of environment" (32). Metalious's narrative terrain shares their thematic preoccupations with sexual repression, religious hypocrisy, corruption, conformity, and small-mindedness. What was new was the novel's treatment of women's sexuality, its assault on class and gender privilege, its assertion of communal culpability in cases of domestic violence and sexual abuse, and the inflections of race within its articulations of sexual desire, anxiety, and threat.

By 1956, Hilfer notes, the revolt was in retreat. Midcentury critical tastes favored Joyce and Proust over Lewis and Masters, and the village rebels "were fairly well snuffed out" (248). In charting the decline and fall of the village revolt writers, Hilfer observes that they "could not provide the fifties critics with the psychological complications, the subtle problems of identity, or the dense symbolic texture that an austere formalistic criticism had been developed to explicate" (248). It is no wonder, then, that *Peyton Place* should have come under fire, because it was, according to these terms, a throwback to a more crude and less aesthetic and thematically nuanced tradition—and, by some estimations, a poorly written contribution to such literature at that. As a defunct and increasingly devalued category, the novel's affiliation with the revolt from the village, along with several other factors, served as a cause for the easy dismissal of *Peyton Place* by critics, who, Cameron suggests, might have seen more in Metalious's work had they seen beyond the perceived narrowness of the revolt tradition. Even so, though some critics used the novel's critique of small-town small-mindedness as a sticking point, *New York Times* reviewer Carlos Baker's linking of *Peyton Place* with Lewis's work seems intended not to trivialize the work as part of a defunct genre. Rather, in mentioning Metalious in the same breath with such literary notables as Lewis, Edmund Wilson, and John O'Hara, Baker grants the work legitimacy and suggests the novel's significance within a category of storytelling that has much to say about American provincialism, hypocrisy, closed-mindedness, and civic habit. *Peyton Place*, then, is as Cameron writes, more than just a revolt from the village tale, as are the other canonical village revolt works. As did *Main Street* and *Spoon River Anthology* before it, *Peyton Place* said something to America about America. Its commentary spoke not simply about the blandness, bitterness, and backwardness of its cloistered village communities, but also about the carefully guarded belief in the nation's small towns as the purest, most upright, and moral places in the land, the "great good place" of the cultural imaginary. Metalious's revolt was against injustices ignored at close range and against the depredations of racism on communities and the national mythos.

## Sex and Race in *Peyton Place*

*Peyton Place* earned its bad reputation as a "sexy" book not only because of its sex scenes but also because it foregrounded the female libido. In addition, as Cameron notes, the novel took a stand on issues of female sexual self-determination, reproductive rights, and domestic and sexual violence a generation before such issues would become the backbone for second-wave feminism (xiii). When *Peyton Place* first arrived on booksellers' shelves, the nation was still buzzing from the revelations of the Kinsey report on female sexual behavior just three years earlier. Among the disclosures of Kinsey and his colleagues was the fact that many women did not enter into marriage as virgins and that marriage did not necessarily prevent them from seeking new sexual partners (Reumann, 22). In other words, most women were sexually misbehaving, in terms of the standards of the times. So were most men, according to volume 1 of Kinsey's research. *Peyton Place*'s men had their peccadilloes as well. For many, *Peyton Place* seemed like a novelization of Kinsey's work.

There is no question that it was *Peyton Place*'s sex that cultural commentators found objectionable. Even so, *Dirty Whites and Dark Secrets* suggests that sex alone does not adequately account for the vigor with which the novel was widely condemned. In her excellent examination of postwar American anxiety about sexuality and national character, Miriam Reumann observes, "The postwar literature of American sexuality— even at its most graphic, pedantic, or alarmed—was never just about sex. Rather, it told and retold stories about gender, the social realities of postwar life, and sexual and national identity, stories through which Americans aired and tried to make sense of the changes that surrounded them" (53). *Peyton Place* is most often said to be "about" sex. I argue that it is also "about" race, and that it is the racialization of the sex that provoked the vituperations against the novel. The chapters that follow posit that *Peyton Place*'s controversial reputation resulted from Metalious's racialized representations of sexuality and the racialization of the spaces in which the sex takes place, the northern New England town in which she sets her story and the homes therein. Peyton Place is a white town with a black founding father, a fact few in the community are willing to disclose. The anxiety produced by this fact is managed through the repression of

Peyton's racial identity, a collective denial that attempts to maintain the facade of the town's whiteness despite its roots, an Africanist presence set literally in stone on a nearby hilltop.

*Peyton Place*'s most quotable lines are perhaps its first two: "Indian summer is like a woman. Ripe, hotly passionate, but fickle, she comes and goes as she pleases so that one is never sure whether she will come at all nor for how long she will stay" (1). It is an image redolent with sex, one that conflates race, gender, and sexuality in ways that set the stage for the novel's explorations of female sexual agency. Chapter 1 situates my project within the historical moment of the 1950s and sets up the theoretical framework that will inform the balance of my discussion. *Dirty Whites and Dark Secrets* is an effort to answer Toni Morrison's call for concerted interrogations of the sources, purpose, and character of literary whiteness (9). It falls under the heading of "whiteness studies," the curiously named subcategory of critical race theory that has produced a fair amount of discussion on its own. I argue that Metalious's notorious novel presents a critique of racial whiteness by presenting it as a pathology deeply rooted in the American psyche, one that is profoundly damaging when it emerges as cultural practice.

In chapter 2, I examine the dystopic view of the American family that Metalious presents at a time when the nation was experiencing what Sylvia Ann Hewlett has called "an orgy of domesticity" (qtd. in Skolnick, 65). No family in *Peyton Place* conforms to the postwar nuclear family ideal of the two-parent, three-child configuration. Many households are missing parents, some lack children, and all have secrets to keep, though some suppress them better than others. It is well known, for instance, that Lucas Cross beats his wife, Nellie, and because "he [pays] his bills" (29), the town accepts this fact as a private matter between husband and wife. What is not known is that Lucas rapes his stepdaughter. When it is later discovered that Selena has killed Lucas, Peyton Place is scandalized by her ingratitude. It is also scandalized by the story of its own origins, a story we learn in full just before Selena's murder trial. This chapter investigates the relationship between the town's unwillingness to admit to its own history and the social pathologies of racism, class prejudice, and patriarchal injustice that *Peyton Place* articulates through the example of the Cross family. Like the Peytons, the Cross family is geographically and socially marginalized. Though she is not black, Selena shares with Samuel Peyton a difference in skin color that further sets her apart from the town's mainstream, white, middle-class community. Similarly, Lucas and Nellie are variously darkened in the narrative. I will examine these shadings and their contingent relations to class and sexuality in the context of *Peyton Place*'s critique of the 1950s family.

The reputation *Peyton Place* earned and still maintains as a sexy book can be credited in part to the fact that Metalious foregrounded female interest in sex. Several of the novel's women are eager participants in self-interested sex outside of marriage, and many of them are able to engage in such behavior at a time when the repercussions and consequences for alleged sexual impropriety were often severe. One of *Peyton Place*'s main characters, Constance MacKenzie, also learns to pursue sex to her own satisfaction by novel's end. Helen Gurley Brown's *Sex and the Single Girl*, Erica Jong's *Fear of Flying*, and Judy Blume's *Wifey* each owe something to *Peyton Place* for its acknowledgment and exploration of women's active libidos, as do recent television programs such as *Sex and the City* and *Desperate Housewives*. While it is therefore true that *Peyton Place* defied convention and courted controversy by giving voice to and legitimating female sexual agency outside of marriage, it would be a mistake to call it a feminist text, or at the very least, to do so without qualification. The sexual re-education of one of its central characters, Constance MacKenzie, is initiated through a rape at the hands of her eventual husband, Tom Makris. Chapter 3 examines the terms of Constance's second coming of age, paying special attention to the articulations of race in Metalious's portrayal of her novel's central couple. The union of Tom and Constance in marriage shortly before the narrative resolves is presented as a good thing, a sign of the healthy reintegration of Constance's libido into her life. It also serves to integrate the community, with the installation of its dark-skinned erstwhile outsider within the family home of a fair-skinned, fair-haired native of Peyton Place. Nevertheless, this progressive position is compromised by the terms under which it is effected.

Following closely on the heels of chapter 3's examination of the rape/redemption of Constance MacKenzie, I shift my focus in chapter 4 from Constance's white body to Tom's dark one. I look at the dependence on race in American culture's definitions of masculinity and femininity, and turn to another famous rape scene in order to explore the nexus of race, gender, and sexuality in *Peyton Place*—Rhett Butler's rape of Scarlett O'Hara in Margaret Mitchell's *Gone with the Wind*. The scenes are similar in terms of the racialization of the men (dark) and the women (alabaster white) and the effect that each rape has on its victims, that of a sexual awakening that retroactively recasts the rape as seduction. The virile darkness of Rhett Butler is opposed to the enervated whiteness of Ashley Wilkes, a character type whom Michael Kimmel calls the "Genteel

Patriarch," whose raison d'être is sacrificed with the Confederate loss of the Civil War. Tom Makris's potent brand of dark masculinity is opposed to that of very nearly all of the white male characters in *Peyton Place*, save, perhaps, for that of Doc Swain, the white knight (in racial and sartorial terms) who saves Selena's life by performing the abortion she seeks in order to rid her of her stepfather's child. Metalious's novel lacks *Gone with the Wind*'s nostalgia for the sort of imperial whiteness embodied by Ashley Wilkes. Instead, *Peyton Place* is frankly critical of the majority of its white male characters. This chapter investigates the relationship the novel suggests between white racial identity and dysfunctional masculinity.

Chapter 5 addresses the repressions of individual and collective secrets in *Peyton Place* in relation to the uncanny. In some ways, the chapter itself may enact a return of the repressed, as I argue that the gothic and the supernatural undergird the narrative from beginning to end. *Peyton Place* is full of uncanny elements: racial, sexual, and class repression; repetitions; doublings; and private and public hauntings, among others. It is also the unlikely site of an actual castle, a structure elemental to gothic fiction.[2] Whereas in chapter 2, I discuss the significance of Peyton's castle in light of the "failed families" in town, in chapter 5, I return to the castle in relationship to domestic architecture and the structuring of space. The castle serves as a fortification for Peyton against the outside world, much as traditional castles do. It is a structure that signifies a presence that is desired as an absence, both at the local and national level. The current residents of Peyton Place wish to ignore the house and its history, a home and a story produced by a nation founded on a white supremacist ideology that denies full citizenship and subjectivity to its nonwhite inhabitants.

Priscilla Wald and Renée Bergland have theorized the implications of the physical and figurative removal of racial and ethnic others from the American landscape in terms of the uncanny. In positing populations who existed within national boundaries but to whom the rights of citizenship did not extend, Wald explains that fully matriculated citizens of the United States "could see [their] own alterity, or alienation, reflected in the fate, and often quite literally in the face, of the racialized other" (65). The presence of nonwhite persons whose status had been legislated as "in but not of" the United States reified the civic identity of the nation's white populace. It also called into question the terms upon which one's status as a citizen was based. Nonwhite, native-born individuals to whom full rights as national subjects did not extend became "uncanny figures who mirror[ed] the legal contingency—and the potential fate—of all subjects in the Union" (59).

Bergland uses the idea of the "national uncanny" to examine the implications of the "ghosting" of Indians, in particular, on constructions of American identity. She writes:

> Ghosts are the things that we try to bury, but that refuse to stay buried. They are our fears and our horrors, disembodied, but made inescapable by their very bodiliness. Ghostly Indians present us with the possibility of vanishing ourselves, being swallowed up into another's discourse, another's imagination. When ghostly Indian figures haunt the white American imagination, they serve as constant reminders of the fragility of national identity. . . . Further, ghosts are impossible to control or to evade. When Indians are understood as ghosts, they are also understood as powerful figures beyond American control. (5)

The construction and internalization of these and other nonwhite phantasms may have been intended as a means to control persons and groups who threatened a white racialized American identity, just as attempts to manage and legislate actual nonwhite bodies out of citizenship were meant to do. Though she does not specifically refer to the uncanny, Amy Kaplan makes a related claim in her work on domestic space and national ideology. Arguing that "domesticity worked as both a bulwark against and embodiment of the anarchy of empire" in nineteenth-century women's writing, Kaplan extends this understanding of the American ideological project to address "how images of the nation as home were haunted by 'disembodied shades' who blurred the boundaries between the domestic and the foreign" (Kaplan, *Anarchy*, 26).

For Wald, Bergland, and Kaplan, then, the uncanny helps to explain constructions and disruptions of national identity. Chapter 5 uses the uncanny to investigate the significance of the hauntings that take place in individual homes in Peyton Place as well as the persistent haunting of the town by its own origins. This exploration takes into account changes in 1950s home design that reflect changes in the uses of space, racially charged patterns of urban dispersal, and the suburban housing boom. Recent scholarship has linked postwar suburbanization to atomic anxiety. Kathleen Tobin has argued that the mass migration away from urban centers in the decade after World War II was in part a result of a government-sponsored push to reduce the overall impact of an atomic attack on the nation's densely populated cities. Because redlining practices prevented blacks and other ethnic groups from moving out of these areas, scenarios that imagined a nuclear exchange with the Soviet Union implied the survival of a white American citizenry ready to reconstruct the nation in its own image. Finally, I will examine how Metalious re-envisions the future of the community and, by extension, the nation by incorporating Selena Cross and Tom Makris into its future.

*Peyton Place* is frequently discussed in terms of its impact on the publishing industry. In addition to its sex, its sales caused quite a stir. Chapter 6, which concludes this study, addresses the book's evolution from sensation to commodity to novel. *Peyton Place* did receive some good notices from well-known critics when it was first released, most notably from *New York Times* reviewer Carlos Baker, who compared Metalious to Sinclair Lewis. In the popular press, however, it received quite a drubbing. I will look at some of these early responses, as well as a few of those occasioned by the novel's re-release in 1999 by Northeastern University Press. *Peyton Place* remains controversial more than fifty years after its initial publication. For this reason, one among many, I argue that the novel is a key cultural artifact that has a great deal to say about Cold War anxieties about race and the American nation.

I

# Dark Past, White Lies

## Reconsidering the Sources of Scandal in Peyton Place

*Peyton Place* famously begins, "Indian summer is like a woman. Ripe, hotly passionate, but fickle, she comes and goes as she pleases so that one is never sure whether she will come at all, nor for how long she will stay" (1). This brazen simile, at once racialized, gendered, and highly sexualized, strikingly, efficiently, and suggestively anticipates the conflation of these discourses that will recur repeatedly throughout much of the novel. Already, in its first sentence, *Peyton Place* has provocatively established its preoccupation with race and sex and, moreover, has raced the sex as "other." Indian summer is a season that isn't a season, one that promises something it will not, because it cannot, deliver: the return of summer after the first chill of fall, a revival of that season's heat and steam, a hint that fosters the hope of a more enduring hot spell in spite of the short while it lingers.[1] In its comings and goings, its flirtatious ambivalence, Metalious sexes up the image in the next sentence, explaining that it is coquettishness and caprice that genders the time of year as feminine. Indian summer is a tease:

> In northern New England, Indian summer puts up a scarlet-tipped hand to
> hold winter back for a little while. She brings with her the time of the last
> warm spell, an unchartered season which lives until Winter moves in with its
> backbone of ice and accoutrements of leafless trees and hard frozen ground.
> Those grown old, who have had the youth bled from them by the jagged
> edged winds of winter, know sorrowfully that Indian summer is a sham to
> be met with hard-eyed cynicism. But the young wait anxiously, scanning the
> chill autumn skies for a sign of her coming. And sometimes the old, against
> all the warnings of better judgment, wait with the young and hopeful, their

tired, winter eyes turned heavenward to seek the first traces of a false softening.

One year, early in October, Indian summer came to a town called Peyton Place. Like a laughing, lovely woman Indian summer came and spread herself over the countryside and made everything hurtfully beautiful to the eye. (1)

New England's "unchartered season" plays as if she will settle in and stay the coming of winter altogether. For all of her steamy exhibitionism, though, her enticements are "a sham" and her visit is never to the satisfaction of those who desire her most.

This womanly season is not a white one; the racialized term that names the season also informs the New England landscape to which Metalious compares it. Though the derivation of the term Indian summer "appears to have had nothing to do with the glowing autumnal tints of the foliage, with which it is sometimes associated" (OED Online), the season is discursively racialized such that it does seem to be affiliated with its coloration(s). The term's origins are not easily traced; its etymology "has been lost in the tangled and tortured history of white America's relationship with the indigenous peoples for whom the season is so enigmatically named" (Sweeting, 9). Among the symbolic meanings conveyed by the season is one arising in the nineteenth century, a "wizened understanding, a period of second (and smarter) youth that follows a hard-won maturity (5).[2] For a novel that depicts the second coming of age of the libidinally bereft Constance MacKenzie, this opening image seems all the more appropriate. The reds of this rogue season may be coincidental to its nickname; however, its gendering is deliberate. And once feminized, a chain of mutually reinforcing associations unfurls that illustrates how subtle and inextricable the interplay of race and gender and sexuality are. Indian summer is sultry and seductive, "a seasonal femme fatale" (Sweeting, 6)—even those who know better are in her thrall and believe, however fleetingly, that she will deliver what she has promised. Only nature itself remains unswayed by her presence: "The conifers stood like disapproving old men on all the hills around Peyton Place" (1–2). And in the end, she will take her leave when winter moves in, a white season figured colloquially as an Old Man.

This potent inaugural image participates to some degree in what Anne McClintock has dubbed the "porno-tropic tradition," in effect, a geography of the obscene. McClintock derives this concept from the fifteenth- and sixteenth-century habit of imaging the lands of uncharted, newly discovered territories in Africa, Asia, and the Americas (the "uncertain" continents, she calls them) as female. Cartographers and those who chronicled these expeditions attributed to these lands sexual deviance and excesses, which transformed them into "a fantastic magic lantern of the mind onto which Europe projected its forbidden sexual desires and fears" (22). This porno-tropic ideology bolstered a discourse of masculine sexual aggression—for example, phallically penetrating the interiors of a "virgin" territory and taking an inventory of the attendant discoveries for the sake of "a visible, male science of the surface" (23)—as a means of asserting "knowledge" of and exercising power over the land. In this complicated "conversion" from uncharted feminized territory to indexed and catalogued masculine knowledge, McClintock suggests that "the imperial conquest of the globe found both its shaping figure and its political sanction in the prior sub-ordination of women as a category of nature" (24). This feminization, she states, is a paranoid and pathological male response to "boundary loss," enacting a logic that justifies the enforcement of a "strategy of violent containment":

> As the visible trace of paranoia, feminizing the land is a compensatory gesture, disavowing male loss of boundary by reinscribing a ritual excess of boundary, accompanied, all too often, by an excess ritual of military violence. The feminizing of the land represents a ritualistic moment in imperial discourse, as male intruders ward off fears of narcissistic disorder by reinscribing, as natural, an excess of gender hierarchy. (24)

Though the "discovery" of uncharted lands and colonial expansion was precisely the goal of these seafaring expeditions, success produced anxiety about the unbounded nature of the land itself. McClintock argues that by imaging the new lands as female, the male expedition members had at the ready a figure they could relate to on the basis of its gendered difference, one element of which was woman's "prior subordination" to male power. The idea of land/nature-as-woman announced a project of aggression, domination, management, and control as imperial adventurers sought to expand their home ports' territorial holdings and sovereign reach.

By beginning her novel with a depiction of a libidinized female (Native) American landscape, Metalious at once reiterates this porno-tropic tradition and subverts it, the first of several instances of simultaneous subversion of and complicity with dominant ideologies in the novel. The discourses of British colonialism have continued to find their voice in the

American imperialist practices and racial ideologies that have persisted into the twenty-first century. Toni Morrison begins her 1993 monograph, *Playing in the Dark: Whiteness and the Literary Imagination*, by announcing her wish to "[extend] the study of American literature into . . . a wider landscape" by "[drawing] a map, so to speak, of a critical geography and [using] that map to open as much space for discovery, intellectual adventure, and close exploration as did the original charting of the New World—without the mandate for conquest" (3). In the several years since Morrison stated her hopes and intentions, much space has indeed been cleared for such discoveries to take place, and an increasing body of work has been amassed in the field of what has come to be known as "whiteness studies," a field to which *Dirty Whites and Dark Secrets* arguably belongs. It is convenient for the present study of *Peyton Place* that Morrison's metaphor is a cartographic one, as the novel uses a place name as its title and opens with a passage that sensually introduces the lay of the land. Furthermore, it is a narrative set against a black history, a history that is repressed within the novel and in the vast majority of discussions about the novel. The town of Peyton Place is named after a black man, Samuel Peyton, who escaped southern slavery but not American racism. It seems fitting, then, that Metalious should eroticize, feminize, and racialize a landscape that introduces a narrative that will have much to say about sexual, racial, and national identity. Unlike the travelogues of mastery and submission McClintock chronicles, Indian summer in *Peyton Place* is invested with the agency to come and go at will. Indeed, it is her whim alone that seems to determine her reign over the land. Though as previously noted, folklorically, it is Old Man Winter who will end her tenure in the town, the intimation in this opening passage is that once the "laughing, lovely woman" has had her fill of mischief, she will depart on her own terms and return again as she wishes the following autumn.

## The Time and the *Place*

Though the action of *Peyton Place* occurs between 1936 and 1944, it is, of course, very much a novel of the 1950s. Its scandalous acknowledgment and portrayal of women's sexuality, its concern with the talk of its town, and the racial shame the community struggles to conceal each suggest something of the tenor of the times. When the novel emerged onto the American cultural scene in 1956, the United States was fully entrenched in its Cold War standoff with the Soviet Union. Foreign and domestic policy were guided by anticommunism. Internationally, the United States sought to prevent the establishment of communist governments worldwide. Domestic policy sought to prevent infiltration and subversion of national interests by communist operatives. "Containment" became the geopolitical order of the day. Specifically, it was the policy with which the United States conducted its battle against the threat of communism. In his 1947 *Foreign Affairs* article, "The Sources of Soviet Conduct," George Kennan's so called containment thesis set the terms of the discussion, calling for the "long-term, patient but firm and vigilant *containment* of Russian expansive tendencies" (qtd. in Gaddis, 29). Elaine Tyler May has argued that "containment," though conceived as an approach to foreign policy, also became the modus operandi for domestic politics and was handily applied as a means of reining in wily cultural forces and populations that threatened to destabilize the status quo, among them, those with a progressive interest in the rights of women, blacks, and homosexuals. In her study of the nuclear family in the nuclear age, May observes, "More than merely a metaphor for the cold war on the homefront, containment aptly describes the way in which public policy, personal behavior, and even political values were focused on the home" (xxv).[3] However, despite the pervasive "defense of masculinity and whiteness" (Breines, 58) that was meant to maintain and contain the postwar American culture of consensus, the 1950s registered mounting discontent on several fronts, laying the groundwork for the rise of youth culture, the women's movement, and the Civil Rights movement. This view of the decade is not a new one. A scant three years after it had come to a close, the title of I. F. Stone's *The Haunted Fifties* (1963) suggested that the era was in fact more traumatic than tranquil. Joel Foreman notes that scholars since the early 1980s have been challenging the cherished American cultural recollection of the postwar era as a time of placid contentment (1–2), as safe and well-preserved as a Christmas fruitcake sealed in rose-colored Tupperware.[4] The decade was instead the seedbed of the cultural rebellions and social upheaval that took hold and flourished in the 1960s and beyond (Lhamon, xiv). There were tremendous tensions at play between the pursuit and attainment of "the good life" and the specter of atomic annihilation; the postwar resettlement in suburbia and white flight from the nation's cities; the comfort and security of the new nuclear family and the breakdown of traditional kinship networks; and the fear of communist infiltration and the long reach of the blacklist. The tendency to recall the 1950s as a confection of carefree Americana, as many pop cultural retreads of the era have done and continue to do, is to fundamentally misunderstand a decade during which appreciable measures of discomfort, discontent, and dissent were stirring only just behind an illusion of complacency.

Despite the social and political conservatism that dominated the early Cold War era, civil rights reform gained ground during the 1950s, owing in part to the emergence of the United States from "the Good War" as a great global superpower. America's enhanced visibility as a model of democracy meant that it was under greater scrutiny by the rest of the world, and the reign of Jim Crow became an international public relations nightmare (Dudziak, 12). The nation's desire to keep communism contained meant that it could no longer practice the isolationism that had characterized U.S. foreign policy following World War I (Oakes, 22). Furthermore, having emerged as the world's defender of democracy, the United States had a reputation to uphold. American domestic policy and practices were closely watched by other countries. According to Thomas Borstelmann, "American foreign relations could not be insulated from the nation's race relations in an era of maximum U.S. involvement abroad" (1). It was believed that America's management of its own internal affairs would have diplomatic consequences that would either affirm or undermine the nation's anticommunist project (Dudziak, 15). Civil rights groups and their allies drew attention to the discrepancy between the United States's international evangelism of democracy and its selective application of political equality only to white Americans.[5] While homegrown discontent was gathering momentum, mounting external pressure to redraw the color line was at least equally influential. When black statesmen from other countries faced discrimination on U.S. soil, the world took notice (Borstelmann, 1). The Soviet Union capitalized on this peculiar hypocrisy, gleefully publicizing incidents in which American practice was at odds with its preachings. International pressure challenged the United States to behave in accord with its declared principles of equality by addressing and correcting its racist and discriminatory practices and ideologies at home. As a result, President Truman was persuaded to incorporate the rhetoric of racial equality in his platform for the spread of democracy (Dudziak, 26–27). Still, even as America began to reckon with the illogic of its "separate but equal" social policies, Dudziak writes, "Civil rights groups had to walk a fine line, making it clear that their reform efforts were meant to fill out the contours of American democracy, and not to challenge or undermine it" (11). At issue was the question of loyalty to America's anticommunist agenda versus loyalty to a civil rights agenda. Adherence to the former bespoke patriotism; commitment to the latter suggested subversion, as racial identity superseded national identity. Discussions of civil rights reform were therefore at once enabled and constrained by the Cold War. "The primacy of anticommunism in postwar American politics and culture left a very narrow space for criticism of the status quo," observes Dudziak. "By silencing certain voices and by promoting a particular vision of racial justice, the Cold War led to a narrowing of acceptable civil rights discourse" (13). While foreign critics of American segregation could make their critique without fear of reprisal, American citizens who criticized the federal government ran the risk of being brought under suspicion of communist sympathy or subversive activity.[6]

The tensions and contradictions of the Cold War are evident in many of the mass-marketed and commercially successful pop cultural products of the 1950s (Foreman, 6). Writing specifically of best-selling novels, Jane Hendler remarks that such works, as in all popular cultural artifacts, register "both hegemonic and counterhegemonic discourses" within individual texts (10). Such an idea would have been anathema to postwar intellectuals for whom there was nothing redeeming in what was passing, so they claimed, for art and literature by the standards of midcentury Americans. Cultural critics rallied against what they saw as the vulgarization of high culture by bourgeois tastes. Middlebrow culture was especially threatening, as it muddied the waters between elite culture and kitsch, critic Clement Greenberg's polarities for high art and those widely circulated cultural products lacking in literary or artistic value. Middlebrow offerings masqueraded as high culture without, the argument ran, the necessary engagement with avant-garde ideas or stylistic nuance. In a remark that strikingly echoes antimiscegenation discourse, cultural critic Dwight Macdonald warned of middlebrow's murky, miasmal effect on culture more broadly. His aggressive disdain for popular culture, or what he called "Masscult" notwithstanding, it is the terrain between high and low that he found most pernicious: "The danger to High Culture is not so much from Masscult as from a peculiar hybrid bred from the latter's unnatural intercourse with the former. A whole middle culture has come into existence and it threatens to absorb both its parents" (qtd. in Hendler, 13). This "peculiar hybrid," also known as "Midcult," aspires to the status of high culture while pandering to the market. Macdonald and Greenberg and others feared for the state of the arts, tolling the alarm bells—what they feared were the death knells—of American culture. The nation's taste for art and literature, they held, was formed and sustained by the bread and circuses proffered from a market-driven, commodity-rich economy. Despite the vehemence with which postwar intellectuals sought to protect and defend high culture from extinction or vitiation, that the distinctions between high, middle, and mass culture were, as Evan Brier points out, "a matter of ideology, not fact" (*Novel*, 3) meant that out-of-hand dismissals of best-selling novels foreclosed sites of significant critique. Later scholars, beyond the reach of the cultural gatekeepers of midcentury, have recognized the critiques embedded in pop cultural products and have recuperated many for study, *Peyton Place* among them. Although it is true that conventional wisdom holds that capitalism and its commodities are traditionally conservative forces that tend to reify the status quo, Foreman suggests that many of the artifacts produced and consumed in mass-media markets in 1950s America were ideologically progressive:

> As highly successful commodifications whose American consumers numbered in the millions, the mass media representations of the fifties are quintessential representatives of their time, and we can say about them (with little doubt or hesitation) that they captured the needs, desires, and expectations of so many people as to provide significant indexes of the changing behavior and the internal tensions of that cultural body we call America. . . . There is no question that capitalism and capitalist markets have enforced conservative codes of behavior. But it is equally true . . . that markets have aided and abetted the production and dissemination of subversive ideologies. (6–7)

The cultural progressivism for which Foreman finds evidence in mass-market products of the midcentury is not idiosyncratic to the time. He notes that while capitalism gives the people what they want, it also at the same time serves as something of a barometer for cultural dissonance.

*Peyton Place* is just such a contradictory commodity, registering its broad appeal on the best-seller lists while at the same time scandalizing the arbiters of good taste by virtue of its subject matter: the sex life and other sordid secrets of a small town. In the month following its publication on September 24, 1956, the novel sold 104,000 copies and remained a best seller for twenty-six weeks (Toth, *Inside*, 131). It also prompted several scathing critical rebukes of its content and its author, along with some relatively positive recognition by a few less offended critics, who believed that Metalious had candidly revealed some measure of truth about seemingly idyllic American communities.[7] It was banned in Indiana and Rhode Island and deemed contraband by Canadian authorities, who, under Tariff Provision 1201, could confiscate copies at border crossings on account of its "indecent and immoral character" (ibid., 132). In spite of the controversy, or indeed, possibly owing to the publicity generated by the novel, *Peyton Place* went on to become a successful Hollywood film starring Lana Turner and a long-running television series, launching the careers of a very young Mia Farrow and Ryan O'Neal.[8]

It has been argued that *Peyton Place* serves as "a valuable corrective to the myth of quiescent domesticity and class consensus" that had previously characterized the 1950s (Cameron, xvi). Within the three years prior to the novel's publication, Alfred Kinsey's *Sexual Behavior in the Human Female* was published; *Playboy* debuted at the nation's newsstands; segregation was declared unconstitutional in the *Brown v. Board of Education* Supreme Court ruling; Rosa Parks took her stand while seated on a bus; and in 1956, the year *Peyton Place* revealed the hidden improprieties of a small New England town, Elvis Presley made his debut from the waist up on the *Ed Sullivan Show*. Jane Hendler suggests that *Peyton Place* resists the era's pervasive containment consciousness "by breaking apart the dichotomy of good/bad girls, by empowering a female victim of sexual violence, by representing female teens enjoying erotic pleasures and sexual experiences" (208). Issues of female sexuality, desire, and agency are indeed central to the novel and have been the focus of the greater part of the still relatively limited but increasing scholarship on it. *Peyton Place*'s frank approach to women and sex has been held responsible for much of the scandal and controversy surrounding the novel from the moment of its publication. To be sure, it was not the only "dirty book" of its time—other postwar best sellers, such as James Jones's *From Here to Eternity*, were similarly explicit and "trashy." Whereas an acknowledged level of vulgarity worked in the service of *Eternity*'s popularity, it caused an uproar when articulated by *Peyton Place* (Hendler, 185). The difference in reception, she suggests, was not simply a general critical disdain for melodrama (or women's fiction); the problem for *Peyton Place* was that "it was 'dirty' in a particular way in that it violated the cultural norms of femininity by focusing on the sex lives—the desires, fantasies, fears, and practices—of 'ordinary' women" (185). Also contributing to its unconventionality is that it issued from the pen of a small-town housewife and mother, one bold enough to pose for *Peyton Place*'s most famous publicity photo wearing a serious expression but casual clothes: cuffed dungarees, a plaid flannel shirt, sneakers without socks, her hair pulled back in a ponytail, a portrait of the artist as a young housewife seated before a typewriter on a kitchen table that came to be known as "Pandora in Blue Jeans." This is the general consensus, with which I agree; however, I would add that it is not just the gendering of the novel that made it so scandalous, its apparent alliance with What Women Want. More than that, and less obvious, is the way the novel conflates sexuality with gender and race, the feature that is at the root of its particular charge in the pre–civil rights era.

## Peyton Place in Academe

As of this writing, only two book-length studies of Peyton Place exist: Emily Toth's literary biography of Grace Metalious and Ruth Pirsig Wood's challenge to the high-middle-lowbrow stratifications of fifties fiction, Lolita in Peyton Place. Very little of the available work on the novel deals with issues of race. A few articles have been anthologized that address some of the cultural work Metalious does in the novel. Other scholars have included chapter-length analyses of Peyton Place as part of studies of growing up female in the 1950s, the uses of fairy-tale elements in the telling of the story, page-to-screen adaptations of twentieth-century best sellers, and the midcentury narrative of cultural decline with which the novel has been credited in hastening.[9] Toth's biography, published in 1981, is useful for its thoroughness in sketching the difficult life of the author of the century's most notorious potboiler. It falters where Toth analyzes the book itself, in that she claims the existence of an empathetic sisterhood within the novel for which there is little evidence. To some degree, Toth's misreading of the relationships between the women in the novel as close, nurturing examples of sisterhood at work may be understood as a by-product of her 1970s' feminist agenda, that is, rehabilitating the book's smutty reputation into a more respectable set of cultural observations and social commentaries. In doing so, she seems to have erred on the side of passionate championship instead of maintaining enough critical distance to adequately contend with the novel's contradictions. If there are characters who come out ahead at novel's end, Toth asserts,

> [t]he winners are independent women like Allison, who pursues her writing, putting an unhappy love affair behind her; Connie, who acknowledges her sexuality—and keeps her career; and Selena, who transcends desertion, rape, and murder and relies on herself—and her female friends. Allison and Selena both find women's friendships the most enduring relationships in Peyton Place. Unlike Grace Metalious in real life, women who succeed in Peyton Place depend less on men, more on a community of women, and most on themselves. (143–44)

Toth's is an upbeat assessment of the situation, but not one that is fully borne out by the text. Neither Allison nor Selena have long-standing female friendships that have weathered their adolescence; in fact their friendship has waned with time. In addition, Selena's most vocal detractor is a woman, Marion Partridge, the wife of her attorney; Allison's relationship with her mother is still mostly frayed though on the mend by novel's end; and Constance's relationship with her eventual husband, Tom Makris, most closely resembles that of a protégé to her Svengali.

In a separate article on Metalious titled "Fatherless and Dispossessed," Toth correctly observes that it is the women of *Peyton Place* who are most affected by the balance of power in town, which is concentrated in the hands of and delegated by the town's wealthiest and most prominent men (31). And it is also true that in the face of this, there are examples of women assisting one another in difficult situations—after overcoming her initial distrust of and distaste for Allison's best friend, Constance's interest in Selena Cross's well-being is perhaps the most illustrative. Toth later goes on to claim, "In *Peyton Place*, the women want independence, sexual expression and security—and they know they need one another, with a sense of sisterhood" (36). Although the first half of her statement seems true enough, the latter again betrays an understandable optimism for which there is very little textual support. The community of women to which Toth refers exists only by virtue of geographic proximity, not through affective bonds.

Ardis Cameron's introduction to the latest edition of *Peyton Place* works hard to redeem a much-maligned novel and its author and offers several good reasons why the academy might reconsider its condescension, noting that scholars in Metalious's own time recognized the value of her cultural commentary (xxiv). Metalious's gritty portrait of a small town is not limited to the seamy sexiness that made the novel's and its author's reputations, but serves also to expose the way in which a community can be complicit in the crimes committed by its citizens. "Both class indifference and patriarchal power relations are held up to scathing attack," Cameron notes. Lucas Cross's panicky and weak confession and defense that he was drunk when he raped his stepdaughter, Cameron observes,

> is matched only by the moral failure of "good" citizens who cloak their indifference in a pseudo-tradition of Yankee toleration and a misguided notion of civic duty. . . . In ways that would foreshadow the modern feminist movement, *Peyton Place* turned the "private" into the political. By reinterpreting incest, wife beating, and poverty as signs of social as well as indi-

vidual failure, Metalious turned "trash" into a powerful political commentary on gender relations and class privilege. (xii–xiii)

Readers and critics who have focused only on the novel's sex scenes and have drawn their conclusions about *Peyton Place*'s value from them alone have missed Metalious's significant and more broadly based sociocultural critique. The novel is not simply an exposé about the sex lives of the residents of a small New England town, Cameron asserts. It is, she argues persuasively, an important critique of social injustice, sexual oppression, and class discrimination.

Like Toth's upbeat approach to the novel, however, Cameron offers a too-rosy reading of the relationship between women and sex in *Peyton Place*, asserting that, "it was not sex per se that made *Peyton Place* scandalous, but rather the extent to which Metalious's characters, especially her women, both enjoyed and gave sexual pleasure. Metalious celebrated female sexuality and positioned women at the center of sexual relations, politicizing both the female body and attempts to control it" (xiv). Although it is true that some of Metalious's women are sexual because it is what they want versus what men want them to be, to say that female sexuality in *Peyton Place* is "celebrated" is to greatly oversimplify a much more complicated issue. With the possible exception of Evelyn Page, whose particular peccadillo it is to give enemas to her son, Norman, men are often still the ones in control of women's bodies. Such is the case when Harmon Carter pimps his fiancée, Roberta, to a rich old doctor in order to enhance their nest egg, and when Leslie Harrington threatens Betty Anderson with a solicitation charge when his son, Rodney, gets her pregnant. Betty, like her sister before her, has to leave town for the sake of propriety, not hers so much as Rodney's. It is also hard to consider Constance's rape by Tom Makris a celebration of women's sexual liberation. Allison's sexual initiation by an older man, while it is indeed something she desires and sets the stage for, is dominated by his paternal patronizing of her inexperience. Cameron also accuses the film and television adaptations of *Peyton Place* of re-centering the town's power in the hands of its men, lamenting that on screens large and small, "[m]en show [women] the way to true happiness, moral courage and safety. The town's women, who become for Metalious an oasis of comfort and a source of support, are reduced to marginal players, their quiet heroism reframed as gossip and helplessness" (xviii). I would argue that this, too, misunderstands *Peyton Place*: the most powerful and influential figures in the novel are its men. For example, Doc Swain saves Selena the agony of enduring a pregnancy brought about by incest and then saves her from the death penalty when he takes the stand in her behalf at her murder trial. More troublingly, given his violent initiation of his relationship with Constance, Tom Makris is positioned as the novel's voice of reason on matters, ironically enough, of healthy sexuality. He takes it on himself to break Constance of her "frigid" exterior in order to expose the "passionate, love demanding woman that she really was" (178), finally freeing her from her long years of sexual repression and making her erotically whole once again. While it is true that by novel's end, Constance initiates sex because she recognizes that it is what she wants, to overvalue this single show of sexual desire at the expense of the violent manner in which it was brought about is to overlook a significant and central issue in Metalious's original work.

In her reading of both the book and the film adaptation of *Peyton Place*, Jane Hendler is more nuanced, acknowledging the conservatism embedded in Metalious's narrative alongside the radical assertion that women can be self-motivated sexual beings. Hendler takes a queer-eyed look at the novel:

> By presenting the difficulties that her female characters experience in taking up culturally prescribed sex roles, Metalious directed attention to the inadequacies of situating gender and sex purely in the realm of nature. . . . [T]he novel shows the possibility that gender and sexual identities are relational and contingent on cultural definitions of marriage, home, and family rather than on any stable or fixed notion of a female self. (188–89)

Although hesitant to call the novel "feminist," pointing out that the balance of power in its eponymous town still tips toward its men in the end, Hendler suggests that *Peyton Place* "clearly decenters the exclusive authorization of male interests and values" by lodging a critique against the narrow parameters of publicly acceptable performances of femininity (195). In presenting Constance as a sympathetic figure who has been made to live a lie as a result of stepping outside of the culturally condoned limits of female sexuality, Metalious argues against American culture's sexually repressive dictates. Rather than moralizing against Constance's youthful involvement with a married man, Metalious instead takes her to task for buying into the dominant sexual ideology that caused her disavow her own desires and vigilantly police those of her daughter (196). By staging the effects of the narrow norms governing sexual practice and gender roles at midcentury, Hendler writes, "Metalious's novel may have laid some groundwork for theorizing female oppression" (200).

Other approaches to the novel have included Ruth Pirsig Wood's book-length analysis of the crossroads of highbrow and lowbrow culture in the 1950s, *Lolita in Peyton Place*. Admitting that *Lolita* loyalists will blanch at the thought of affiliating themselves with a novel as earthy as Metalious's, Wood observes "the two novels give reflexive accounts of the same moral concern: the effects of sexual self-indulgence and of sexual repression" (5). She does, however, note that it is the invisibility of Nabokov's craft and Metalious's sometimes heavy-handed approach to hers that distinguish each coming-of-age narrative as high- and lowbrow, respectively. *Peyton Place* is closer to fantasy than is *Lolita*, Wood argues, citing Nabokov's tacit admission of the limits of socially acceptable behavior, Metalious's melodramatic flourishes, and her promise of a happy ending (8). Yet she does not dismiss *Peyton Place* as pure fantasy, contending that "contrary to popular assumption that lowbrow fiction sweepingly and irresponsibly erases the chasm between desire and possibility or reality and fantasy, *Peyton Place* acknowledges the breach by splitting characters and by balancing the ill fortune of minor characters with the unlikely good fortune of main characters" (9). Similarly, in *Insatiable Appetites* Madonne Miner considers *Peyton Place*'s relationship to fantasy and fairy tale. Miner posits that Metalious is engaged in a critique of several of the literary forms that she borrows for use in *Peyton Place*. Unlike the bodice rippers peddled to women by publishers like Harlequin, in which the boundary between character and reader is said to collapse almost completely, Miner sees Metalious as "[promoting] a policy of critical evaluation and assertive individuation in the face of fantasy" (59), at once commenting on and questioning the building blocks of the genre "which glorify passivity, dependency, and self-sacrifice as a heroine's cardinal virtues" (Rowe, 210). In *Peyton Place*, Miner tells us, Metalious offers a counterreading of such narratives, suggesting that there are options for women beyond the generic impotence of female characters in fantasies and romances.

Miner is one of very few scholars who have noted the way race works in the novel. In a footnote, she offers a cursory reading of the story of Samuel Peyton as a cautionary tale to female readers. In Peyton's castle, Miner sees the structure at the heart of the novel—identifying it, correctly, I believe, as having been borrowed from the gothic tradition. As for the danger being articulated, Miner writes, "dark men, fair women, castle walls—lovely, but for women, lethal" (77). Elsewhere she addresses the matter of Constance's fairness and Tom Makris's darkness and the fairy-tale antecedents of each type, drawing on the stories of "Snow White" and "Beauty and the Beast." Though she considers the significance of Selena's difference from most other girls in town, Miner misreads her as "fair" in charting the parallels between Selena's rape by Lucas and Constance's rape by Tom Makris (70). Selena is drawn darkly by Metalious, explicitly but inexplicably so; her honey-tan skin sets her apart from the rest of Peyton Place, an othering that is foregrounded early on in the novel. Miner's comparison of Selena and Constance on the basis of fairness forces a likeness that does not exist.

Two discussions of *Peyton Place* address the issue of race within the novel. Wini Breines's exploration of postwar white girls' attraction to African American cultural forms highlights the novel's preoccupation with race. Her survey of postwar literature points out the fact that beyond its soft-core sexual content, *Peyton Place* demonstrates a consistent concern with race in the characters of Samuel Peyton, his white wife, Selena Cross, and Tom Makris. The article that most directly examines race in *Peyton Place* is an eleven-page conference paper by David Jones, "Blacks, Greeks and Freaks: Othering as Social Critique in *Peyton Place*." Here, Jones considers Metalious's characterization of Selena, Tom, and Samuel Peyton as evidence of her "interven[tion] in the matrix of representations that cast African Americans and ethnic minorities as marginal 'others'" (par. 3). Jones's work is an excellent starting point for an analysis of how race operates in *Peyton Place*, and it seeks to correct earlier misapprehensions of where the novel's charge and controversy lie.[10] My own analysis begins in full agreement with Jones's observations about how darkness is written into Metalious's work and extends the concerns with difference to include how *Peyton Place* uses and critiques whiteness against the dark backdrops it presents. I suggest that the relationship Jones sees between Samuel Peyton's castle and the novel's dark/ened characters is not limited to those characters alone but applies to her white characters as well. Adherence to America's cultural construction of race in all its forms produces pathological responses in its attendant project of vigilant and anxious boundary maintenance—the process of inclusion and exclusion by which national subjects are constituted. As an ever-present memorial to the dark history of the town's origins, a narrative the town actively represses but that is articulated by the Gothic structure on town's highest hill, Peyton's castle marks the story that Peyton Place will not tell about itself but can neither erase nor escape. The town's failure to incorporate its foundational narrative is coextensive with America's failure to fully acknowledge its own black identity by denying full subjectivity to its black citizens. Writ small upon the lives of the residents of a New England small town, the white supremacist culture that produced Samuel Peyton's anger and, in turn, his castle repeats its perversions upon Peyton Place's citizens. The town's anxiety about its civic origins arises from the same racist ideology that led Samuel Peyton to New Hampshire in the first place. The damage that results from a fear-induced impulse to deny that a black identity inheres within civic identities both local and national produces the multiple repressions and denials, the abuses and dysfunctions that characterize its citizens, its families, and the community as a whole.

## Approaching *Peyton Place* through Whiteness Studies

The problem for the town of *Peyton Place* is not that Peyton was black. The problem is that the town's white populace cannot deal with the fact that he was black. Nor do they seem to be able to deal with his having married a white Frenchwoman and his rumored willingness to aid the Confederate cause after having been shut out of the Boston housing market. The issue, then, is not Peyton's race, but the ideology that produces him and his story as a threat to whites, in other words, whiteness.

The pathological response to Peyton's story, the repressions it inspires, infiltrates the homes and lives of all of Peyton Place's residents. In its ability to produce such strains of shame and anxiety, it is emblematic of the "misery" to which David Roediger refers when he writes that his landmark study, *The Wages of Whiteness* "provid[es] some ways to consider not only how racial identity leads some whites to deal out misery to others but also how it leads them to accept misery for themselves" (xv). Whiteness, as a concept, "both names and critiques hegemonic beliefs and practices that designate white people as 'normal' and racially 'unmarked'" (Hartigan, qtd. in Garner, 5). It refers both to the phenomenon of being white and all that such a happenstance entails *and* to the analytical approach through which being white may be understood. More simply, the former is a state of being, the latter is a way of seeing, what Steve Garner calls the "whiteness problematic" (174).[11] The present study of *Peyton Place* examines how the various miseries of Metalious's characters are engendered by their positionality within a system of social practices and relationships that characterizes them according to white racial status, a system that damages them as a by-product of maintaining whiteness as a dominant/dominating paradigm.

Whiteness has been typically understood as the "unmarked marker" of race—to be white is to be associated with the one race distinguished for being widely characterized as not a race at all, for being a-racial. Whereas other figures throughout literary history have been written into positions of alterity through direct reference to the colors of their skin, white characters have been understood as white precisely because they are not otherwise described. Richard Dyer has theorized the paradox of whiteness, the race that represents itself as a-racial, and offers an explanation that suggests a reason for this habitual sin of omission:

> Whites must be seen to be white, yet whiteness as race resides in invisible properties and whiteness as power is maintained by being unseen. To be seen as white is to have one's corporeality registered, yet true whiteness resides in the non-corporeal. The paradox and dynamic of this are expressed in the very choice of white to characterise us. White is both a colour and, at once, not a colour and the sign of that which is colourless because it cannot be seen: the soul, the mind, and also emptiness, nonexistence and death, all of which form part of what makes white people visible as white, while simultaneously signifying the true character of white people, which is invisible. (45)

The frequency of this presumption in Western literature has secured, elevated, and reified the status of whiteness as norm. Considerable scholarship since Morrison first issued her call to action has sought to lay bare the politics of this assumption and has worked to interrogate how whiteness is de-racialized. Whiteness, Ruth Frankenberg writes, never functions on its own terms; rather it operates in tandem with, but not as an equivalency to, class and gender. This imbricated relationship is, she observes, "fundamentally asymmetrical, for the term 'whiteness' signals the production and reproduction of dominance rather than subordination, normativity rather than marginality, and privilege rather than disadvantage" (*White Women*, 236). This asymmetry has caused several scholars interested in interrogating whiteness as race no small amount of anxiety in their efforts to deconstruct whiteness without inadvertently (or inevitably, some would argue) re-centering it (as Frankenberg puts it), specifically, as the subject of the study of race and, more generally, reinvigorating its hegemonic power. In *The Color of Sex*, Mason Stokes catalogues a few of the qualifiers that accompany academic discussions of whiteness studies, perhaps the most curious of which was issued in 1997 by the editors of *Off White: Readings on Race, Power, and Society*. In carefully considering the impact of their project in the wider world, they write, "We worry . . . that there will follow a spate of books on whiteness when, in part, we (arrogantly? narcissistically? greedily? responsibly?) believe that maybe this should be the last book on whiteness" (Fine et al., xi). This sort of "end-of-discussion" proclamation, however earnest and qualified, is indeed worrisome in its presumption that their collective work should rise to the level of the last word on the matter. Only a decade earlier, Hazel Carby had called for "more feminist work that interrogates sexual ideologies for their racial specificity and acknowledges whiteness, not just blackness, as a racial categorization" (*Reconstructing*, 18). In *Playing in the Dark*, Toni Morrison suggests that an understanding of the uses of "literary 'blackness'" may best be understood through a careful interrogation of "the nature—even the cause—of literary 'whiteness.' What is it *for*? What parts do the invention and development of whiteness play in the construction of what is loosely described as 'American'?" (9). Stokes acknowledges that, to be sure, nothing is to be gained through an "unselfconscious approach" to interrogating whiteness, one that would certainly replicate the very problem it presumes to address. He wonders, however, about the consequences of too sharp a focus on the pitfalls of "whiteness studies"—an excess of self-reflexivity that also runs the risk of recapitulating the dominance of whiteness and that fails to take the conversation much beyond the problem of focusing on whiteness as a problem:

> what does it mean that the solution to this problem brings with it a reinscription of the problem itself—that our attempt to displace whiteness triggers a need to talk about the problems of such displacement, resulting in, at best, a narcissistic critical practice and, at worst, the critical paralysis called for and displayed by the editors of *Off White*? Is it really time to cease this talk of whiteness, to send whiteness back to the invisible center from which it came? Wouldn't that simply be the latest trick up whiteness's sleeve, a supremely ironic manifestation of its continuous ability to avoid the glare of the spotlight? (187)

Stokes eloquently foregrounds the double-edge of such acute self-consciousness, and I share his concern about such calls to inaction.[12] It is hard not to be aware of the challenges that go along with the academic study of whiteness. It is harder still to imagine that recoiling from the subject would serve any scholarly purpose beyond the retrenchment of the original terms of the conversation about race, which focuses exclusively on the significations of blackness at the expense of any critical investigation of how whiteness is a necessary partner in the construction, maintenance, and perpetuation of racial categories and differences.

Frankenberg, Carby, and others have suggested the importance of understanding race in conjunction with other social forces and phenomena often mentioned in the same breath but habitually treated as discrete from one another.[13] Race, sexuality, gender, class, ethnicity, and nationality neither operate in a vacuum nor independently of one another but interact as part of a concatenation of cultural forces at work in the world. Attempts to "read" or analyze women and blacks, for instance, as independent and monolithic categories fail to illuminate "the articulations of racism within ideologies of gender and of gender within the ideologies of racism" (Carby, *Reconstructing*, 25). Similarly, Vron Ware in *Beyond the Pale* observes, "black men, black women, white women, white men are all categories that have both racial and sexual connotations which can be further transformed or complicated by class" (11).

By the same token, just as race, class, and gender inflect and inform, influence and intersect with each other, a countervailing tendency also exists: to bring together concerns of race and class, to see them as more closely aligned with each other to the exclusion of gender. This, too, is problematic: it blurs the differences between race and class, and suggests that gender is of a higher order of concern. Not so, contends Anne McClintock, for whom race and class are not "sequentially derivative of sexual difference, or vice versa":

> Rather, the formative categories of imperial modernity are articulated categories in the sense that they come into being in historical relation to each other and emerge only in dynamic, shifting and intimate interdependence. The idea of racial "purity," for example, depends on the rigorous policing of women's sexuality; as an historical notion, then, racial "purity" is inextricably implicated in the dynamics of gender and cannot be understood without a theory of gender power. (61)

Following Kobena Mercer, McClintock reminds us to remain attentive to the various ways each category influences and alters the differences to which it ostensibly speaks. The risk otherwise is to "flatten out the complex and indeterminate spaces *between* relations of race, gender, ethnicity, and sexuality," thus denying additional richness and complexity in our awareness and experience of who we are (Mercer, 324).[14]

This middle grounding of these concerns—understanding race, class, gender, as well as ethnicity and nationality as inextricably linked to but still identifiable from one another—opens up a space for the productive examination and rich readings of the texts, a point foregrounded in the works of McClintock, Gayle Wald, and Stokes. Moreover, in his study of the powerful confluence of whiteness and heterosexuality, Stokes asserts "that whiteness works best—in fact, that it works only—when it attaches itself to other abstractions, becoming yet another invisible strand in a larger web of unseen yet powerful cultural forces" (13). This book also seeks to read by turns the construction, maintenance, deconstruction, and reconstruction of whiteness and its engagement with those other invisible forces to which Stokes refers. *Dirty Whites and Dark Secrets* investigates how these tropes are invoked in order to reveal how *Peyton Place* registers and intervenes in the construction of whiteness as a racial category.

The community of Peyton Place abides according to the terms of what Charles Mills has called the "racial contract," a social contract produced by and for white people, that structures, produces, and regulates a polity based on white hegemony. According to Mills, the racial contract "explains how society was created or crucially transformed, how the individuals in that society were reconstituted, how the state was established, and how a particular moral code and a certain moral psychology were brought into existence" (10). It also racializes space, "depict[ing] . . . space as dominated by individuals (whether persons or subpersons) of a certain race. At the same time, the norming of the individual is partially achieved by *spacing* it, that is, representing it as imprinted with the characteristics of a certain kind of space" (41–42). Persons are raced, space is raced, and raced space reifies the racing of persons in the first instance. An individual may be included or excluded from the raced identity of a space or place depending on the extent to which that individual embodies the characteristics of the place in question. The ex-slave Samuel Peyton, his story, and his castle appear to be "out of place" within the context of a New Hampshire town and its history. The artifacts of the New England village aesthetic, the white clapboard buildings, white picket fences, white church spires for which the region is well known, signify the "certain kind of space" to which Mills refers, a specific character or quality of space and place that is then imagined to be absorbed and reproduced by the inhabitants therein. These architectural features of small-town New England have served as symbols of the civic virtue, Yankee industry, and moral uprightness of local residents. According to Joseph Conforti, they

encoded the racial landscape of New England, which excluded slavery and blacks from the narratives of regional distinctiveness and republican ascendancy. . . . New England was consistently imagined as America's preeminent republic of free white industrious Yankees, a regional perception that rested on the counterimage of an indulgent, enslaved Africanized South. (200)

Peyton Place has the architecture and the landscape of a New England idyll and a New Hampshire small town; however, the lives portrayed within its pages speak to a more complicated set of circumstances than those contained in tourism bureau brochures. By deploying the standard markers of New England regional identity in the service of an African-ized North, Metalious races and spaces Peyton Place—its town and its characters—and in so doing, calls attention to the construction and main-tenance of racial identity at the individual, regional, and national level. In effect, Peyton Place's black history is not a regional anomaly but a product of America's racial contract, established within its foundational constitutional framework. Andy Doolen has argued that slavery and rac-ism were in fact enabled by the vision of America and American national identity enshrined by the Founding Fathers within the Constitution. "Slavery . . . is so thoroughly a part of the system that it is both the logi-cal effect of American constitutionalism and its sine qua non" (xvi), writes Doolen. The historical fact of slavery and the persistence of racism are evidence not of hypocrisy but rather irony and paradox. Doolen explains, "[T]he American rhetoric of equality was articulated not simply over and against an imperial logic of racial domination, but within that very logic. In the new republic, whiteness declared independence, using terror as its founding vocabulary" (xvi). White supremacy, then, is encoded in the DNA of American national identity. Peyton Place suggests that the repressions necessary for a program of racial dominance and exclusion of this scope, that is, the founding and functioning of a national republic, are damaging and give rise to a variety of dysfunctions. Within the novel, racism pro-duces the slavery that produces Samuel Peyton as a slave. It is responsible for his exclusion from the Boston housing market as a free black man and, in turn, leads Peyton to build the castle as his hermitage from white men. Furthermore, racism elicits the shame that the town exhibits over its black history, the shame that produces the tacit understanding that Pey-ton Place's story must not be told in order to reify the fiction, what Mills calls "an invented delusional world," of a fully white civic identity (18).

## Selena and the Slave Girl

In one of the several instances of illicit observation in the novel, Allison MacKenzie witnesses through a kitchen window the rape of her friend Selena Cross by her stepfather Lucas. Falling from the wooden crate on which she had been standing, and unable to "fight off the blackness that threatened her from every side," Allison becomes sick and passes out (57).

The scene remains unspeakable to her—she says nothing to Selena of what she knows; however, it is vividly recalled for her by an eye-catching illustration, "a book with a paper jacket showing a slave girl with her wrists bound over her head, naked from the waist up, while a brutal-looking man beat her with a cruel-looking whip. That, she concluded, was what had been in Lucas Cross's mind on the afternoon that she had stared through his kitchen window" (92). The comparison is a provocative one. It would be easy to assume that the girl depicted in the illustration is a black slave; and it is fair to suggest that in an American context this is a safe assumption. Based on what evidence exists within the given description, however, that would be assuming too much—no mention at all is made of the color of the slave girl's skin or that of her antagonist. Within the broader context of the novel, however, such a supposition would follow, as it is one of several associations the narrative makes suggesting the literal and figurative darkness of Selena Cross.

From the first chapter of *Peyton Place*, Selena is figured as dark and exotic, possessing a "dark, gypsyish beauty, her thirteen-year-old eyes as old as time" (7). Already, her skin color is made to suggest both ethnic difference and sexual allure, this despite the fact that she's white and thirteen. Women notice this, too. Allison's mother Constance had not fully understood what unsettled her about her daughter's friendship with Selena Cross. One afternoon in her dress shop, she discovers the source of her discomfort and disapproval when Selena appears in a gown Constance gave her to try on. "'She looks like a woman,' thought Constance. 'At thirteen, she has the look of a beautifully sensual, expensively kept woman'" (40). Constance attributes to Selena the sexual availability and awareness stereotypically associated with the combination of dark skin, femininity, and low-class status. Together, these position Selena outside of a moral code, which might in turn lead her to become someone's mistress, therefore threatening to the social order. Written into this position of alterity, Selena is the town's figurative, dusky other. Recalling the violent scene on the book jacket that attracts Allison's attention after witnessing Selena's rape, when Allison imagines Selena as the stand-in for the figure of the bare-breasted and bound slave girl portrayed in the illustration, the original figure is reified as black by association. The implicit darkness of the slave girl on the book jacket, when filtered through the logic constructed by the narrative and its references to the figurative (and relative) darkness of Selena Cross, becomes explicit through the complex chain of associations that lead Allison to imagine Selena in the slave girl's stead. If the figure on the cover was not necessarily black before the moment of Allison's imaginative fancy, she has become so in its wake, which in turn reiterates Selena's darkness and perpetuates a sort of closed circuit of darkening representations. And when Metalious describes Lucas as waxing rhapsodic about tying Selena up the first time he raped her (the episode Allison observed), the recursive relationship between Selena and the slave girl obtains.

Although it is quite clear throughout *Peyton Place* that a great deal of sympathy is given to Selena, Metalious is drawing on a long history and tradition of affiliating darkness with prurience. In *The Myth of Aunt Jemima: Representations of Race and Region*, Diane Roberts notes, "The white world drew the black woman's body as excessive and flagrantly sexual" (5), opposing it to the white woman's body, which was contained and aggressively chaste. In Edith Wharton's *The Age of Innocence*, for example, another novel about how a small community deals with its subterranean improprieties, a similar dichotomy is constructed between the Countess Ellen Olenska née Mingott and her cousin, May Welland. Ellen and May are cast as dark and light respectively, and in a dynamic not unlike that between Selena and the slave girl, Ellen's darkness is reiterated and reified through her affiliation with ethnic others throughout the novel. Anne MacMaster notes several instances of what she calls the "subtle replacement" of the novel's female protagonist, Ellen Olenska, with dark-skinned maidservants (195). On more than one occasion, when Newland Archer expects to meet Ellen, instead he finds "swarthy" and "foreign-looking" women in her place (Wharton, 44). The effect of these moments is a kind of darkness by association. Ellen has already been cast in the novel as "dusky" as compared to the alabaster whiteness of her cousin May. By replacing Ellen with these darker women, Ellen returns to the narrative darkened as a result of her affiliation with these "foreign" bodies. She becomes less figuratively and more literally the novel's dark heroine, drawn in sharp contrast to May's diaphanous lightness.

Like *The Age of Innocence*, *Peyton Place* opposes Selena to the more fair-skinned women around her. As the book darkens Selena, it also works to lighten Allison. There is what strikes me as a curious and frankly awkward moment attached to the earlier scene, an instance that works to iterate Allison's not-darkness against Selena's darkness, something of an obverse to the dynamic described above. Just after Lucas has torn Selena's shirt leaving her bare-breasted (like the slave girl in the illustration), and just before it registers with Allison what it is that is about to take place, Allison wonderingly notes to herself, "Why the ends of hers are *brown. . . .* And she does not wear a brassière all the time, like she told me!" (57).

Here, Allison seems to be seeing Selena's body in contrast to her own, one that isn't "brown" where Selena's is. The implication is that, for Allison, Selena's body is the anomaly where her own is the norm—normative enough in fact that its shadings and tintings need not be directly addressed. It is this point that is central to my argument. This project investigates what is at work in these and other moments that articulate racial difference. Part of this consideration will take into account the disturbance produced by such moments in the text. Returning to the example above, rather than expressing alarm at the escalating violence of the scene and Selena's vulnerability, Allison engages in an inappropriate interrogation of her friend's body and does so in an inappropriate way. In this critical instant, Allison assesses the physical difference between herself and her friend rather than sympathetically identifying with Selena, a girl cornered by a sexual predator.

The intrusive timing of Allison's base and self-absorbed response is unsettling, as is the distance it effects between herself and Selena. At least as discomforting is the apparent maleness of Allison's gaze, the evaluative scrutiny of her voyeurism. Metalious connects Allison's observation to Lucas's own during his forced confession to Doc Swain. Dreamily recalling for the doctor some of the details of the rape, Lucas tells him, "She's pretty, Selena is. She's got the prettiest pair of tits I ever seen, and the little ends was always all brown and puckered up" (160). However briefly, Allison and Lucas share in the same fixation on Selena's body. Although Lucas's observation comes about a hundred or so pages after Allison's, the reiteration of Allison's gaze in Lucas's recollection refers back to the rape scene Allison watched through the window. Again, where Allison should have been more closely identified with the imminent danger facing Selena, she instead inhabits a position closer to Lucas's point of view. The cumulative effect of such moments may account in part for the lack of critical attention given to *Peyton Place* so far. Though the scenes and dialogue given over to the actual sex in the novel are of the softest core on the continuum, the subtext with which it is conflated is edgier, more perverse, and more damning to readers who confront the pleasure they take in the novel. Similarly, the racial subtext of the novel and the manner through which it unmasks the production of racial categories may have disconcerted white readers of *Peyton Place* at the time of its original publication. Taking this into consideration, I suggest that *Peyton Place* functions as a cultural critique of the construction of whiteness. By exploring how characters are raced as white and not-white, with specific attention to how blackness becomes the repository for white anxieties wound tightly around sexuality, class, and gender, I aim to show how the scandal for which *Peyton Place* is renowned—its sex appeal—is inextricably linked (bound, if you will) to issues of race and its construction within the novel.

Although Metalious's characters operate under the assumption that whiteness is the norm and that darkness is the exception, the novel points to the constructedness of all racial categories, not just that of "others." As Ruth Frankenberg has noted,

> Jewish Americans, Italian Americans, and Latinos have, at different times and from varying political standpoints, been viewed as both "white" and "nonwhite." And as the history of "interracial" marriage and sexual relation-ships also demonstrates, "white" is as much as anything else an economic and political category maintained over time by a changing set of exclusion-ary practices, both legislative and customary. (*White Women*, 11–12)

The color line, as Frankenberg suggests, has a history of instability. Thomas Borstelmann illustratively demonstrates the vagaries of racial clas-sification through the Supreme Court's 1923 decision to classify persons from India "Caucasians" but not "white persons," a distinction that pre-vented Indian immigrants from achieving American citizenship (7). It is this very characteristic, its ability to recast and recognize groups formerly considered "nonwhite" into a category of white privilege that reveals that race is a cultural construct.[15]

In *Peyton Place*, the most prominently "raced" characters, Selena Cross, the olive-exotic, overripe beauty from the tar-paper fringe of town, and Tom Makris, the Greek interloper who comes to town to take over as principal for the Peyton Place schools, are not banished to an out-of-town oblivion by novel's end but rather are incorporated into its future. It is in the breaking down and remaking of Constance Mackenzie's character that *Peyton Place* most fully reveals the construction of whiteness. What Constance sees in Selena in the dress shop, "the beautifully sensual, expen-sively kept woman" is the truth of her own past, and what she finds suspi-cious about Selena is what she has ceased to acknowledge in herself—any trace of sexual being at all. Having returned to Peyton Place after the birth of Allison, the love child of her liaison with a family man whom she ad-mits she did not love, Constance manufactures and lives by a fiction of her own prudence and purity that removes her from the reach of potential suitors. Her reconstituted virginity, which the novel reveals as such early on by disclosing the history of her return, is annihilated by Tom Makris through what is essentially rape, an issue I will explore in more detail in chapter 3. After this point, Constance is effectively made whole in her dawning recognition that she likes and even desires sex. That the transformative moment is a sexual assault and its agent is a "dark-skinned, black-haired, obviously sexual" man (100) whose shoulders leave Constance "terror stricken" (111) reveals the ambivalence in the novel's cultural critique. *Peyton Place* seems, on the one hand, to offer a progressive alternative to the repressive cultural dictates that have coerced Constance into renouncing her sexual desire. In addition to rediscovering her libido, Constance marries the dark-skinned agent of her sexual reinitiation, legally altering her Anglo identity by replacing it with a Greek surname. On the other hand, the novel makes use of, in fact depends on, familiar tropes of white female virtue and oversexed and violent dark masculinity in order to effect Constance's sexual liberation. The chapters of *Dirty Whites and Dark Secrets* explore *Peyton Place* as a text that aggressively critiques cultural constructions of race. At the same time, they examine those moments in which the narrative is implicated in the racist discourse it attempts to critique.

By writing her story in the literal and figurative shadow of Samuel Peyton's castle, the hilltop ruins that served as Peyton's refuge from northern racism, Metalious seems to be, in Morrison's terms, "playing in the dark," participating in the white author's prerogative of establishing and manipulating a dichotomy of white and black. In her work, Morrison has attempted to tease out "signs, the codes, the literary strategies designed to accommodate this encounter" between whiteness and blackness and to understand the end result of this play upon a text (16). What she discovers is "the obvious": "the subject of the dream is the dreamer. The fabrication of an Africanist persona is reflexive; an extraordinary meditation on the self; a powerful exploration of the fears and desires that reside in the writerly conscious. It is an astonishing revelation of longing, of terror, of perplexity, of shame, of magnanimity. It requires hard work *not* to see this" (17). Here Morrison considers the white American writer's use of blackness, be it through characters or connotations, as a way of iterating and establishing the terms of white identity. Metalious does just this, writing her white characters in high relief against the black backdrop of their town's history. Following Morrison's lead, I maintain that *Peyton Place* is an American dream about white identity, a kaleidoscopic swirl of sexual anxieties and desires that are inexpressible on their own terms but displaced and reenvisioned through black or dark figures.

As much as *Peyton Place* is about sex, its sex is about race, which is about sex. I contend that by presenting a black backdrop against which the naturalness of white identity is investigated, *Peyton Place* is not simply participating in the long-established literary habit and history to which Morrison calls attention, but rather that the novel intervenes in the practice and questions the supposed truth behind such assumptions. For example, while Metalious uses "blondeness" to suggest "fairness" and all that it connotes, as she does when describing Constance MacKenzie, to be seen as "white" in her estimation appears to be a liability. The "white hands" of mill magnate Leslie Harrington and the "sheet of white paper" that characterizes the face of the town's cat lady, Hester Goodale, are each associated with the "emptiness, nonexistence, and death" that Richard Dyer understands as partly constitutive of the condition of being racially white. And yet, while *Peyton Place* frustrates the received wisdom of white identity at the time of the book's publication in 1956, Metalious is still caught up in the uses of black stereotypes in her attempts to do so. In this study I will show how individual characters in *Peyton Place* exhibit those "white" habits of longing, terror, and shame of which Morrison writes, and how the book itself became known for being a compendium of these elements among others. It is for this reason that I would argue that trafficking as it does in flesh, sex, and perversion, *Peyton Place* was so scandalous to readers and reviewers because of the extent to which it examines and exposes the artifice of race through those same soft-core taboos that enticed its readers between its sheets.

2

# The Color of Incest

## Sexual Abuse, Racial Anxiety, and the
## 1950s Family in Peyton Place

*Peyton Place* refers to three things at once: the blockbuster best-selling novel with the racy reputation, the town in which that novel is set, and the castle ("the Peyton place") that gives the town its name. Though the full telling of the story of the latter is held in abeyance until very near the novel's conclusion, the English castle erected on a New England hilltop by the escaped slave who founds the town haunts the narrative from beginning to end. As a permanent fixture of the town's landscape, Peyton's castle is the town's collective secret hiding in plain sight. The Peyton place memorializes the dark history, literal and figurative, that marks the town's origins. Castles, despite their size and architectural flourishes, are at heart family homes, and the Peyton place is no different. It was within the walls of this fortification that Samuel Peyton defensively established himself and his European wife after having been prevented from buying into the Boston housing market because of his race. Like the castles of gothic literature, Peyton's dwelling is indicative of a "failed" family (Ellis, ix); indeed, there are no Peyton offspring to inherit the castle following his death. As a result, it is willed to the state of New Hampshire and becomes a mighty husk of a home on the town's horizon. As the beneficiary of Peyton's property, the state becomes a legal surrogate for next of kin. In the absence of a next generation of Peytons, the families that propagate in the shadow of the looming gray edifice inherit the founding family's secret and find themselves troubled by all manner of their own. Scandalized by its own origins, the town collectively seeks to stanch the storytelling the castle threatens to inspire. Unable to do this, it betrays its own anxieties about civic ancestry and family relationships by similarly "failing" in the way of its families.

Samuel Peyton's castle acts as a floating signifier, registering the town's anxiety about the community's nonwhite history, threatening to speak the secrets of its failed families, refracting the idiosyncratic dysfunctions of individual Peyton Place residents. Though the repression that characterizes responses to the castle's enduring presence is produced by white racial anxiety to a black civic history, the structure itself is a product of the very anxiety it provokes within the community. Samuel Peyton, his story, and his castle are all products of the logic of a national program of white hegemony, as is the town's compulsion to maintain the fiction of its own whiteness by evading questions about its long-ago past. Peyton Place restages the racism that produced the story of Samuel Peyton in the first place by repressing that very narrative. The community of Peyton Place works to keep up appearances of a racially pure history by not acknowledging its progenitor, by eliding the details of his history and its own. The nature of this disavowal, the community's refusal to admit into public discourse what it knows to be true about itself, is of a piece with its unwillingness to address the familial dysfunction in town. Peyton Place's commitment to its white mythos is coextensive with its commitment to its domestic mythos.

Although we are told that there are no heirs to the Peyton estate, no reason for Peyton's lack of progeny is offered. We learn only that the state of New Hampshire inherits his property upon his death. Samuel and Violette Peyton's childlessness sets the stage for subsequent generations of Peyton Place residents for whom reproduction seems to have been hampered. Despite being a product of the 1950s, Peyton Place presents no examples of the iconic white nuclear American family of the decade. Instead, its small-town world offers an unsettling critique of the nuclear family ideal, what Stacey Stanfield Anderson has called "toxic togetherness," in which Metalious suggests that neither happiness nor safety nor security is ensured by the structure of the family or the space of the home. Considering Peyton Place within this context, I examine in this chapter the relationship between the racial anxiety motivating the town's repression of its foundational narrative and a reading of the Cross family and their racialization. I am particularly interested in Selena's darkness, her rape, her silence, and her return to the community in the wake of a very public spectacle of very private matters. Though Peyton Place is home to other families existing at a subsistence level, the Crosses are Metalious's case study of the inextricable effects of social and familial dysfunction. They are perhaps the most tragic portrait Metalious offers of a failed family, their household becoming the site of a long list of pathology and dysfunction that includes domestic abuse, alcoholism, incest, suicide, and homicide. The Cross family's disintegration and the public reckoning it entails as a result of the nature of its undoing—a jury trial for the killing in self-defense of an incestuous sexual predator within the home itself—catalyzes the community's confrontation with its class prejudice and, more subtly, but still significantly, its anxieties about race. Selena's murder trial is associated within the narrative with the final telling in full of the story of the town's origins, revealing its roots in racism, miscegenation, and treasonous subversion. By linking these two stories, Metalious intimates the danger with which each threatens the community while managing the threat of racial otherness in the end by assimilating Selena Cross into the future life of the town.

## Still Life with Family: The Fifties and the American Domestic Ideal

*Peyton Place*'s entrée into American culture coincided with the ongoing glorification of family life that had taken its unique shape following the end of World War II. As the bedrock institution in the Cold War against communism, the white American nuclear family ideal was very nearly an imperative for men and women who came of age during and immediately after the war. As the popular advice book *The Woman's Guide to Better Living* (1958) warned its many readers, "Whether you are a man or a woman, the family is the unit to which you most genuinely belong. . . . The family is the center of your living. If it isn't, you've gone far astray" (qtd. in Miller and Nowak, 147). To go astray in the 1950s was a dangerous undertaking indeed, as one risked being painted by the broad brush of deviance if one's lifestyle fell outside the narrow definitions of "normal." To a large extent, "the family" and one's relationship to it became the standard-bearer of normativity in the postwar era. Roles or behaviors that could not be reconciled with one's duties as a husband/father or wife/mother (e.g., homosexuality, extramarital or nonmarital sex, overly ambitious women in the workforce) cast an individual under a cloud of suspicion for subversion of the institution of the family itself, an act tantamount to treason.[1] The new and looming threat of nuclear war may be partially credited for this fortification of the American family and the collective retreat into the fortress of its homestead, along with anticommunist anxieties about infiltration and domestic subversion. "A home filled with children," Elaine Tyler May writes, "would create a feeling of warmth and security against the cold forces of disruption and alienation. Children would also be a connection to the future and a means of replenishing a world depleted by war deaths" (17). Similarly, Miller and Nowak attribute the "extreme exaggeration" (175) of postwar domestic ideology and practice to the atomic aftershocks of Hiroshima and Nagasaki. "[S]o resonant of Hitlerian evil," they write, the dawn of the atomic age "promised a long shock-filled future," one that came to pass in the form of the Cold War and its nuclear arms race; the development of the hydrogen bomb and its acquisition by the Soviets; and the loyalty program established in March 1947 by President Harry Truman's executive order, expanded by Dwight Eisenhower, and exploited along the way by Joseph McCarthy (152).[2] In addition to developments on the international stage, the recent memory of Depression-era and wartime domestic upheavals and the postwar prosperity that helped make homeowners of millions of Americans caused the nation's citizens to seek sanctuary within the family home, a space whose shape had shifted to enable and encourage more interaction among family members while sheltering them against a volatile Cold War world.

Marriage at this time was the sine qua non of normative adult behavior, and the family was the "most basic institution in society" (Coontz, 24). The extraordinary number of men and women who did get married during these years indicates the powerful cultural push to walk down the aisle: "96.4 percent of the women and 94.1 percent of the men" who grew up and/or out of adolescence in the immediate postwar era exchanged vows (May, 14). Newlyweds of all racial, ethnic, and class backgrounds married at younger ages and bore their children sooner and more closely spaced together than families of previous generations (May, i). Of course, it is the vision of the blissfully happy *white* nuclear family of the 1950s that has held tenacious sway over the American national imaginary ever since the days of Ozzie and Harriett, Donna Reed, the Cleaver family and *Dick and Jane*. The iconic image of a gray-flannel-suited husband and his unruffled wife in shirtwaist dress, heels, and pearls along with their contented and well-scrubbed, well-heeled children has been the calling card of moralists in recent years who have intoned that the so-called breakdown of the American family might be readily redressed if only we returned to the way it was then—the "traditional" family of the 1950s. In her important work debunking this mythic midcentury domestic past, social historian Stephanie Coontz has demythologized the postwar American family and revealed that nostalgia for "the way things used to be" has misrepresented the way they actually were for the nation's families at this time. Contrary to popular opinion, Coontz muses, " 'Leave It to Beaver' was not a documentary" (29).[3] Instead, the demographic shifts of the postwar era were a freak phenomenon that was not a return to tradition but rather a novelty that ran counter to patterns in marriage and childrearing that had established themselves over the course of the first half of the twentieth century. Both women and men married at younger ages. The average age of brides in 1950 was 20.3, down from 21.3; that year's crop of new husbands was on average four years younger than it had been twenty years earlier, saying its "I dos" by 22.8 (Weiss, 4). These new "young marrieds" entered parenthood sooner and had more children in shorter time than did previous generations: there were twice as many three-child families in 1960 than there had been in 1940 and three times the number of fourth children (Coontz, 24). The enthusiasm for founding and forming families was mitigated by tacit standards dictating at what age married couples should begin to reproduce. Similarly, the "boom" factor had its limits: too many (as well as too few) offspring were regarded with disdain (Coontz, 26; Weiss, 35).

This relative rush down the aisle and into the maternity ward led to a traditional domestic division of labor, the "neo-Victorianism" for which the 1950s is widely known, in which husbands fulfilled the breadwinner function and wives tended to children and housekeeping. The conservatism that the re-gendering of domestic labor and the demographic reversals speaks to is complicated by elements of domestic ideology that are often masked by the iconic "still life with family" image that informs popular (mis)conceptions of the midcentury American nuclear family. Although the drop in marital age may have been in part an effort by children of the Depression to find stability early in their young adult lives, it has also been suggested that early marriage enabled these men and women to satisfy their sexual desires legitimately, which is to say as husband and wife (Coontz, 39).[4] Encouraging young couples to tie the knot sooner rather than later would theoretically reduce the incidence of premarital sex and in the end encourage the American libido to behave in accordance with family values. According to this new ideological framework, "wives in the postwar era were recognized as sexual enthusiasts whose insistence on conjugal satisfaction would contribute to erotically charged marriages. Sexual containment—unlike sexual repression—would enhance family togetherness, which would keep both men and women happy at home and would, in turn, foster wholesome childbearing" (May, 89–90).[5] Once the marriage knot was tied, the cultural prohibitions against sexual expression and satisfaction were lifted for the nation's husbands and wives, and a well-exercised libido was encouraged for the overall health of the family unit. Though the ideology of sexual containment was powerful and pervasive and alternatives to the marriage imperative were virtually nonexistent, May suggests that many of the men and women who exchanged marriage vows at this time believed in what married life could offer them: "domestic security and happiness" and "a positive alternative to the lonely life of a single person" (22). Public opinion toward singles echoed the beliefs of social scientists, which held that such women would live and die "unfulfilled and miserable" and that single men were "psychologically damaged and immature" (22). Contrary to the decade's stuffy and thoroughly repressed reputation, the 1950s advocated and encouraged sexual intimacy (a pursuit that advances in birth control enabled by reducing the risk of unwanted pregnancies) as long as it was within bounds, circumscribed by the vows of marriage.[6]

While it is true that propaganda campaigns helped get white women into the workforce in the service of the war effort and then ushered them out again at war's end, Arlene Skolnick cautions against viewing these women as "passive victims" of media suggestion and cultural persuasion (67). Rather, Depression-era memories of fathers without jobs and mothers supporting the family lingered long in the lives of the nation's young adults after the war such that the topsy-turvy family configurations of the 1930s and 1940s, when husbands and fathers were overseas and women joined the war effort and the workforce, were "righted" in the 1950s. What might have resulted in a more balanced redistribution of domestic duties and responsibilities led instead to a more defined gendering of work within the family (67).

And yet, as this retrenchment of gender roles was under way, by 1952 there were more wives in the American workforce than at the height of Rosie the Riveter's renowned wartime reign. The caveat to this gesture toward sexual equality was, of course, that the work women were allowed to do was neither high-powered nor high-paying; nor was it permitted to be undertaken for the sake of career advancement or personal satisfaction. It was expected that a middle-class wife working for wages was doing so selflessly for the sake of the greater good of the family (Coontz, 31). The women Weiss refers to as "breadwinning brides" often worked to support their new husbands as the latter pursued higher education degrees. It was often the case that young women had to put their own educational aspirations on hold for many years of their family life as childrearing responsibilities that followed soon after marriage often prevented them from finishing college early in their adult lives. As a result, whereas women had been on a path to closing the education gap with men until World War II, the gap began to widen in the years immediately following its end. Furthermore, minority and working-class women had no choice but to work in order to make ends meet, as they always had. The role of stay-at-home wife and mother was not open to them.

These apparent contradictions belie the conventional wisdom regarding the postwar American nuclear family. Marriage at this time became the site of what Weiss has called "contested egalitarianism," the attempt of couples to negotiate familial roles and responsibilities that hearkened back to gendered spheres of influence while at the same time attempting to establish more democratic partnerships along the lines of the couple-centered companionate marriage ideal of the 1920s (16–17).[7] The gravitational pull of domestic life involved not just mothers in childrearing but fathers as well. The uniting of both parents in pursuit of recreation, fun, and fulfillment as a family unit was encapsulated in the idea of "togetherness." First introduced into the national lexicon in the May 1954 issue of *McCall's*, "togetherness" was both the key ingredient in the recipe for a happy family and the doctrine by which the American family was advised to abide. The editorial that coined the term took note of the decline in the marriage age, the increase in fertility rates, and the affluence that elevated more Americans into middle-class status than ever before, declaring that the nation's families had embarked on a "new and warmer way of life, not as women *alone* or men *alone* isolated from one another but as a *family* sharing a common experience" (Wiese, 27, emphasis in original). The family had become a centripetal force, drawing its members closer to one another, enjoining them in the pursuit of a common bliss through the practice of mandatory fun as an ensemble. The bounty of material comforts and recreational enhancements that were becoming standard within the postwar home—modern kitchens, television sets, time-saving appliances, and, for the suburban homeowner, backyard barbeques—enabled the 1950s family to meet very nearly all of its physical, emotional, and recreational needs within the parameters of its own picket fence (May, xxii).

Togetherness, however, had its downside. The pursuit of romantic partnerships in marriage had been displaced by the demands of raising young children, often several at once (Weiss, 116). In addition, togetherness placed the burden for personal happiness and satisfaction almost entirely within the domestic sphere (and upon women to make it happen) while diminishing the importance of extrafamilial relationships: "When the family cannot make good on its promise," social historian Laura Miller writes, "all its members can do is hope to join a new and better familial unit" (411). The isolationist impulse of togetherness took its toll: tranquillizer use, which had barely registered on the cultural radar in 1955, skyrocketed to 1.15 million pounds by 1959 (Coontz, 36); and in 1956, the same year that *Peyton Place* arrived on the nation's bookshelves, "at the peak of togetherness, the bored editors of *McCall's* ran a little article called 'The Mother Who Ran Away.' To their amazement, it brought the highest readership of any article they had ever run" (Friedan, 50). In its most damaging form, togetherness provided a smokescreen for domestic violence and child abuse, exploiting its isolationism for the sake of tyrannical abuses of power. Women and children were often victims of the extreme privacy that such an approach to family life espoused. In *Peyton Place*, "the home is no shield from the dangers of the outside world, but a tightly sealed trap" that threatens its captives with physical and psychological harm (Anderson, par. 9). Indeed, the "tender trap" of marriage and family proved to be a site of treachery for many.

## Domestic Dissonance: *Peyton Place*'s Failed Families

*Peyton Place* emerged in the thick of the postwar exaltation and embrace of nuclear family life and presented an alternative to those visions of the white, middle-class American family that were being beamed into the nation's living rooms during prime time. Although the novel spans nine years from the Depression into World War II (1936–44), it challenged the overarching ideology of Cold War domesticity by lacking any traditional examples whatsoever of the version of the white nuclear family ideal that rose to prominence in the 1950s. The world of *Peyton Place* is one of damaged and broken or incomplete families. This domestic dysfunction is pervasive, running along a continuum from bad to worse and cutting across the town's socioeconomic lines, from mill owner Leslie Harrington to the Cross family in the town's shack district. Mothers and fathers are missing or dead, and few parents have more than one child. A survey of the novel's most prominent characters reveals the following: Leslie Harrington has driven his wife to an early death and shares single-parent status with Constance MacKenzie and Evelyn Page; the union of Nellie and Lucas Cross is an ill-starred second marriage for both of them, each having lost their first spouses to early deaths. Charles and Marion Partridge are childless, as are Doc Swain (a widower) and Kenny and Ginny Stearns (the town drunk and the town's good time girl). Schoolteacher Elsie Thornton; newspaper editor Seth Buswell; and Hester Goodale, the town's gothic cat lady, have led ever-single lives. And Allison, Norman Page, Rodney Harrington, Ted Carter, and Kathy Ellsworth (Allison's best friend following Selena's pairing off with Ted Carter) are all only children. The striking lack of large families in town suggests a breakdown in the postwar domestic imperative. Metalious notes this unusual state of affairs almost as soon as she introduces the town's moneyed class, the Harringtons, Doc Swain, the Partridges, and Seth Buswell among them:

> "Seems funny, don't it?" said the townspeople, some of whom lived, with many children, in cramped quarters, "that the biggest houses on Chestnut Street are the emptiest in town."
> "Well, you know what they say. The rich get richer, and the poor get children." (20–21)

Indeed, the Cross family, among the poorest of the town's citizens, inhabits "cramped quarters" on the other end of town from Chestnut's stately homes; however, the children living there number only two: Selena and Joey. Of the families Metalious presents, the Crosses are the only one whose numbers nearly approximate the typical postwar family average of 5.4 members: two parents, Lucas and Nellie; and three children, Lucas's son Paul (who leaves home early in the novel), Nellie's daughter Selena, and Joey, their son together. Betty Anderson, the daughter of a mill hand, is the only other sibling in the novel; her sister is mentioned only in passing as an example of a girl who "got into trouble." While the Cross and Anderson families may be the most populous of those discussed in the novel, even marked as they are by their socioeconomic status, they defy the classist stereotype of the quip above by falling below the total number of members for the average American family during the baby boom years.

A good case has already been made for Metalious's critique of the 1950s family ideal by Stacey Stanfield Anderson. "Toxic Togetherness" suggests how the national impulse to huddle at home with one's closest kin left a door open to various perversions of family relations. *Peyton Place*, Anderson writes, reveals "the ease with which [togetherness] concealed destructive family dynamics from the outside world" (par. 1), a dynamic destruction manifest most tragically in the case of the Cross family.[8] Although the forces that conspired in togetherness ideologically circumscribed the family as a social unit against the outside world and enabled domestic and child abuse, it may be a mistake to suggest that they "concealed" family dysfunction from outside observers. One female participant in a long-range study of American family life from the 1950s to the 1980s was a victim of domestic violence who tried, often unsuccessfully, to shield her children from her husband's abuse. She recalled the reluctance of her neighbors to intervene, remarking, "I can't say I blame the neighbors. They wouldn't come. They didn't want to get involved" (qtd. in Weiss, 137). The town of Peyton Place is very well aware of Lucas Cross's debauchery; his participation in a six-week basement drinking binge ends with his capture above ground in the presence of a crowd of local onlookers. The town expresses pity for Selena and Joey, who are on hand for the scene; however, its acknowledgment of their hard lot fails to mobilize any assistance or protection in their behalf, dismissing their endangerment with the summary judgment, "Well, that's the shackowners for you" (87). And the scene is all too easily forgotten in the tumult surrounding Selena's confession to Lucas's murder: the pendulum of the town's inert sympathies swings from Selena to Lucas, whose role as a "provider" for the family outweighs the open secret of his violence against Nellie and his legendary intemperance. Rather than guaranteeing the mutual protection of its members, the Cross family's geographic and economic marginalization among the town's tar-paper shacks favors Lucas rather than assuring protection to Nellie, Selena, and Joey. The family's "privacy" is a side effect of the town's unwillingness to directly address the dangers posed to minors in the care of a known wife batterer. The view into the Cross family, then, is only partially obscured, and the collective turning of a blind eye to the troubles that occasionally spill into public view leaves room for the violence of the Cross household to escalate to the level at which one of its members is compelled to kill in self-defense.

## Darkness on the Edge of Town

Like Samuel Peyton's castle, the Cross home is geographically marginalized on the fringes of town and is the object of a collective repression that seeks to deny its existence as part of the community. This denial of both Peyton and families like the Crosses is linked also to the fact that both threaten the ideological whiteness that is at the heart of Peyton Place's vision of itself. Though they are in fact racially white, Richard Dyer explains,

> Working-class and peasant whites are darker than middle-class and aristocratic whites. . . . Colour distinctions within whiteness have been understood in relation to labour. To work outside the home—literally out of doors but also away from the values of domesticity—is to be exposed to the elements, especially the sun and the wind, which darken white skin. In most hierarchi-

cal social systems, however much the toiler may be lauded in some traditions, the very dreariness and pain of their labour accords them lowly status: Thus to be darker, though racially white, is to be inferior. (57)

The Cross family has not been singled out for erasure. Rather, it is a matter of course to ignore the crushing poverty of the town's poorest residents, the standard midcentury practice of rendering the most socioeconomically disadvantaged "socially invisible" (Harrington, 3). Commenting on the contrasts between the nation's postwar haves and have-nots, one economist observed that while "[m]ost Americans never had it so good . . . [p]ossibly 15 to 20 percent have it as bad as ever" (Lekachman, 190). Lack of social programs to help the poor meant that the nearly fifty million people in the United States who lived below the poverty line in the mid-1950s were left to fend for themselves (Coontz, 29). Metalious observes this attitude and its effects in her small town, remarking, "If a child died of cold or malnutrition, it was considered unfortunate, but certainly nothing to stir up a hornet's nest about. The state was content to let things lie, for it never had been called upon to extend aid of a material nature to the residents of the shacks which sat, like running sores, on the body of northern New England" (29). Metalious's comparison of the shacks to open wounds on the body of the local landscape suggests both their unsightliness and their susceptibility to infection. It is a situation that, if left untended, could spread to the rest of the "body of northern New England." It is precisely this danger that prompts Doctor Matthew Swain to support newspaper editor Seth Buswell in his opinion that zoning the shacks would benefit the community as a whole. "They're cesspools," he declares, "as filthy as sewers and as unhealthy as an African swamp. . . . No toilet, no septic tank, no running water, eight people in one room and no refrigeration. It's a wonder that any of those kids ever live long enough to go to school" (23). The public health risk is too great to ignore, Swain insists: an outbreak of disease on the order of typhoid or polio in the shacks would endanger the entire community (23–24). Swain's pointed comparison of the shacks to "an African swamp" racializes them, linking these homes and their inhabitants to darkness, danger, disease, and disorder.

Located on the margins of town, existing on the lowest socioeconomic rung of the community, the Cross family is an abject entity, "something rejected from which one does not part" (Kristeva, 4). Like the anonymous others to whom Doc Swain refers above, the Crosses are at once cast out of and caught within the community's outermost limits of space and of civic life, privileged to pay their bills and their taxes but not necessarily protected by the law. Selena cynically makes this point to herself as she reviews her decision to remain silent about her sexual abuse: "[A] shack dweller never goes to the law. . . . A good shack dweller minds his business and binds up his own wounds" (337). Abjection incorporates repression as constitutive of its condition. It is by definition denied and displaced, cast out and yet inhabiting and marking the margins of society:

> Abjection traces the silhouette of society on the unsteady edges of the self; it simultaneously imperils social order with the force of delirium and disintegration. . . . [T]he expelled abject haunts the subject as its inner constitutive boundary; that which is repudiated forms the self's internal limit. . . . Abjection . . . is that liminal state that hovers on the threshold of body and body politic. (McClintock, 71–72)

The Cross home itself is an abject space directly "imperiling the social order with the force of delirium and disintegration," with the force of the secrets that breach its boundaries and become a public scandal. Kristeva states that "abjection is above all ambiguity" (9). The surname *Cross* itself suggests ambiguity and hybridity, as well as a burden to be endured. In addition, it suggests traversal, a crossing of borders and boundaries. Lucas, Nellie, and Selena variously embody these definitions in their contingent racializations, their variant whiteness and darkness, as does the domestic space they inhabit.

The Cross dwelling is as much a hovel as it is a home: a one-room shack without indoor plumbing or refrigeration. With neither a septic system nor sewerage, Lucas, Nellie, Paul, Selena, and Joey Cross live by the light of a single incandescent bulb (23, 161). Allison MacKenzie, though a longtime friend of Selena, has never been invited into Selena's home. When Allison does get an accidental peek into the interior through the kitchen window, she is riveted:

> So *this* is what the inside of a shack looks like, thought Allison, fascinated. Her eyes took in the unmade cots and the sagging double bed and the dirty dishes which seemed to be strewn from one end of the room to the other. She saw a garbage can in one corner which had not been emptied for a long time, and on the floor next to it was an empty can that had once held tomatoes and one that had contained beans. Lucas was sitting at a table that was covered with a streaked oil cloth so old and filthy that the pattern in it was no longer discernible, and Selena was filling a coffeepot from a pail of water,

with a long-handled dipper. Allison thought of the houses in town that Nellie Cross kept spotless, and she remembered the food she had eaten in various homes that had been cooked by Selena's mother. (54–55)

The space is disordered, unclean, unsanitary. It is open, without boundaries and therefore without privacy. This room, which constitutes the whole of the Crosses' living quarters, lacks proper domestication, as there are no physical divisions designating public versus private space. All of the family's activities, including sex between Lucas and Nellie, take place in the open room. This is the antithesis of the "felicitous space" of house and home, "the space we love," the "eulogized space" upon which Gaston Bachelard's meditation *The Poetics of Space* is based (xxxv). Minrose Gwin writes against Bachelard's idealized vision of the relationship between domestic interiority and psychological interiority by drawing attention to the dangers that the home can contain and filter from the view of the outside world. "What happens," she asks, "when the space of 'home' becomes nonfelicitous? The space of the unspeakable? What happens when the unspeakable is spoken? When the house's ideology of purity is contaminated by another story?" (75). Instead of protecting and nurturing its inhabitants, at its worst, "the notion that the 'home' signals safety and protection is a claim that is not only wrong but complicitous with sexual violence" (Alcoff and Gray, 276 ). The conditions under which the Crosses live provide a partial answer to Gwin's question. Living too much together in impoverished circumstances, the cramped and boundariless interior of their home creates an excess of inappropriate intimacy between family members and enables what ranks among the most improper of domestic relations, the incestuous sexual assault of a parent upon a child. The unboundedness of the Cross home has tragic consequences for Selena especially, as she is unable to escape Lucas's rapes when they begin in her early adolescence. Lucas's disregard for both personal boundaries and the incest prohibition lead him to target Selena as an appropriate victim of his violent sexuality. The home's lack of privacy provides him ease of access.

In addition to the metaphor of contagion with which the Cross home and others like it are racialized through Doc Swain's "African swamp" simile, members of the Cross household are also shaded by the extremity of their poverty. Because she and her family live well below the poverty line, Nellie Cross must work outside of her home in order to survive. She earns her living as a housekeeper in the town's middle- and upper-class homes, and her proficiency at domestic work has earned her the reputation of being "the best house worker in Peyton Place" (131). Her work sends her across class lines and into the living spaces of the town's more privileged residents, where her labor orders and organizes these interiors. The process of setting other homes in order may be understood as part of a larger project of "boundary maintenance." As Anne McClintock explains, "Cleaning is not inherently meaningful; it creates meaning through the demarcation of boundaries. Domestic labor *creates* social value, segregating dirt from hygiene, order from disorder, meaning from confusion" (170). The bodies that mediate dirt, those that are charged with its removal, both establish boundaries and thwart them, as their mobility challenges the fixity of the "limits" of cleanliness, order, and meaning. Dirt itself is neither good nor bad—dirt just is. As Mary Douglas has famously reasoned, "There is no such thing as absolute dirt: it exists in the eye of the beholder. If we shun dirt, it is not because of craven fear, still less dread of holy terror. Nor do our ideas about disease account for the range of our behavior in cleaning or avoiding dirt. Dirt offends against order. Eliminating it is not a negative movement, but a positive effort to organise the environment" (2). It is in the process of organizing the environment and establishing boundaries in order to manage dirt that its value "develops," that dirt becomes dirty. Writing of the Victorian era, McClintock finds that the presence of hired help within the home was evidence of multiple crossings "of private and public, home and market, working and middle class." Such traversals inspired an anxious response by the middle-class to the contacts that these arrivals and departures produced. Domestic workers became affiliated with "images of disorder, contagion, disease, conflict, rage and guilt," leading, McClintock asserts, to the racialization of the home "as the rhetoric of degeneration was drawn upon to discipline and contain the unseemly spectacle of paid women's work" (165).

Given the description of the Cross home as littered with empty tomato cans, trash bins blossoming with garbage, and grimy tabletops, it would be hard to argue that it couldn't use a good tidying up. However renowned for her work of ordering and cleaning other people's homes, Nellie's efficiency does not transfer to her own housekeeping, a detail Allison notes as she gazes through the kitchen window. Allison's view of the unkempt chaos of the Cross interior contrasts with her memory of the well-scrubbed homes Nellie is paid to keep clean. The dirtiness and disorder of Nellie's own home is matched by her appearance: her body bears the traces of her labor, transporting the dirt she accumulates in other people's homes from those spaces into her own. Metalious describes her as "short and flabby with the unhealthy fat that comes from too many potatoes and too much bread. Her hair was thin and tied in a sloppy knot at the back of her not too clean neck, and her hands, perpetually grimy, were rough and knobby knuckled, with broken, dirty fingernails" (31). She is soft (the result of a subsistence diet), sloppy, unclean, and poorly manicured. Her body resembles the Bakhtinian grotesque in its "open unfinished nature, its interaction with the world" (Bakhtin, 281). The dirt with which Nellie comes into contact affixes itself to and travels with her; however, it does not seem to trouble the interiors in which she is employed for wages, only her own. Her body's lack of closure is rather graphically manifest in the manner in which she imagines her body as she loses her mind. Nellie thinks she is suffering from gonorrhea, which she believes she contracted "off her husband, like any decent woman should" (228).[9] There is some uncertainty as to whether or not Nellie is, in fact, afflicted as she claims, as she begins to lose her mind shortly after overhearing Lucas's graphic confession to Doc Swain of his rapes of Selena. Her descent into madness is signified in part by the position she assumes on the floor of the MacKenzie kitchen on what becomes her last day of work, the day she hangs herself in Allison's closet. To Nellie, "it seemed perfectly natural to her to sit calmly on the kitchen floor . . . resting her feet which ached from standing too long in one place" (227). This position of abasement also marks the extent of her abjection: dirt-laden on a clean floor. Caroline Hellman reads this scene as further evidence of Nellie's othering, as she might have chosen to rest in a room designed for such purposes had she felt she deserved it (par. 40). Nellie's physical and visual appearance contrast with the order of the rooms and the cleanliness of the surfaces around her, organized through her own labor, and mark her difference through dirtiness, which Hellman links to dark otherness (par. 38).[10] Nellie's body remains unbounded even after her death. The Catholic church will not bury her because she has committed suicide, and the Congregational church refuses to do so for the same reason (although in this case it is because the Reverend Fitzgerald is a closeted Catholic, who, soon after refusing Nellie a proper burial, makes his confession to Father O'Brien, resigns his position, and leaves town). Risking putrefaction from remaining above ground, Nellie is rushed to rest under the auspices of the newly established Pentecostal church in town. Fittingly enough, the proximity of her grave to Peyton Place's factories means that "[s]moke and soot hovered over it continually and the ground was hard and bare" (244). Nellie's burial marks her permanent marginalization from, and final degradation by, the community.

## "A Corruption of Public Discourse"

In the short list that Metalious provides of a small town's three sources of scandal, "suicide, murder, and the impregnation of an unmarried girl," incest is not among them (241). Strikingly, all four of these take place within the Cross family. The absence of incest on *Peyton Place*'s list of scandals may be explained by the long-held belief that incest was a "one-in-a-million occurrence" (Cameron, xi) and that, given the fraction of that number of people who make up the population of Peyton Place, that "one" was not likely to live among them.[11] The rarity of incest is, of course, a fallacy. Studies since the mid-1950s have revised the number significantly, such that more recent data place the incidence of father-daughter incest at a rate of 1 in 22 females (Wilson, 36). This radical revision testifies to the widespread denial of incest in U.S. culture. Stories of incest have long been among the hardest to tell and the least likely to be heard. Incest is clearly scandalous; however, there is no cause for scandal if the stories are silenced. The cultural denial of incest, the unimaginable unmentionable of family life, enables the community to exist under the false assumption that "it can't happen here." But, in fact, it does, and not just in the Cross home. For example, Allison MacKenzie "nurs[es] an unnatural affection for her deceased father" while Evelyn Page "fosters an abnormally intimate attachment to her son" (Anderson, par. 9).[12]

Incest is not, Metalious suggests, an automatic by-product of poverty; it is, rather, the result of a cultural consensus that conspires to deny that such things happen at all. As Anderson observes, "the story that a town like Peyton Place tells about itself has no space for disturbing counternarratives that define families like the Crosses. Indeed, the wholesome cultural narrative of family togetherness relies on girls like Selena to suffer in silence rather than risk public humiliation" (par. 41). And it is this same collective impulse to repress the "disturbing counternarratives" about the family that motivates the town's repression of race in Peyton Place. The "wholesome cultural narrative" that Selena's story disrupts is also violated by the town's originary family: an interracial couple who produced no children. In both cases, the community pursues and maintains a fantasy of its own white identity, past and present.

When victims of sexual abuse did step forward, their stories were frequently dismissed as the product of overactive imaginations or, when viewed through a psychoanalytic lens, that of wishful thinking, the manifestation of a daughter's desire to sleep with her father (Coontz, 35). For a short time around the turn of the twentieth century, however, before the dominance of psychoanalysis, child welfare workers did listen to and hear what victims of incest had to say. Linda Gordon's work, which investigates case histories of incest in the Boston area from 1880 to 1960, reveals that girls and women did bring incidents of sexual abuse to the attention of local social workers. Ignoring cultural codes that encouraged female passivity and docility, these women actively sought intervention on their own behalf, and, in some cases, the offenders were punished. By 1960, however, female incest victims were caught in the crosshairs of the dominance of psychoanalytic interpretations of incest as well as the postwar sex panic in which perverts and perpetrators were imagined as anonymous others existing outside the home, and not as family members inhabiting a common and too-intimate space. As a result, girls who brought charges of incest were recast as "sex delinquents," themselves the agents of perversion, because such reports assailed the culturally mandated harmony of the home and struck at the heart of the family (Doane and Hodges, 20).

Freud's theory of infantile sexuality had the pernicious effect of suggesting that all underage victims of sexual abuse invited the violations they claimed to have suffered. In cases of parent-child incest, children, according to acolytes of psychoanalysis, were considered culpable and bore responsibility for their involvement in the incestuous relationship. In a 1936 report recommending the psychiatric evaluation of those victims of sexual abuse who reported their experiences, the American Bar Association warned that "the erotic imagination of an abnormal child of attractive appearance may send a man to the penitentiary for life" (qtd. in Pleck, 156). Psychiatrists alleged that in many cases of incest, "the child may have been the actual seducer rather than the one innocently seduced" (Bender and Blau, 514), in which case the logic held that "there was no moral or legal problem" and offenders were effectively blameless, leaving them in a position to continue their assaults virtually risk-free (Pleck, 157).

Psychoanalytic explanations of incest as oedipal fantasy and fabrication did not, of course, change the fact that sexual abuse was a reality in many families. The typical family dynamic in cases of father-daughter incest was that of an exaggerated patriarchy in which the father wields an excess of dictatorial power within the household; the mother is "absent" either literally or figuratively, leaving her children vulnerable to the father's whims; and the female child is forced into the role of surrogate wife (Doane and Hodges, 19). Writing against the belief that female incest survivors were Lolita-like nymphets whose nubile sensuality invited sexual advances by adult males unable to resist their temptations, Judith Herman and Lisa Hirschman emphasized the indisputable fact that in a patriarchal society, the power differential "between father and daughter, adult male and female child, is one of the most unequal relationships imaginable. It is no accident that incest occurs most often precisely in the relationship where the female is most powerless" (47). By the 1970s, feminists began to argue that because incest was much more common than once imagined, the prohibition against it was clearly not in its commission but in the telling (Fischer, 96). More than the act itself, Louise Barnett writes, "bringing it to light was the greater scandal, a corruption of public discourse" (22).

The belief that the problem of incest was represented disproportionately among poor and nonwhite populations was well established among the white middle class in the postwar era and contributed to the silencing of such stories at many levels. The myth that incest was a domestic affliction of the poor meant that there was little urgency devoted to dealing with it. In addition, in ascribing its incidence to an underclass and to racialized others, the white middle class reaffirmed its moral superiority over such groups, whose purported predilection for incest and other forms of sexual deviance was taken as evidence of inherent and categorical degeneracy. For the white middle class, then, reports of incest were freighted with the threats of class degeneracy and racial contagion; to acknowledge them would challenge its moral high ground as well as its claims to promoting and protecting children's welfare. "Incest charges," writes Elizabeth Wilson, "undermine these claims and therefore constitute a threat from within" (41). Significantly, Diana Russell's important work in the early 1980s on the incidence of incest revealed that incest is no more likely to occur in low-income homes than in middle- and upper-class homes. Moreover, Wilson states, "depending on how class is calculated, incest is either evenly distributed over the class spectrum or it is relatively *more* frequent in the middle- and upper classes" (41).[13] The actual "location" of incest notwithstanding, the tenacity of the misinformed assumption that intrafamilial rape is characteristic of marginalized populations also has the effect of repressing charges of incest within those communities. Doane and Hodges write that stories of incest in black families were often silenced by blacks in order to avoid corroborating stereotypes of African American sexual depravity: The "social discretion" that suppresses these stories is a "form of silence . . . that tacitly supports racialized, patriarchal prerogatives," the prerogatives that enable the incest to occur in the first place (32). As in the white middle class, resistance to hearing reports of incest suppresses the telling of those stories, which in turn reinforces the power structure that protects abusers instead of the abused. In lower-class or African American households, female victims are even less likely to gain protection against incest owing to the articulations of class and race upon the gendered position of the girl in American society. Thus, according to Cheryl Wall, "In a society ordered by hierarchies of power based on race, class, and gender, no one is more powerless, hence more vulnerable, than a poor black girl" (3).

## The Color of Incest

Though she is not in fact black, Selena Cross's perpetually "honey tan" skin, the darkness of her hair and eyes, and the "startling" whiteness of her teeth emphasize her difference from the normative whiteness of Peyton Place's residents. Her darkness is not simply a social anomaly; it is apparently a genetic anomaly as well. Neither Nellie nor her half-brother Joey shares her skin tone, and the brief mention of her biological father suggests nothing whatsoever to connect her tawniness to him (130). Selena is, in fact, the darkest-skinned resident in town until the arrival of Tom Makris, after which time she remains Peyton Place's duskiest female. It is also widely agreed that Selena is stunningly beautiful, with the exoticized features of "everybody's idea of a perfect gypsy" (31). She is also physically mature for her age, "with the curves of hips and breasts already discernible under the too short and often threadbare clothes that she wore" (31).

Coupled with the difference of her darkness, Selena is further marked as "other" by virtue of her class status. She is a resident of the town's shack district whose homes are "tumble-down, lean-to, makeshift" affairs lacking in many of the most basic of modern conveniences. The shacks are structures reputed to be bursting at the seams with too many people in too small a space, where alcoholism and domestic violence and child abuse are said to be the norm (29). With the exception of its average size, Selena's family is marred by these things: her stepfather's drinking is legendary; her mother is the frequent target of his violent temper; and Selena is sexually assaulted, violently and repeatedly, by Lucas beginning at age fourteen. Following Cheryl Wall's observation above, then, Selena Cross is the most vulnerable to abuses of power and least likely to find assistance given her position as a wretchedly poor, dark-skinned girl.

Selena's sensuality is natural and unaffected, and she herself seems unaware of her beauty. Unlike Betty Anderson, a mill worker's daughter not quite as abjectly poor as Selena but physically mature and sexually active, Selena is chaste. She enters into a steady romance with Peyton Place's golden boy, Ted Carter, and though she jokes about being a hot-blooded girl from the backwoods (aware of the class-based stereotype), she and Ted have decided to wait until they marry to have sex (139). Constance MacKenzie's impression of Selena after seeing her in the white party dress—that of a "beautifully sensual, expensively kept woman" (40)—is in fact much closer to the truth of Constance's past as the mistress of an established New York family man than to Selena's present.

The scene of intimate violation that Allison MacKenzie observes through the Cross's kitchen window, discussed in chapter 1, is set in a domestic dystopia of material want and despoilment, dingy with neglect and messy with matter out of place. She senses in Lucas a "sly and evil something" (55) as she watches him watching Selena preparing a pot of coffee in a domestic tableau that is consistent with the roles mapped out in families where incest takes place. His repeated pronouncement that Selena has become "quite a gal" hints at his sexual desire for her. It is Selena's expressed disapproval at his throwing a freshly drained liquor bottle on the floor, her affront to his paternal authority, that sends him into a rage. If there was any doubt as to the intention brewing behind Lucas's observation that Selena was "gettin' to be quite a gal," his predatory designs seem certain when Selena breaks free of his grip and accidentally tears her blouse, a move that leaves her naked from the waist up. As he closes in on her, preparing to bear down on her with his "grimy hands" and "grotesque smile," Selena screams, a summons answered by the seven-year-old Joey Cross, who rushes in to protect her. He, like Selena, is clearly outmatched in size and strength, "and like a horse swishing his tail, Lucas Cross swept him away" leaving Joey lying "still on the floor of the shack." Lucas repeats his now overt sexual assessment of Selena, "Yep. Gettin' to be quite a gal, ain't you honey" and the scene fades to black, literally, with Allison's rush of nausea as she stumbles from her perch into unconsciousness (57).

When Lucas's repeated rapes of Selena result in her pregnancy, Selena turns to Doc Swain for help in the form of an abortion. Doc Swain is the moral center for the community, a beloved and curmudgeonly elder who believes in protecting lives, not taking them. When Seth Buswell jokes that an epidemic would rid Peyton Place of its tar-paper blight, stating with some conviction that "perhaps the town would be better off without the characters who live in those places," Swain retorts without hesitation, "There is nothing dearer than life, Seth. Even the lives being lived in our shacks" (25–26). Selena's urgent and tragic predicament pits the Doc's professional ethics against his moral priorities, and after weighing his options against hers, he chooses Selena's life over that of the child she would have borne to Lucas. Swain's moral outrage leads him to confront Lucas at home while Selena recovers from her "emergency appendectomy" in the hospital (he does, in fact, remove her appendix). The showdown effectively matches white knighthood against a darkened rapist, a confrontation whose racialized undertones are underscored when the white-haired, white-suited, blue-eyed denizen of the most privileged avenue in town invokes the threat of a lynch mob of the town's fathers as retribution for Lucas's assault on his stepdaughter.

Lucas, like Selena, is racially white. As I note in my earlier treatment of this scene, when Allison MacKenzie is reminded of Selena's rape by a dime-novel boasting a picture of a man beating a slave girl bound at the wrists with a "cruel-looking whip" (92), Selena's figurative darkness becomes enhanced and Lucas's whiteness provides the contrast. Lucas's job as a woodsman "of a now-and-then variety common to northern New England," intermittently employed in order to earn wages enough to drink and meet his debts, places him at the lowest end of the town's socioeconomic spectrum. "[H]ad he lived in another section of America," Metalious observes, "he might have been called an Okie, a hillbilly, or poor white trash. He was one of a vast brotherhood who worked at no particular trade, propagated many children with a slatternly wife, and installed his oversized family in a variety of tumble-down, lean-to, makeshift dwellings" (28–29). Lucas lives on the discursive edges of racial whiteness, and his equivalence to "poor white trash" enunciates his whiteness while marking its outer limit. John Hartigan finds "two critical dimensions" associated with the "white" in "white trash": it names those whose behavior violates the tacit codes of "white" propriety, and it is reserved for white people whose socioeconomic status and/or locale places them literally and figuratively closest to socioeconomically disadvantaged African Americans. Hartigan explains, "[T]hese are the whites who make the arbitrariness of the 'color line' apparent by the way their predicaments undermine racial conventions. Hence it is with 'white trash' that the opportunities for deconstructing whiteness become most tangible" (105–6).

Such is the case with Lucas, whose variable whiteness depends on that of those around him. The sexual brutality with which Lucas tyrannizes his dark-skinned stepdaughter is so steeped in an imbalance of power hegemonically maintained by white patriarchal norms that to Allison, the white man wielding the whip on the pulp novel's front cover is a clear analog for him. Similarly, the refrain both Lucas and the town sound regarding Lucas's generosity toward Selena despite her not being "his own" indicates his sense of proprietorship over both Selena and the family as a whole: "I been decent to you just as if you was my own. Kept a roof over your head and food in your belly," underscoring each word with a heavy slap across her face (57). The insistent, recursive attention to Selena's status in relation to Lucas suggests to Stacey Anderson that "in the vernacular of the day, Selena is owned by and thus obligated to a man who both is and is not her father" (par. 31), as if Selena was his property secured through his labor for wages. The issue of ownership and obligation affirms again the analogous relationship between the figures Allison sees on the book cover and Lucas and Selena Cross. Though it is not clear whether the white man in the picture is the slave girl's master or a lesser ranked administrator of discipline and punishment, within the Cross home, Lucas's head of household status entails Selena's abject submission to his abuses of power.[14]

At the same time that Lucas is represented as abusing white male power, Metalious also shades his depravity darkly, particularly in relation to the aforementioned confrontation with Doc Swain. I address this scene at length in chapter 4, where I examine constructions of white masculinity in *Peyton Place*, but it bears a close reading within the present discussion as well. In her analysis of the novel's fairy-tale elements, Madonne Miner calls Lucas "dark" (70); however, this is technically incorrect. Unlike the description of Selena's skin as "never fad[ing] to sallowness in the long months of the harsh New England winter" (31) and the characterization of Tom Makris as "that big, black Greek" (132), Metalious never explicitly mentions Lucas's skin tone.[15] She does, however, signify his darkness by marking his difference against Doc Swain's indomitable whiteness: the Doc's shock of white hair, the blueness of his eyes, and his habit of wearing white suits. When Swain enters the Cross home to confront Lucas, he appears "tall, white suited, looking larger than he really was." Lucas, by contrast "was sitting at the kitchen table, dressed only in a pair of greasy dungarees. The black mattress of hair on his bare chest looked as if it might be a hiding place for lice, and his skin was shiny with sweat" (156). When Swain presents Lucas with his knowledge of Selena's sexual abuse, Lucas drops back into his chair, with "sweat dripping from [his] face now, and its odor [rising] from him in hot waves" (157). When Swain threatens him with mob violence, Lucas "star[es] at the matted black hair on his forearms, with the smell of sweat rising from skin that was roughened now with the tiny bumps of fear" (158). Lucas's essential immorality is signaled by his bodiliness, which is made explicit in his hairy, sweaty drunkenness and his lack of impulse control. His sexual deviance is linked in part to the material conditions under which Lucas lives, in a hovel so filthy that its inhabitants might be covered in vermin.

Swain's white-knightness obscures and recasts Lucas's racial whiteness as not-quite-white, and it may be this effect that motivates Miner's reading of Lucas. Lucas is not black, exactly, but located at the darker end of the continuum of racialized morality, a color-coding that illustrates Dyer's point above about how members of the white working class are symbolically darkened by dint of their labor, which positions its members at a greater symbolic distance from the home because "the very dreariness and pain of their labour accords them lowly status" (57). Significantly, however, Metalious challenges Swain's moral superiority when he issues the ultimatum that extracts Lucas's admission that he raped Selena: "Lynching seems to be something an outraged man always knows how to do" (158). Swain, too, is fully embodied in this scene. He sweats heavily from a combination of his righteous anger and the hot summer night air in the tar-paper shack that "wet his shirt through in seconds and trickled down his sides" (156). He looks at Lucas with "crazy blue eyes" (158); his breath is audible (160); and, having issued his order for Lucas to leave town, Swain departs with "a tiredness in him such as he had never known" and "the taste of tarnished silver" on his tongue (161). Metalious writes, "It took a long time for the sickness and the rage that comes to a man when he realizes how thin the layers of civilization on another man can be, to abate in Dr. Swain" (160). Although Swain is thinking of Lucas here, the layers of civilization on Swain, too, get stretched thin in his encounter with the stepfather who raped and impregnated Selena. The difference between them is that rather than giving in to baser impulses, as Lucas does with Selena, Doc Swain manages them. Even though he seems to mean it when he threatens Lucas with vigilante justice, Swain holds himself in check long enough to drive Lucas out of town, still extralegally, but through manipulation and coercion rather than racialized ritual torture. The threat of lynching has been invoked, however, which positions each man along a racialized continuum in relation to power: Swain as an agent of white righteousness and Lucas as a not-quite-white surrogate for black stereotypes of sexual depravity and perversion. The difference between the two men is gauged along a continuum of morality. Swain represents a man of high moral ground while Lucas lacks the ability to distinguish right from wrong on the most fundamental level.

Lucas remains away long enough for Selena to renovate the tar-paper shack so that it becomes, to borrow from Bachelard, felicitous. With its interior walls, indoor plumbing, and a fireplace, it now possesses the comfort, privacy, and domesticity proper to a home (Rybczynski, 77). Lucas's intrusion into this space late one winter night and his renewed appeal that she "be good" to him move Selena to defend herself by bludgeoning Lucas to death. When the murder is discovered, Selena confesses to having killed Lucas; however, she remains steadfastly silent on the matter of why. Selena's silence is twofold. She keeps silent about Lucas's sexual assaults until she becomes pregnant, at which point she seeks help from Doc Swain, the only man in town in a position to actually give her the assistance she needs. Selena knows that reporting Lucas to the local authorities would neither protect her nor serve her interests. Instead, she abides by the aforementioned shack dweller's code: "A good shack dweller minds his business and binds up his own wounds" (337).[16] In addition to her acute awareness of the futility of speaking up when her stepfather's attacks first began, Selena remains silent as to her motive for killing Lucas, a muteness that threatens to silence her for good should she be found guilty of first-degree murder and hung. On the matter of her refusal to offer a motive in her own defense, Selena's silence becomes a complicated matter, one that belies the simple explanation that Selena had given "a solemn promise of silence" to Matthew Swain in order to protect his professional integrity (337). Having performed an illegal abortion, the doctor has put his medical license on the line. Selena also believes with good reason that no one would have believed her had she disclosed her sexual abuse. She is defiant in her refusal to say why she killed Lucas, stating plainly that she did it, knew exactly what she was doing at the time, and does not regret it (334). Despite pressure by her defense attorney and her boyfriend Ted Carter to defend herself against the charges, Selena keeps her own counsel. Her insistent silence suggests her acute awareness of her abject position within the power structure of the community, a position Metalious underscores by likening her to a slave girl at the mercy of a sadistic, predatory master.

Selena's silence extends into the courtroom, where the testimony that saves her from the gallows is not her own but that of the town's most privileged white male, who speaks in her behalf. When Swain testifies and confesses to aborting Selena's pregnancy by Lucas, a female newspaper reporter from out of town inhales a scandalized gasp. Her response is not one of sympathy for Selena's struggle and what she has been made to endure, but rather for the fate of Swain's career, exclaiming in disbelief to a colleague, "This doctor has ruined himself!" (347). The attention to what Swain is risking versus what Selena has survived and has lost reflects the relative esteem each holds in the community. For the residents of the town, the loss of Swain as its moral center and its medical professional would have a much greater impact on their daily lives than would Selena's loss of life in the event of her execution for Lucas's murder. As the community's most privileged personage, Swain's testimony on the stand also performs the function of modeling for the town how Peyton Place's citizens might care for the least privileged and most vulnerable among them. The judge hearing the case takes Swain's word as evidence and leads the jury toward its verdict: "'There's not one of you on the jury who don't know Matt Swain,' said the judge. 'I've known him all my life, same as you, and I say that Matt Swain is no liar. Go into the other room and make up your minds'" (349). Within ten minutes, Peyton Place has issued its acquittal of Selena Cross.

## Redressing Incest

The most significant change to the manuscript of *Peyton Place* that Metalious was asked to make by her publisher, Kitty Messner, who edited the book herself, was to recast Lucas from Selena's biological father into her stepfather, out of concern that the former would be too hot for a 1950s reading public to handle. The result, according to Metalious, was that Peyton Place had become "trash rather than tragedy" (qtd. in Cameron, xii). That Metalious drew on the real-life story of a local girl who killed her father and buried him in the sheep pen after enduring years of sexual abuse made no difference. Metalious's concession to her initial vision seems to have been recorded in Doc Swain's judgment, "Lucas Cross was guilty of a crime so close to incest that the borderline was invisible" (157). In fact, feminists would later succeed in broadening the definition of father-daughter incest to include father surrogates such as step- and foster fathers (Fischer, 107). Today, Lucas's rape of Selena does belong to the same category of sexual abuse that the editorial change from biological parent to stepfather was intended to circumscribe for 1950s readers. The "close[ness] to incest" that renders the distinction between incest and Selena's rape "invisible" to Doc Swain has in fact become invisible during the years since the novel's publication. Once feminists succeeded in holding father surrogates and biological fathers equally accountable for sexual abuse, incest reasserts itself into the narrative under the same terms that forced the midcentury repression and revision of Selena's story as Metalious had originally written it. In other words, for present-day audiences, Lucas's crime *is* incest, according to current legal definitions. In addition, whereas Swain's abortion of Selena's pregnancy would have been more readily justifiable in the case of Selena's rape by her biological father, the fact that Swain decides to follow his conscience and operate for "humanitarian reasons" rather than for reasons of consanguinity (Toth, *Inside*, 106) makes his choice, and Metalious's narrative, all the more radical for its logic. The ironic end result of the emendation from biological father to stepfather is that the story is a more powerful critique of incest and the community's failure to prevent it. The beneficence with which the town credits Lucas for "taking care" of Nellie's kids seems that much more outrageous in light of the manner in which he stakes his absolute claim to the household and to Selena's body, as if Selena owes her sexual submission to Lucas in exchange for his having "provided for" her.

By reinstating Selena within the Peyton Place community and to what philosopher Gaston Bachelard would call a more "felicitous" home space, a shack renovated to include the comfort and privacy so destructively lacking under Lucas's rule, Metalious presents a more inclusive alternative to the pathological racializations of citizens and spaces. Furthermore, *Peyton Place* critiques the rationale behind the cultural presumption that locates incest primarily in the homes of the poor and those outside the purview of white privilege. While the most explicit case traces the familiar cultural bias that maintains that deviance is elemental to socioeconomic disadvantage, the novel nevertheless challenges such received wisdom. Instead, *Peyton Place* forcefully argues that poverty is not constitutive of immorality, and the novel articulates a clear difference between material deprivation and moral depravity. Metalious connects national anxieties about white racial identity to the project of civic boundary maintenance in a small town. The pathologies such defensive policings of whiteness and repressions of darkness produce are exposed in part through the dysfunction they cause and the damage they do to Peyton Place's families. Content to let Lucas alone on account of his practice of the twin virtues of minding his own business and paying his bills, despite the collective agreement that he was "always the crooked one in that family" (324), the town enables the sense of wage-earning, property-owning entitlement that Lucas possesses over Selena's body, which invites him to exploit his stepdaughter violently and sexually. Lucas is more like one of the town's mainstream inhabitants than Selena is: he is a property-owning, white male who makes good on his debts despite his "now-and-then" employment. As the most marginalized of Peyton Place's citizens, a minor, dark-skinned female, Selena's situation becomes Metalious's object lesson of the risks entailed in maintaining the status quo. The failure of those in the community in a position to actively protect and empower its citizens against the endangerment enabled by the collective, casual dismissal of the signs of violence, abuse, neglect, and need is symptomatic of a deeper cultural dysfunction steeped in racialized anxieties delimiting insider and outsider status. The attempt to maintain such distinctions, *Peyton* Place demonstrates, produces the greater measure of destruction and moral disintegration.

3

# Domestic Disturbances

## *Rape, Race, and* Peyton Place

In a scene considered by many teen readers at the time to be the "quintes-sence of romance" (Toth, *Inside*, 138), *Peyton Place* ushers the fair, blond, and Anglo Constance MacKenzie out of her sexual repression at the hands of the dark, virile, Greek, Tom Makris. This act of libidinal rehabilitation leads her into a sexually satisfying marriage and suggests that the novel takes issue with more than the cultural mandates against women's sexu-ality. It also calls attention to how whiteness and darkness have been used to construct and maintain definitions of sexual character. The resolution of Constance's central conflict through her relationship with Tom, a rela-tionship that rewrites her legal identity with a decidedly non-Anglo sur-name, indicates that Metalious sees something limiting and pathological in white cultural sexual mandates and finds something liberating in alter-natives to it. While *Peyton Place* presents the dark, ethnically Other Tom Makris as the harbinger of sexual health and well-being, his role is com-plicated by his violent method of bringing Constance back to sex and sex back to Constance. The ambiguities and contradictions inherent in *Pey-ton Place*'s shared moments of sex, resistance, and violence engage with what Sabine Sielke has termed the rhetoric of rape. In this chapter, I in-vestigate the manner through which the novel appears to resolve the problem of Tom's rape of Constance through Constance's marriage to Tom, a contractual union that serves to justify the violent initiation of the romantic relationship.

## Wives and Lovers

Though *Peyton Place* is well-known for marking a significant shift in at-titudes toward female sexuality by presenting the stories of women who seek and gain varying degrees of control over their sexual destinies, it would be wrong to suggest that sexual pleasure was denied to women as a matter of course in the 1950s. On the contrary, a seemingly new attitude toward sex emerged around this time, one that on the face of it suggested a measure of freedom for women. Whereas white, middle-class American women had previously been discouraged from expressing sexual desire, so that their virtue would make them more marketable as would-be wives, the new experts on family life in the postwar era were openly in favor of women's active participation in sexual relations. This sexual liberation had its limits, however: only women who were *wives* were allowed this freedom. Barbara Ehrenreich and Deirdre English note, "Marital sex was not only permissible, it was obligatory" (267). What's more, wives were instructed to have sex selflessly for the sake of their children and their husbands. In his 1943 book *Maternal Overprotection*, for instance, psychiatrist Dr. David Levy prescribed sex to mothers as a bulwark against overmothering. Theorizing that a mother's pent-up and unsatisfied sexual energies are at risk of misdirection toward her child, a child who then "must bear the brunt of the unsatisfied love life of the mother," Levy posits that "a woman sexually well adjusted could not become overprotective to an extreme degree" (122).[1]

The clinical recommendation that mothers have more sex with their husbands did not guarantee them sexual pleasure. Rather, it was a prescription that, if followed, was meant to keep the family together and, in particular, the husband happy. One 1952 medical textbook suggested that doctors advise their female patients as to "the advantage of *innocent simulation* of sex responsiveness" in matters of connubial bliss. Now that women *could* enjoy sex, if it so happened that they did not, it had also become the case that they *should*, or at least engage in expertly advised "innocent deception" for the sake of marital harmony (qtd. in Ehrenreich and English, 268, their emphasis).

These newly sexually liberated wives were many of the same white, middle-class women who had been raised to treat their chastity as a kind of currency in the marital marketplace. The years of training that girls and single young women received in vigilant virginity were often at cross purposes with the shift into sexual readiness expected in marriage. In *Preparing for Marriage* (1938), new and soon-to-be husbands were counseled to expect the "unconscious resistance of the bride" to sex: "She has all her life been taught that the one thing she must not do is surrender to any man, and she cannot, in every case, cast off the effects of this teaching in a moment, even in the arms of her husband" (qtd. in Bailey, 93). Beth Bailey notes that while women were held responsible for men's bad behavior should premarital petting get out of hand ("A man is only as bad as the woman he is with," warned one 1932 advice book), they were equally at fault for not surrendering themselves freely once they were safely ensconced in marriage (90). As one commentator warned, "the person who is over-inhibited, excessively prudish, or unresponsive to the extent that he or she cannot or will not tolerate overt expressions of affection from a member of the opposite sex has just as great a problem as the person who aggressively goes as far as possible in petting on all dates" (qtd. in Bailey, 94). The strategies deployed to keep girls' and single women's chastity intact were dysfunctional once a woman crossed the threshold of marriage. An excess of either sexual reticence or sexual readiness was a liability, depending on one's marital status.

The rhetoric of virtue sometimes drew on a racialized and gendered discourse of the marketplace. A white woman's purity was commodified in exchange for a husband, financial security, and, according to some writers on the subject, her personal liberty. In 1932, *Parents* magazine cautioned its readers, "In other countries women are bought and sold in the marketplace as other commodities that satisfy men's appetites. . . . [T]he girl who holds herself cheap will force herself back into the marketplace" (qtd. in Bailey, 96).[2] Sexual availability on the part of white American women, this line of reasoning argued, would in the end debase them, forcing them into sexual slavery. Having renounced their chastity and thus losing their value to potential husbands, such women would be responsible for stimulating men's baser instincts, which, unleashed and unchecked, would in the end lead only to their physical and sexual domination (Bailey, 96).[3] It was every woman's responsibility, therefore, to guard both themselves and society from this sort of cultural devolution in which white American women would share a subjugated position with darker-skinned women at home and abroad.

In the postwar era, the perceived link between sexual behavior and national security led to something of a sex panic in the 1950s in which any nonnormative sexual behavior or anything that took place outside the bounds of a legally recognized marriage was considered a threat to both American society and its dominance on the world stage.[4] According to Elaine Tyler May, "Nonmarital sexual behavior in all its forms became a national obsession after the war" (82). Any act that undermined the strength and centrality of the family (e.g., homosexuality, extramarital, or nonmarital sex) was taken to be indicative of the sort of moral weakness that could lead to communist sympathy and infiltration. In this way it was necessary to keep sex under control, to domesticate it, May has argued, in order to "contain" the threat that it, like communism, posed to national security and well-being. Sexual containment was part of the anticommunist agenda, involving a narrowly defined set of mores and behaviors meant to keep the American public dutifully in line with the national interest. Whereas the geopolitical application of containment sought to prevent the further expansion of communism overseas, sexual containment sought to neutralize the threat of subversion on the American home front by U.S. citizens.

Women in the 1950s were in an untenable position. On the one hand, motherhood was meant to be the ultimate ongoing achievement in a woman's life, heralded as the state of being meant to bring her closest to bliss and complete fulfillment. On the other, it was also, according to social commentators and experts, a minefield for the making of mistakes that could potentially ruin a child.[5] Bad mothers were to blame for much that was said to be wrong with American society. *Momism*, Philip Wylie's term for the scourge of excessive maternalism that results from women's outliving their biological usefulness, was very nearly as dangerous as communism, especially as it was a threat to the American social fabric from within. It was widely held that too much mothering would damage children irreparably (Coontz, 32), thus jeopardizing the future of the nation.

The linked endeavors of marriage and maternity were widely considered a woman's highest calling. In fact, not embarking on these two projects called a woman's very womanliness into question. Furthermore, some respected experts on female psychology stated unequivocally that it was only by embracing one's destiny as wife and mother that a woman could reach sexual fulfillment. Orgasms were reserved, so it was argued, for those women who believed in their heart of hearts that their greatest happiness was to be found in married maternity. While it was true that some sexually active women who were neither wives nor mothers did achieve orgasm, the authors of *Modern Woman: The Lost Sex* (1947) decried such pleasure as an abomination, calling it "the malicious orgasm" (qtd. in Miller and Nowak, 158).[6] This category of sexual pleasure articulates the antisocial and pathological valence that nonmarital sex entailed.

Following the end of World War II, concerted efforts were made to urge women out of the workforce and back into the home, once their usefulness during wartime production had dissipated. Government and social science "experts" discouraged women's continued employment in the Cold War era, charging that wives and mothers were neglecting their civic duties if they were not busy at home raising the next generation of cold warriors. Ignoring the census figures evidencing an escalating birth-rate nationwide, the rallying cry of "race suicide" was injected into the discussion in an effort to encourage white, middle-class women (and men) to reproduce (May, 87). Alfred Kinsey's studies of human sexual behavior confirmed what many were beginning to suspect: sex was "out of control" in America (88). The average sexually active American violated not only the nation's moral codes, the Kinsey reports revealed, but its laws as well (Reumann, 1). One commentator noted that based on the data Kinsey reported, when matched against state and federal laws governing sexual activity, most Americans were de facto sex criminals (Reumann, 29). Rather than trying to get the genie back into its bottle, May observes, "efforts to achieve sexual repression gave way to new strategies for sexual containment," especially early marriage (88). Twenty-one was considered the ideal age at which to get married. If a woman was twenty-three or older and unmarried, according to advice books of the time, she had best take stock of herself and develop an aggressive strategy for making herself "interesting and attractive" in order to land a husband (qtd. in May, 89). Though the marital age did drop for both men and women in the postwar era, encouraging early marriage did not necessarily ensure it, a situation that was particularly problematic for young women for whom premarital sex led to pregnancy. For many, early marriage was the most expedient solution to an unplanned pregnancy, thus retrofitting illegitimacy with containment within a hastily founded family and curbing rates of teen single-motherhood. Because many young women in their teens were married when they gave birth, the moral hazard of teen pregnancy was managed through an exchange of vows. Stephanie Coontz wryly observes, "Young people were not taught how to 'say no'—they were simply handed wedding rings" (39). Illegitimate pregnancy in the pre–*Roe v. Wade* era meant that a young unwed mother-to-be found herself in a devastatingly public predicament. Her options included risking her health should she choose an illegal abortion, moving away from her hometown before the pregnancy came to light, or risking ostracism in the event that her "trouble" was discovered.[7] And it was in this situation that a young and single Constance Standish finds herself. Constance's life as an unmarried mother begins in New York City; however, despite the distance from Peyton Place, her mother lives in fear that her daughter's secret will find its way home and make outcasts of the whole family. Following the deaths of both her lover and her mother, Constance returns to Peyton Place to live. In order to do so safely, she must conceal her sexual transgression from the conventional and judgmental eyes of the town.

The level of social stigma attached to unwed motherhood in Peyton Place is severe. It is the reason for Constance's vigilance with regard to her secret. As a native of the town, she knows exactly the sort of fate that would have befallen her long ago and understands that her hard-earned financial security and carefully cultivated social standing would suffer in the event that her past were to become public. The defamation that accompanies illegitimate pregnancy governs the abstinence of committed couple Ted Carter and Selena Cross, who have pledged to wait until marriage to have intercourse. In a flashback to an intimate moment between them, Ted insists that Selena not touch him lest he lose control of himself. "What if I ever got you into trouble? It happens, you know. No matter how careful people are, it happens." He dampens things considerably when he invokes the court of public opinion and recalls the fate of Betty Anderson's sister. "You know what this town is like," he warns. "You know how they treat a girl that gets in trouble. Remember when it happened to the Anderson girl, Betty's sister? She had to move away. She couldn't even get a job in town" (139). The town's strict code of sexual morality punishes girls and women who embark on sex lives outside of marriage not only through the shame it affixes on them for their behavior, but also by withdrawing from them the financial means to support themselves and their children in the absence of a working husband. In carefully constructing the "respectable fiction" (16) in which she has lived since her daughter's birth, Constance has worked the system rather cunningly, although at considerable cost to her sexual self (and to her digestive system, as she medicates her libido and its periodic rumblings of discontent with stomach-settling palliatives). Constance has managed to attain a level of self-sufficiency that traverses gendered boundaries and leads her into the masculine world of the marketplace. Not only is she a single working mother, she is a female entrepreneur, a small-business owner whose refined sense of style has made her clothing boutique a success in Peyton Place. Such success, however, would not have been possible without the necessary construction and perpetual maintenance of the false front of her premature widowhood.

Having committed herself to this project since her return to town, Constance becomes an exemplar of Mikhail Bakhtin's "classical body," a "strictly completed, finished product," one that is "isolated, alone, fenced off from all other bodies" and that does not reveal or disclose its capacity for performing strictly bodily functions (29). Although the presence of her daughter indicates that Constance's body has experienced entrances and exits, intercourse and birth, Constance has indeed finished, not just with reproduction itself, but with sexuality altogether. This disavowal of her body symbolically enhances her already evident "fairness" of complexion and draws itself in distinction to the darkened racializations of the fully embodied and domestically unbounded Nellie Cross. Constance manages her home as she does her body, ordering the space through canny decor and careful presentation so that her past remains a secret from the town. Ironically, this is managed through the presence of her former lover's portrait on the living room fireplace mantle. The photograph performs and maintains Constance's social respectability at its post in her home's most public room but also provides her with a daily reminder of the danger of stepping, or sleeping, out of bounds. Whereas the lack of physical barriers in the Cross home means that "only by eradicating the oppressive, destructively intimate presence of the father can the Cross home reach any semblance of normalcy" (Stacey Anderson, par. 27), Constance has domesticated herself and her home to excess. As a result, Metalious suggests, she must be broken of the habit and her body broken into. Plainly stated, she must be raped. Furthermore, whereas the rapist must be purged from the Cross home in order that domesticity's constituent elements of comfort and privacy may be established, in the MacKenzie home, the rapist must break in. And he does, in the "big, black Greek" figure of Tom Makris (132), who brings to Constance sexual wholeness and forces her to relax her too-rigid physical boundaries. Having successfully guarded herself against widespread suspicion of sexual misconduct, Constance is left with a deep sense of self-loathing, an internalization of the community's moral censure of women who stray from the narrow codes of female sexual conduct. In addition to enabling sexual pleasure, Tom's rape of Constance serves as the provocative and deeply troubling mechanism that enables Constance to free herself of her past, of her shame, and of the destructive judgment she imagines would be cast upon her in the event that her truth be discovered.

## Sexual Agency or Sexual Assault? The Trouble with *Peyton Place*

Like Selena's rape in Book One, Constance's rape by Tom Makris in the second third of *Peyton Place* is problematic, both at the level of content and form. Critics have long categorized the scene as one of seduction and not rape. When Emily Toth dared in the 1980s to take *Peyton Place* seriously by undertaking a book-length study of the novel and its author, she did not address the complications evident within Metalious's celebrated liberation of female sexuality from the rigid confines of 1950s societal norms. Instead, she offers that for teenage readers of the time, the scene represented "an adolescent urgency about sex that appeared in nothing else teenagers could read" (138), as evidenced by Tom's demand that Constance bare her breasts for him so that he can feel them against his chest when he kisses her. In her reading of the scene, Toth offers no qualification of Tom's demands and no suggestion that what he asks for is inappropriate. Furthermore, she says nothing whatsoever of the rape itself: that when Constance is back in her own home and threatens to have him arrested for rape, Tom backhands her, demands that she keep quiet, and forces himself upon her. Writing more recently, Cinda Gault directly addresses the contradictions of the scene, remarking that "feminists who would later redefine rape as an act of violence rather than sexuality would be horrified by such a narrative solution to the social contradictions associated with gender inequality" (989). The idea that Tom does Constance the favor of assaulting her back to her sexual senses is indeed horrifying, especially in light of the novel's reputation for being the opening salvo in the sexual revolution. Whether or not this encounter was intended as the "quintessence of romance," it functions as a pivotal moment in the development of Constance's character. It is this brutal act that begins the unmaking and unmasking of her reconstituted virginity. The language Metalious uses bears the mark of a masculinized discourse of rape fantasy. Despite her earlier protestations, Constance succumbs to a "red gush of shamed pleasure" (150) before falling unconscious during Tom's attack. It is this second point with which I am most concerned here. Challenging those readings of *Peyton Place* that would position it as a paean to female sexual agency, I maintain that in writing the initiatory moment of Constance's sexual reawakening as a rape, Metalious endorses the idea that women want and need to be raped in order to achieve a healthy libido. Furthermore, in enlisting the figure of a "dark-skinned, black-haired, obviously sexual" ethnic Other to perform the task of both raping and redeeming the fair Constance from her self-imposed second maidenhood (100), Metalious re-enacts an American narrative habit of writing dark Others as sexually rapacious. By novel's end, Tom Makris has been installed as a permanent resident within the MacKenzie home in the role of Constance's husband. In her attempt to have it both ways, Metalious exposes the dysfunction that results from a program of white cultural repression of female sexuality (e.g., the "indigestion" Constance suffers upon Tom's arrival in town and her self-loathing for having succumbed to adulterous sex and an illegitimate pregnancy sixteen years earlier) while at the same time employing the very stereotypes she claims to critique.

One plausible explanation for the popular (mis)reading of Tom and Constance's midnight swim and the sexual assault that follows as a seduction scene instead of a rape may have to do with its placement in the novel. The scene occurs as a flashback in the narrative after it has been made clear that Constance and Tom are a steady couple of two years who are planning to marry, though their plans are not yet public knowledge. At this point, only Selena knows of their engagement—Constance has resisted telling Allison out of concern for Allison's response. Constance has also demurred in setting a date—privately, she wants to tell Tom the truth of her past before she fully commits to a future with him. Constance loves Tom, Metalious writes, "in the only way a woman of thirty-five can love a man when she has never loved before—wholeheartedly, with all her mind and body, but also with fear" (140). With fear, indeed—though there are two years between the rape and Constance's recalling of it, fear has always been an element of her regard for Tom. Her present fears have apparently to do with the secrets she still keeps from Tom (that is, the truth of her daughter Allison's illegitimacy), but Constance's earliest responses to Tom are marked by visceral uneasiness, evident in the shivers of terror inspired by something about him she cannot quite name. During an early dinner date, "[h]e had made her feel uncomfortable in a way she could not explain" (147), and at the lake, Tom's nearly naked and looming presence causes Constance to "[quiver] with fear" (149). Recalling the night's events from memory two years later as they drive past the lake where her long, hot summer night began produces a similar caliber of fright: Constance "shivered again as uncontrollably as she had shivered that night" (149). Metalious cannily inserts the story of the date, which is meant to be understood as the inaugural moment of Tom and Constance's romance, only after it has been well established that they have been a steady pair for two years and intend to be so for the rest of their lives.

With the promise of marriage on the horizon, Metalious in effect sanctions the rape with which the relationship began. So, if the coupling scene was, in fact, understood as the "quintessence of romance" by a significant segment of its readership, one might also argue paradoxically that it is a seduction without consent, a rape with a happy ending.

## The Rhetoric of Rape

The question of whether or not a rape has taken place is determined by establishing the victim's nonconsent—a factor ultimately more important than the perpetrator's intention. In "Rape and the Rise of the Novel,"

Frances Ferguson explains that the male intention to have sexual intercourse quite literally takes the same shape (i.e., that of an erect penis),
whether or not the other participant in the act is willing. Thus, the matter
of determining the willingness (or lack thereof) of both parties relies on
the explicit articulation of consent because "only the intention to have
sexual intercourse has any nonverbal clarity. The law has repeatedly maintained that the capacity for sexual penetration in the act of intercourse
establishes intention (although at least one defense maintained that intercourse had been 'accidental'). The act itself thus indicates intention" (90).
Since intention to have intercourse does not certify the intention to rape,
determining whether or not a rape has taken place rests on establishing
the alleged victim's consent or nonconsent:

> The victim's nonconsent revalues the shape of the act of intercourse, and
> converts what could conceivably be merely an intention to have intercourse
> into a criminal intention to have intercourse despite the nonconsent of the
> other party. Thus, while critics of rape law have plausibly objected that victims
> are more aggressively interrogated than rape suspects themselves, that very
> attention to the victim bespeaks the fact that rape has progressively been
> defined as a crime that is constituted as one by the victim's nonconsent. (91)

This issue of nonconsent has been a notoriously tricky one to assess
and affirm for a couple of reasons. Nonconsent and intention are what
Ferguson calls "mental states," and it is the mental states of the parties
involved that become the basis upon which rape cases are ruled: reduc-
tively, did he intend a rape or an act of consensual intercourse? Did she
say no when she really meant yes? In addition to the ambiguities that
accompany assertions and assessments of psychological states, there are
inherent contradictions within laws governing consent and intention, specifically at the level of statutory definitions. Whereas the age of intention
protects males under a given age from charges of rape, the age of consent
establishes in absolute legal terms the nonconsent to sexual acts for those
individuals under a given age. The contradiction arises in those cases
when a young, sexually aggressive male participates in what would otherwise be considered rape were it to have been committed by someone
older and, similarly, when a person under the age of consent does in fact
agree to engage in sexual intercourse. Ferguson's point is that in both
cases, though the law seeks to establish absolutely that such things cannot happen, there have been times when they do happen. And when they
do, Ferguson continues, where the law says there is no intention, facts may

dictate that intention exists and the same holds true for consent. Such definitions "thus create the categories of consent that is not consent (for some hypothetically consenting female who has not reached the age of consent) and intention that is not intention (for some hypothetically intending and physically competent male who has not reached the age of legal discretion and competence)" (95).

The certainty that is legally ensured by the juridical ages of consent and intention has significant ramifications for rape cases not governed by statutory law. The clarity and absolutism that is meant to be formalized and guaranteed by statutory rape law, observes Ferguson, insist that explicit consent must be legally denied, a paradox that has implications for nonstatutory rape: "If in statutory rape *yes* is always taken to mean 'no,' in other kinds of rape *no* is frequently taken to mean 'yes.' Thus, rape law continually suggests as a paradigmatic interpretative strategy the reversibility of the terms that seem to be asserted by the charge of rape itself" (96). In other words, she later clarifies, "the law generates a fictitious certainty—or the certainty of fiction—by defining rape in formal terms that specifically involve the possibility of self-contradiction" (98). The idea here is that if the legal parameters for the ages of consent and intention are said to be firm but belie the facts, then establishing the mental/psychological states for alleged victims and perpetrators is even trickier.

One way in which the law has, until recently, been alarmingly unambiguous is in its granting of the marital rape exemption. The year following *Peyton Place*'s publication saw the following declaration on the matter by an American legal scholar: "A man does not commit rape by having sexual intercourse with his lawful wife, even if he does so by force and against her will" (qtd. in Ryan, 941). The English jurist Lord Matthew Hale is credited with establishing the marital rape exemption in both English common law in the 1600s and as precedent in the American court system by asserting that "the husband cannot be guilty of a rape committed by himself upon his lawful wife, for by their mutual matrimonial consent and contract the wife hath given up herself in this kind unto her husband, which she cannot retract" (qtd. in "'To Have and to Hold,'" 1255–56). Long before Hale's judicial opinion, ancient law held that marriage could transmute a rape into consensual sex even if the assault took place prior to the marriage. Ferguson reports that ancient Saxon law provided a stay of execution to the rapist whose victim was willing to marry him (provided she was a virgin prior to the attack) (92). Hebraic law had a similar mechanism, which involved the payment of a fine by the assailant and the marriage of the assailant to his victim (92). Marriage thus ensured and secured consent for sexual intercourse at any time for all time. As Ferguson notes, "Marriage recasts rape, so that marriage is a misunderstanding corrected, or a rape rightly understood" (92).

Because rape laws evolved based on the premise that women were chattel and therefore lacked legal standing, the sexual assault of a man's daughter or wife was, by law, an attack on his property and not her person. Rape laws "protected a father's interest in his daughter's virginity and a husband's interest in his wife's fidelity" ("'To Have and to Hold,'" 1256). Virginity ensured a woman's value on the marriage market, and fidelity guaranteed a husband's paternity of his wife's children. Because women-as-property were tied to the acquisition of property, such practices as "bride capture" and "stealing an heiress" enabled men to lay claim, as it were, to women through rape (which, as *bride* in the former term suggests, would eventuate in a marriage) (ibid., 1257). A man might then legally gain his entitlement to a woman and could elevate his rank and potentially enhance his property holdings through rape. The practices that endangered women's safety and security were thus prosecuted as property damage and/or resolved and legitimated through the subsequent marriage of the victim and her assailant. This "correction" enacted by marriage is of a piece with the marital rape exemption, the loophole that disallowed a charge of rape to be brought against a husband by his wife because of the "implied consent" of the marriage contract. Marital rape law "served to complete the conceptual framework by establishing a man's sexual entitlement to a woman within the marriage contract" (ibid.). Under common law, rape could be decriminalized through marriage, and within marriage, it would never again be acknowledged as such. Matrimony in essence annulled rape.[8]

The novel, Ferguson reminds us, is particularly adept at representing internal psychological states (99). Several studies of the rise of the novel correlate its emergence with enlightenment ideas about individualism, identity, privacy and the body, and the inalienable rights that attend full personhood.[9] Where the novel excelled or innovated was in giving (or gaining) readers access to a sense of the interiority of particular characters. As a genre of literature, the novel could offer readers a character's inner experience of conscious states of thinking and feeling, rather than the report of that experience as a dramatic soliloquy might. Because the novel provides a formal structure and the space through which to explore states of mind such as consent and nonconsent, it thus presents an opportunity to investigate female subjectivity within representations of rape (Sielke, 18). In her interrogation of the rhetoric of rape in American literature and culture, Sabine Sielke extends traditional readings of literary sexual violence beyond that of "rape and silencing" to "rape, silence, and refiguration" (4–5). This silence results from both propriety (literary decorum expurgates the graphic details of an assault before it passes through the pen onto the page) and from a lack of female subjectivity (Bal, 142).[10] In positing refiguration as a third term, Sielke asserts:

> we acknowledge that texts do not simply reflect but rather stage and
> dramatize the historical contradictions by which they are overdetermined.
> At best, readings of rape therefore reveal not merely the latent text in what
> is manifest, explicit, and thus produce a text's self-knowledge; they will also
> evolve a new knowledge pertaining to the ideological necessities of a text's
> silences and deletions. (5)

The narrative representation of rape is not a fait accompli within a given tale but speaks to something ongoing and contemporaneous with the text's emergence from and back into a particular culture. A reading of a text's silences leads to and engages in this process of refiguration by way of "displacement and substitution," through the uses of metonymy and metaphor (5).[11] Rather than "read[ing] the violence back into the texts" (which is one way she suggests a great deal of feminist criticism has "insinuate[d] this silence can be broken"), Sielke investigates the discursive ellipses for the broader cultural meanings they articulate, cautioning that "readings of rape cannot be reduced to the study of a motif" (4–5).

Refiguration, Sielke holds, has much in common with the development of cultural identity. In both, there exists a sort of reconciliation of sameness and difference without a resolution of one into the other (which would necessarily be that of difference into the same, which would in turn erode the concept of identity). Literary narratives do this, too. Through the production and interpretation of a nation's stories about itself, "they both form and interfere with the cultural imaginary" (6). Scenes of rape in literature can alternately "'naturalize' sexual violence into seemingly consensual views on gender, sexuality, and the world at large" and/or suggest approaches to reading a literary rape. In each case, Sielke argues, literary rape narratives "refigure, re-present, repoliticize, and thus reinterpret previous literary interrogations of rape and sexual violence, and in this way inscribe themselves into a tradition of readings of rape, a tradition they simultaneously remember and interfere with" (6). Literary rape narratives revisit established representational patterns of sexual assault in order to understand the matrices that produce them and the mechanisms that enable their articulation. By reproducing narrative sites of sexual violence, scenes of and about rape can act as important critiques of the violence they enact.

*Peyton Place* does just this, recasting a somewhat familiar scenario (e.g., dark stranger ravishes fair maiden) with a fresh twist (e.g., she's more "old maid" by the day's standards). An analysis of the novel's rape rhetoric at once recapitulates timeworn ideologies about sexual violence while somewhat paradoxically critiquing a cultural regime that represses healthy sexual expression. In her intervention into the literature of seduction, Metalious on the one hand rewrites the outcome, moralizing in the opposite direction of earlier texts, advocating for the acknowledgment and integration of sexuality into women's lives rather than penning a cautionary tale urging restraint and chastity. At the same time she uses racialized sexual violence as the means by which sexual self-actualization takes place.

This is especially evident where the issue of female self-determination is concerned, as a closer look at the rape scenes in *Clarissa*, *Charlotte Temple*, and *Peyton Place* will demonstrate. As discussed above, rape raises questions about subjectivity because the designation of an act *as* rape depends on the issue of consent. In *Clarissa* and *Charlotte Temple*, the eponymous heroines of each faint at the moment of crisis, foregrounding the issue of consent through withholding it by default. Neither Clarissa nor Charlotte is awake for her ravishment. In *Peyton Place*, however, Metalious muddies the issue by casting Constance into a swoon only after she is aware of what has taken place and, perhaps more significant, after she has experienced pleasure from the assault.

## Of Consciousness and Consent: *Clarissa* and *Charlotte Temple*

Frances Ferguson offers a fascinating reading of the problem of subjectivity in *Clarissa*, an analysis that rewards sustained attention. Clarissa's assailant, Lovelace, is troubled by her nonconsent, Ferguson tells us. He longs for her to have remained conscious in order to consent to his "complet[ing] his wishes upon the charmingest creature in the world" (Richardson, 888). Clarissa's conscious awareness of Lovelace's actions would give closure to his predations by confirming them as rape. At the same time, Clarissa's consent would recast the act as seduction, because by definition there can be no rape with consent. By virtue of her having a will to exercise, she would, in that case, be possessed of subjectivity. The wrinkle arises in that Clarissa's subjectivity is, according to Ferguson, neither confirmed nor denied as a result of her swoon. She explains, "If the question in any rape case is, 'What was the victim's mental state? Did she consent?' then the answer *Clarissa* seems to give is, 'She had no mental state.'" Clarissa cannot defend herself against Lovelace because she is unconscious, and, being unconscious, she cannot withhold consent or, as Ferguson puts it, "her resistance to the rape has been made impossible." Still, Clarissa's lack of subjectivity, her insensibility owing to her swoon, automatically writes the act as a rape according to rape law. Writes Ferguson, "The stipulation that unconsciousness is nonconsent—even though it necessarily cannot manifest itself as physical resistance—thus provides that Clarissa's nonconsent continues even in her absence, even in her unconsciousness" (100). In a footnote, Ferguson points out that in this case, where some scholars have suggested that Lovelace does not rape Clarissa, the law unequivocally insists upon it, which, in turn, brings Ferguson (and us) back to rape law's potential for inconsistency. The assertion that Clarissa "had no mental state" leaves open the possibility that, had she maintained awareness, she *might* have said "yes," whereas her lack of consciousness yielded an inarticulate but legally viable "no" (100–101).

The circumstances in which Richardson places Clarissa before Lovelace has his way with her introduce competing understandings of subjectivity. Lovelace and Clarissa are each vying for access to and mastery over her will. Because Clarissa is belated in her resistance to Lovelace, Ferguson notes, she has, as far as Lovelace is concerned, abdicated her autonomy. Even prior to the rape, Lovelace understands her will as having always already been under his control. Clarissa, on the other hand, believes it is still hers to act upon. Lovelace's sense is that "consent has always implicitly been given," while Clarissa's is that "consent can only be given freely and thus the act of deciding the value of an action—the interpretation of it—is itself a kind of prospectiveness, a claim that 'the action' is never over" (Ferguson, 102). In addition to his *post factum* pining for Clarissa's consent, Lovelace connives to persuade Clarissa that they have married, which would settle the matter of her rape (by retroactively assigning Clarissa's consent) and render it right (102–3). Clarissa does not, however, succumb to this attempt at rhetorical coercion, a continuation of the physical coercion through which Lovelace gained his prize, so, in the end, Lovelace's rape of Clarissa ensures her ruination, thus leading her into madness and finally death.

Language and discourse are also responsible for Charlotte Temple's fall from grace in Susanna Rowson's popular novel of the early American republic. Because it would have been conventionally indecorous for Rowson to offer a graphic representation of the encounter between Charlotte and Montraville, Sielke proposes that "[i]n *Charlotte Temple* . . . the invasion of the heroine's privacy, directed at her private parts, is metaphorized as the penetration of her mind by rituals of persuasive rhetoric more powerful than physical attraction" (17). Montraville's approach to Charlotte is written "as a conquest of the mind through speech, through forceful rhetoric—as opposed to physical force" (18). As such, without direct reference to force or violence or the body, Sielke argues that this discursive representation of sexual violation supports the understanding of rape as "'a crime on the level of mental states' (Ferguson, ["Rape"], 91), a crime 'against the will,' an act that is violent because it overrides ambivalence or nonconsent" (18).

Equating persuasion with invasion, Sielke reads the encounter between Charlotte and Montraville as both a seduction and a rape. It is, she asserts, a seduction that the novel itself rewrites as a rape. Of the moment that seals Charlotte's fate, when she is faced with the decision to remain in England or depart with Montraville, Sielke observes that Charlotte poses but never answers her own question, "How shall I act?" Ever the opportunist, Montraville seizes the moment (and Charlotte, "lifting her into the chaise"), saying, "Let me direct you" (Rowson, 48). Once contained within the carriage, Charlotte falls unconscious and, in turn, from grace. Unlike Clarissa, who remains unconscious throughout Lovelace's attack, Sielke notes that we do not know when Charlotte regains her senses. Foregrounding Rowson's characterization of the event as "tempestuous" (67), Sielke suggests that Charlotte might have eventually regained awareness (Sielke, 18). What we know or do not know about Charlotte's state of mind at the height of her crisis does not matter in the end, as Montraville's success in gaining his way and Charlotte's sexual initiation are connoted by her pregnancy and, notes Sielke, "such loss of virtue and honor, whether enforced or not, leads only one way: downhill" (19).

Whereas Rowson does not resolve the issue of coercion and resistance herself, Charlotte's wavering response signals seduction. Her ultimate inability to respond at all (recalling Ferguson) signals rape. Sielke intriguingly suggests that the novel itself rewrites the seduction as rape by signaling Charlotte's silence and underscoring her nonconsent. The novel shifts course in part through Montraville's repentance, as he too (like Charlotte), goes a bit mad when he learns of Charlotte's fate. Having avenged himself on the ironically named Belcour (in whose trust he ill-advisedly places Charlotte when he abandons her), Montraville himself suffers something of a nervous breakdown. Rowson leads him from "agitation of [the] mind," "insensibility," and "a dangerous illness and obstinate delirium" to "rav[ing]," "disorder," and "severe fits of melancholy," all catalogued within the same paragraph (130). Montraville's guilty prostrations before Charlotte's father and his subsequent mental collapse admit his part in her fatal fall and, according to Sielke, "thus echo[es] Charlotte's own deterioration, which itself figures the violence she was subjected to" (21). By enduring a pregnancy without the legal and social protections of marriage, Charlotte's original vulnerability is redoubled into violation. Having been "robbed of innocence" (Rowson, 67) and thus her social and economic capital, Charlotte's pregnancy signals her lost virginity and honor. Her abandonment by Montraville and subsequent descent into madness speaks to the violence of their sexual encounter (Sielke, 18). There is a curious paradox, however, that inheres within this reading. On the one hand, it is Charlotte's goodness and innocence that motivates Montraville to choose her as his victim, thus resulting in what Sielke (following Jan Lewis) calls "the seduction of a man by a woman's virtue" (21). In this case, female innocence sows the seeds of its own destruction, in short, blaming the victim for her lost honor. On the other, the fallout from the carriage ride (Charlotte's pregnancy, her abandonment and decline, madness and death; Montraville's reckoning and repentance, *his* madness and melancholy) flags the sexual encounter as an assault. In either case, Sielke offers, Rowson's unwillingness to resolve the issue is irrelevant. Like Clarissa Harlowe before her, Charlotte's ruination is guaranteed by the encounter.

## From Brutality to Bliss: The "Shamed Pleasure" of Constance MacKenzie

Whereas *Charlotte Temple* is the story of a seduction that the novel rewrites as a rape, *Peyton Place*, I would argue, presents us with a rape that Metalious recasts as a seduction. My disagreement with other readers of *Peyton Place* as to the nature of what transpires between Constance MacKenzie and Tom Makris just after their midnight swim may be in part a result of the ambivalence written into the scene itself. What begins as a straightforward sexual assault in Constance's bedroom is represented within the same scene as her initiation into sexual pleasure. The end result of this inaugural liaison (an apparently happy and sexually fulfilling marriage) suggests that Metalious endorses the idea that Tom's use of force in his conquest of Constance is necessary in order to restore the former "ice maiden" to a state of libidinous health, rendering her the "passionate, love demanding woman" he knew her to be all along (178). Furthermore, in uniting by novel's end the Waspy Constance Standish MacKenzie with the "big, black Greek" Tom Makris, the narrative exploits stereotypes of black male sexuality in an attempt to offer a progressive critique about whiteness as sexual pathology.

Tom's rough-and-ready approach begins while still at the lake. After he handily removes her suit top, Tom kisses Constance "brutally, torturously, as if he hoped to awaken a response in her with pain that gentleness could not arouse." His hands hold her head immobilized; his mouth is "bruising, hurtful" (149). When they arrive back at the MacKenzie house, Constance is "still crumpled, half naked, on the front seat" (149). At the moment of crisis, when she struggles to reclaim and protect her body and her home from further trespass or injury by threatening to have Tom arrested for "breaking and entering and rape," he violently and explicitly silences her "with a stunning blow across the mouth with the back of his hand":

> "Don't open your mouth again," he said quietly. "Just keep your mouth shut."
>
> He bent over her and ripped the still wet bathing suit from her body, and in the dark, she heard the sound of his zipper opening as he took off his trunks.
>
> "Now," he said. "Now."
>
> It was a like a nightmare from which she could not wake until, at last, when the blackness at her window began to thin to pale gray, she felt the first red gush of shamed pleasure that lifted her, lifted her, lifted her and then dropped her down into unconsciousness. (150)

Metalious's intervention in the seduction tale tradition repeats the mode of the novel's critique of racist discourse. In attempting to do something new with an old form, Metalious refashions the seduction narrative while slipping into its old habits. Though there is no evidence to suggest that Metalious had read or was familiar with Richardson's *Clarissa* or Rowson's *Charlotte Temple*, there are striking likenesses between the scenes of sexual violation in all three. And, of course, there are differences. Unlike Clarissa Harlowe or Charlotte Temple, Constance is not a virgin at the moment of Tom's attack. However, like Charlotte, Constance's pregnancy and the birth of her child publicly attest to her sexual experience and threaten to annihilate her social respectability and honor. Constance's affair with her lover, Allison MacKenzie, does not prove fatal, as do the sexual initiations of Clarissa and Charlotte. Nevertheless, Constance does pay for it with her life. She must remain vigilant in maintaining the pretense of "respectability" by hewing to the plausible fiction of her daughter's birth and her "husband's" death. Though she is a sexually experienced adult, Constance is able to enact a second maidenhood. With the sudden death of the father of her child soon after her daughter's birth, Constance is afforded the time, money, and opportunity to return home to Peyton Place, toddler in tow. The town in its collective voice recognizes the challenge facing Constance as a single mother:

> "It's a shame," said Peyton Place. "And him so young."
> "It's hard for a woman alone, especially trying to raise a child."
> "She's a hard worker, Connie MacKenzie is. Stays in that shop of hers 'til six o'clock every night." (17)

Because the community believes in Constance's virtue, it expresses sympathy for her situation and respect for her efforts to do the best she can for herself and her daughter.

With her ever-present awareness of the social death she would experience should the truth ever become public, Constance denies having taken any sexual or romantic pleasure in her past. She claims it was neither love, nor sex, but "loneliness" that landed her in the bed of Allison MacKenzie, and she actively represses whatever libidinous desires have haunted her since. In her rewriting of the seduction tale, Metalious's heroine is revirginized in advance of her ravishing: the "first red gush of shamed pleasure" Constance experiences suggests both orgasm and a kind of second deflowering through language that evokes the tearing of a female virgin's hymen.

The issue of Constance's "shamed pleasure" is what complicates the naming of this scene as one of rape or seduction. Tom's initiatory gestures at the lake are unwelcome and startle Constance to the point of inaction. Back at her house, having threatened to cry rape in advance of the act itself, Constance's consent is never explicitly offered. Metalious embeds an ellipsis into the scene in place of the violence of the act itself, providing an example of the pattern of "rape, silence, and refiguration" that emerge from the rape narratives Sielke reads. Between Tom's declarative "Now" and Constance's orgasm are several hours of an ongoing assault that Constance recalls as a living nightmare. Metalious also interjects the whole episode as a flashback. There are two years that go unchronicled between Constance's first night with Tom and her established romance with him.

Like Clarissa Harlowe and Charlotte Temple before her, Constance, too, falls unconscious coincidental with her violation. The interesting difference here is that the blackout occurs progressively later in each case. Clarissa is unconscious throughout Lovelace's assault; Charlotte swoons with indecision only to revive *in medias res*; and Constance remains awake throughout the encounter, and it is the power of the simultaneous shame and pleasure she experiences that "[drops] her down into unconsciousness." The repetition of the loss of consciousness and its links to the question of subjectivity and consent suggest rape. To repeat Ferguson, in Clarissa's case, "she had no subjectivity"; in Charlotte's, she had some subjectivity; Constance's full subjectivity is negated with the back of Tom's hand. Her literal silencing prefigures her loss of consciousness instead of coinciding with it. She is fully aware of what is happening and her shame recalls what she has *already* experienced, her first sexual initiation, rather than what is to come. Unlike Clarissa and Charlotte, both of whom offer neither consent nor nonconsent to the villain's advances, Constance both resists and relents, losing consciousness with an awareness that there was "at last" pleasure in Tom's assault.

A pause to consider intratextual comparisons within *Peyton Place* by looking at this scene alongside the rape of Selena Cross helps to illuminate Metalious's approach to Constance. The ambivalence in her troubled treatment of Constance's rape is enhanced by her clear understanding that Selena's assault by Lucas is a rape without qualification or emendation. The novel condemns both the act and Lucas's attempt to shift the blame to Selena and the suffering to himself. Lucas's murder and Selena's acquittal of the crime, along with Metalious's downright radical position on abortion (as a quality-of-life-saving measure on Selena's behalf) profess her moral certainty on the matter. The alternate resolutions of each event, namely, death for Lucas and marriage for Tom, belie their similarities and expose an odd and unfortunate chauvinism in *Peyton Place* that compromises the progressive stance on female sexuality for which it is famed. Both scenes are mediated: Selena's rape is presented through Allison's point of view and Constance's is a flashback two years later. Both scenes share a loss of consciousness: Allison passes out from the horror of what she observes; Constance faints as a result of what she experiences; and Selena is later revealed to have fainted during Lucas's attack (160). Finally, Metalious uses similar language as she brings both scenes to a close: Allison stumbles from her perch at the Cross's window and "pant[s] with the effort of fighting off the blackness that threatened her from every side" (57); it is when "the blackness at her window began to thin to pale gray" that Constance has her moment of pleasure. In Allison's case, the darkness is descending and closing in, whereas in Constance's case, it is dispersing, lifting. One might read the opposition here as indicative of the difference between the two incidents. The former is clearly a rape and the latter, less clearly so.

The bedroom scene marks the site and moment of Constance's refiguration. Tom's rape begins the process of breaking and unmaking her identity, resynthesizing it into a healthy whole. Where Clarissa and Charlotte Temple come apart, Constance comes together. Two years pass between this night and the evening during which Constance thinks back to it, yet little information is presented that details the rising of the romance out of this incident. We are given the fact of their relationship (that it exists, that they plan to marry), the origins of their relationship (the night of their swim), and then an assurance of a kinder, more tender Tom when the narrative returns to its present, a man who kisses Constance "gently," and tells her he loves her when they arrive at a restaurant for a dinner date (151). At this point in the novel, the truth of Connie's wayward youth and her illegitimate pregnancy are still a secret to Tom. Even though he does not know about Constance's past, Tom recognizes that she (like other notable Peyton Place fixtures such as Leslie Harrington and the closet Catholic Reverend Francis Fitzgerald) has constructed a "tedious, expensive [shell]" behind which she hides for the sake of self-preservation, covering the "passionate, love demanding woman that she really was with the respectable garments of the ice maiden" (177–78). Without fully understanding (or apparently caring) why Constance struggles to maintain this image, Tom makes it his mission to shatter it, to "destroy completely the need for protection" (178) and smash her frosty false front to bits.

In a conversation about the news of Betty Anderson's illegitimate pregnancy, Constance calls teenage preoccupation with sex "abnormal" while Tom argues the opposite case, that a lack of libido in young adults would be cause for concern. Tom then dares Constance to convince him that she had nary a thought of sex before her reputed marriage to Mr. MacKenzie and that her intimacies with her husband lacked "eagerness." Constance takes the bait and responds that there was no pleasure in sex for her during her "marriage"; instead, she says it was "always something [she] allowed [her husband] as a sort of favor" (218). When Tom calls her a liar and challenges her to say the same of their sex life, she concedes (nervously, for fear he can smell her fraudulence) that it is different with him. Interestingly, in this conversation, Constance is convinced of Allison's obliviousness to sex ("She always has her nose in a book and her head in the clouds"), and Tom cautions Constance against such wishful thinking, suggesting that there are many books full of compelling ideas about sex. As evidence, he responds, "As one fourteen-year-old who developed a crush on me once said, 'After all, Mr. Makris, Juliet was only fourteen'" (219).

Constance's deep shame and self-loathing for what Metalious suggests is a freely chosen affair in her youth[12] make a raging return from the repressed in the form of ill-founded suspicions of how her daughter Allison has spent her Labor Day afternoon with Norman Page. When Allison returns home late, Constance imagines a worst-case scenario in which Allison has been sexually violated by Norman or, alternatively, that she has raised a daughter just like herself. In front of Tom, Norman Page, and his mother, Evelyn, Constance chastises Allison upon her return home for her "cheap" behavior and threatens to charge Norman with rape if, after a medical examination by Doc Swain, Allison is not "the way she should be," that is, with her virginity intact (236). After Norman and Evelyn have retreated and Allison declares her complete embarrassment at her mother's behavior, Constance explodes with sexually repressed rage. Despite Tom's attempt to prevent her from saying any more, Constance slaps Allison and reveals her illegitimacy. Accusing Allison of being "just like [her] father," she proclaims their one characteristic in common to be their preoccupation with "Sex! Sex! Sex!" and explodes with the truth:

> It is the only thing like him about you! You don't look like him, or talk like him, but you certainly have acted like him. It is the only thing of his that belongs to you. Not even his name belongs to you. And after the way I've sweated and slaved to bring you up decently, you go off into the woods and act like a goddamned MacKenzie. The bastard daughter of the biggest bastard of all! (237)

With this revelation, "[Tom] realized in this moment what he had tried unsuccessfully to discover for two years. He looked down at Constance's bowed head and fancied that he could see the pieces of her broken shell lying around her feet" (237). Later that night, when Constance attempts to defend her behavior to Tom by claiming it was motivated by her interest in protecting Allison, Tom confronts her with the truth about her self-disclosure. Her anxiety about Allison is misplaced guilt about her own conduct sixteen years earlier. He "brutally" confronts Constance with the lies she tells to herself, calling her "noble" excuses "a lot of crap." He exposes her motives for the self-preservation they belie: that Constance was girding her own reputation, not Allison's, against the talk of the town (275). When Constance continues to defend her conduct in such a way that imputes Allison's guilt and criticizes Tom's belief that teenage sexual experimentation is perfectly healthy, Tom insists once again that she lacks the evidence to make such claims and reads Constance's persistence in this line of reasoning as further evidence of her own shame. Constance fears not that Allison will take after her father; rather, she's frightened that Allison will take after her (275).

While it is true that Allison is innocent of the charges leveled at her, Constance is not completely incorrect in her intuition that Allison wants something more than she's getting from Norman. Allison does, in fact, get rather impatient with Norman's soft, reticent kisses and his intellectualizing about sex during an earlier outing. In a scene that recalls and recasts the violence of both Selena's and her mother's rapes, and that likens Allison to Constance for her posturing, Allison slaps Norman for calling her a liar after she boasts of her experience with other boys (194). In this case, Allison administers the smack: she's had no experience beyond an unwelcome kiss from Rodney Harrington at her thirteenth birthday party, a kiss that in its aftermath inspires her masturbatory fantasies (91). When Allison admits her lie, in part owing to Norman's use of force (he pins her down on the picnic blanket until she does so), Norman asks her if she would like him to kiss her. Allison assents, her face flush, and rejoins, "Except that I don't like you to ask me, Norman. For anything." When Norman complies, stoking her impatience with his careful manner, "Allison wanted to burst into tears of frustration. That wasn't the way she wanted to be kissed at all" (194). As in the first sex scene between Tom and Constance (and in Lucas's rape of Selena), this moment between Allison and Norman bespeaks an ideology of sexuality in general that favors violence as a mode of foreplay. Specifically, it suggests a sort of female sexuality that desires and prefers a rough-and-ready approach to sexual expression, one that advocates a denial of female subjectivity. Allison does not want to be asked what it is that she wants. She wants it to be assumed and acted on accordingly.

Tom's dominance over Constance's sexuality is redoubled in the scene of Constance's abjection, the raging return of all she has repressed. He is judge, jury, and jailer during Constance's confession of her past, significantly locking the front door behind him (just as he did the night of the rape), cross-examining her on the inconsistencies in her tale, and catching her in her omissions. Following the full telling of her illicit history, Constance is finally freed of the weight and threat of her secrets and is reborn into a new life of sexual desire and pleasure:

> It was not until much later that Constance realized fully what Tom had done for her. In the weeks which followed it was as if she were a new and different person who walked freely and unafraid for the first time. It was never again necessary for her to take refuge in lies and pretenses, and it was only when she finally realized this that she knew what Tom meant when he had spoken of the dead weight of the shell she had always carried. But that night there was no realization. There was nothing but a terrible need, a hunger that caused her to reach forward for the first time in her life. (277)

Tom's efforts to break down and remake Constance's identity prove a success. Unburdened of "the falseness of her existence" (237) and no longer in thrall to the danger sex poses to her equanimity and social standing, Constance initiates the encounter and enjoys herself, unafraid.[13] Within weeks they are engaged, and shortly thereafter they marry. But we knew this already, as their engagement is revealed prior to Constance's flashback to the rape scene, and their wedded bliss is established before the narrative flashback to their reconciliation on the night of Constance's truth telling.[14]

This ordering of information—engagements and marriages disclosed before rapes and reconciliations—confounds the nature of the moments that cinch and secure Constance and Tom's existence as a romantic and married couple. At first coerced into her involvement with Tom through physical force, Constance is at last granted the freedom to choose her sexual destiny and take pleasure from it because of a rape that begins the process of her redemption from repression. As I have attempted to show, Metalious follows the pattern of "rape-silence-refiguration" that Sielke foregrounds (and in having done so, I am suggesting that the first term correctly applies to their first bedroom scene), and Metalious cannily re-casts Tom's rape of Constance into a seduction in several ways. The scene at the lake and later, in her bedroom, may indeed be violent, but by presenting it as a flashback, Metalious suggests that Constance has always, already given her consent to Tom. The narrative's use of coercion and surrender problematizes the popular contention that *Peyton Place* freed women from the chains of an oppressive midcentury ideology of female sexuality. Although Metalious does offer her female characters a greater measure of pleasure than perhaps readers had been used to, in Constance's case, sexual self-determination is effected through sexual assault. And if Tom's assault inaugurates the refiguration of Constance's identity, their marriage finalizes it when she becomes Constance Makris. Whatever boundaries he crossed that night have been redrawn such that what was rape has been retrofitted as rough and redemptive sex. The circumscribing of the past with the promise and fulfillment of marriage between Tom and Constance endorses a theory of implied consent and right of access. In this way, Metalious recapitulates the chauvinism of ancient biblical and Saxon laws, which corrected rapes through marriage such that what *was* a rape in fact is eradicated through juridical practice that neutralizes and rewrites a rape retroactively as consensual.

"What Tom had done for [Constance]," Metalious implies, was to emancipate her from a punitive second maidenhood and enable her to take pleasure in sex. The mechanism by which this metamorphosis is catalyzed is Constance's sexual assault. In her attempt to say something radical about female sexual desire (that it exists and its acknowledgment and expression is a far healthier approach to life than its repression), Metalious says something equally reactionary: that Constance wants and needs to be raped in order to experience the wholeness of an identity that comes with a fully integrated and functioning libido. Furthermore, in critiquing the oppressive mores that punish white women for acknowledging their sexual appetites, Metalious invokes cultural stereotypes of black masculinity that are equally problematic, a matter I explore at some length in the next chapter. Constance would not or could not respond orgasmically to Tom's predation if it was not what she secretly (desperately, Metalious might have us believe, given the depth of Constance's need the night she shares her past with Tom) wanted or needed. Her physical responsiveness to Tom on that first night when he institutes his program of renovating her sex life alters the rape by coloring it as consensual. This recalls the belief that conception signals consent, that a pregnancy that results from an alleged rape belies a woman's secret wish to have been ravished, regardless of what she might have said at the time or claimed thereafter. Metalious presents Constance's rape by Tom as "intercourse" and as an "act of discovering what [she] really wanted all along" (Ferguson, 102). Had Tom paid heed to Constance's (now) empty threats of rape charges, Constance would not have developed into the sexually fulfilled, at-peace-with-her-past Mrs. Makris that she is by novel's end.

# 4

# The Good Rapist, the Bad Rapist, and the Abortionist

## Peyton Place's *Crisis of Masculinity*

Tom Makris's rape of Constance MacKenzie in *Peyton Place* is singular within their relationship in its show of sexual force. It is not singular, however, in Tom's experience. His sexual initiation, we later learn, demonstrates a similar strain of aggression. As in the first sex scene with Constance, the issue of consent is made to seem ambiguous: Tom "took" a girl whose name he cannot quite remember in the bathroom of a tenement building. Her desires and reactions are never mentioned, only his revelry in the experience. This vignette is presented in a discussion with Constance on adolescent sexuality in which Tom works, unsuccessfully at the time, to persuade Constance that it is perfectly natural for teenagers not just to think about sex, but to try it out. From the night of the midnight swim onward, Tom emerges as the voice of reason on many matters, most importantly on the matter of libidinal health. His program of rehabilitation enables Constance to integrate her estranged sexuality into her identity and, in the end, to have a more honest relationship with her daughter.

This chapter shifts the focus from Constance to Tom in order to investigate racialized constructions of masculinity within *Peyton Place*. I begin with Tom Makris—the novel's dark hero, its rapist/redeemer figure—and end with Doc Swain, its white, southernized moral center. This inquiry moves from an analysis of the novel's uses of dark masculinity into its critique of white male sexuality by way of the novel that *Peyton Place* dethroned as the top-ranked best seller: *Gone with the Wind*. Margaret Mitchell's Civil War epic is useful to this discussion for many reasons. Like *Peyton Place*, it is a female-authored text with a strong-willed heroine at its center. Furthermore, *Gone with the Wind* contains a very famous rape scene that resolves into a seduction. And in both novels, the rapists are darkly drawn strangers-to-town that the narratives develop into heroes of a sort. Perhaps most important, in both works, white masculinity is taken to task. As I will show, in *Peyton Place*, the idiosyncratic dysfunctions and perversions that Metalious catalogues among the male members of the community are symptomatic of the pathological investment in whiteness that structures the town.

## Tough Love: Tom Makris and the Right Kind of Rape

I have maintained that although Metalious's sexual politics might have seemed progressive at the time, they also trade on a timeworn masculinist ideology that articulates a discourse of rape fantasy in the same moment that her novel seeks to give voice and vitality to the fact of female sexual agency. In a similar vein, *Peyton Place*'s endorsement of Tom's role as the agent of Constance's liberation is troubling because of the manner through which the conversion from "ice maiden" to erotic helpmeet is effected. On the one hand, Metalious's installment of the town's newly arrived dark other as the bedrock for Constance's domestic stability and as an important figure in the community as the schools' new principal is a progressive gesture, particularly in 1956. However, her attempt at balancing Tom's logic, rationality, and occasional tender gesture toward Constance with a sexually violent tendency undermines her critique of race by repeating the terms of the self-same discourse of bigotry.

The scenes at the lake and in her bedroom stand alone in their violence against Constance. The romantic interludes between the lovers that follow their first encounter are peppered with nuzzles and sweet nothings as if to justify the stormy initial contact by way of demonstrating the committed coupling it produces. Constance herself is occasionally mystified by the anomaly of Tom's tenderness:

> He could do little things like kissing her finger tips or the inside of her wrist with a complete naturalness and sincerity that kept them from seeming planned or contrived. Once, he had kissed the sole of her bare foot and she had been aroused to the point of powerful and immediate desire. At first, she had been embarrassed by his unorthodox expressions of tenderness, for they had reminded her of love scenes in rather effete novels. They seemed incongruous coming, as they did, from a man of Tom's size and temperament. (181–2)

Their relationship has remained sexual as well as romantic. We learn that Constance "had done [Tom] the favor, in over two years, of sleeping with him perhaps a dozen times" (181). He is, by his own admission, "hog-tied and completely swozzled" by Constance, and Tom's devotion is manifest in his patience in the face of her reticence to marry on account of Allison (181). That Tom is more gentleman than brute in the wake of his first foray into Constance's bed may be Metalious's manner of reha-bilitating his reputation for her readers while still sanctioning the rough-ness of his initial approach as a necessary step in rehabilitating Constance's identity.[1] Constance's occasional surprise at Tom's sweetness, informed perhaps by her own history with him, allows her to accept the story about his sexual initiation without objecting to his role in it, one that bespeaks a consistency in his bedside manner. The context for this revelation is a discussion about teenage sexuality, brought on by the news about town that Betty Anderson is pregnant by Rodney Harrington and has been "left with the short end of the stick": she has been sent away to Vermont to have the baby or an abortion, and she can expect little to no financial support from the Harringtons (215). Where Constance finds it "awful" that teenagers might think about, not to mention engage in, sexual acts of any stripe, Tom argues that it would be abnormal for them *not* to. He clarifies his position, telling Constance that he does not "[advocate] for-nication on every street corner and an illegitimate child in every home"; however, physical maturity, social conditioning, and a "basic drive for sex" suggest to him that teenage sexuality is completely natural and not at all abnormal (217). When Constance dares him to convince her that he was driven by "this tremendous basic urge at the age of fifteen or sixteen," Tom responds:

> "Fourteen," . . . and laughed at the look on her face. "Fourteen I was. She was a kid who lived in a tenement on the same floor as I, and I caught her in the toilet at the end of the hall. I took her standing up, with the stink of potatoes boiled too long in too much water, and filth and urine all around us, and I loved it. I may even say that I wallowed in it, and I couldn't wait to get back for more." (217)

Constance is bothered by the crudeness of his manner but not the sub-stance of his story. Tom defends his rendering by prioritizing truth over niceness: "Some of the things I say may not be particularly 'nice,' but they are true. It was, perhaps, not particularly 'nice' of me to have intercourse with little Sadie, or whatever the hell her name was, in a hallway toilet, but it is true," he retorts (218). The objection that Constance makes in this case, and that Tom dismisses, is not that Sadie may not have welcomed

Tom's advances; rather, it is that the locale perhaps left something to be desired. This remark *almost* grants Tom the benefit of a more enriched hindsight. Instead, it is less a matter of Sadie's wishes, and more a matter of where Tom was most readily able to satisfy his own sex drive.

What is especially interesting about the Sadie story, in addition to how it recalls the dominance of Tom's sexual will over Constance's on their first long night together, is how Metalious uses it to critique Constance's willful naïveté, her aggressive amnesia for her own late-adolescent sexual history, and her present-day prudence. Tom's earthy encounter with Sadie, who may or may not have been a willing participant, is meant to exemplify a healthy young libido in action. Sexual desire, Tom argues, is healthy, and sexual intercourse is normal. Sex is to be celebrated, as Tom's "wallowing" suggests, not suppressed or shamed. And this is what he teaches Constance over the course of their courtship. By novel's end, her sexual desire has resurfaced, and she has been remade by Tom's tutelage into a woman who enjoys and initiates sex. Tom's attitude toward sex is promoted by Metalious as the most enlightened the novel has to offer and as a welcome alternative to the tyranny of repression and resultant dysfunction that haunts Constance until she fully unburdens herself of the secret of her past. Tom's approach is not simply an antidote to Constance; Metalious installs him as the healthy alternative to white sexuality. He is the foil to Leslie Harrington's irresponsible paternity; Rodney Harrington's oversexed, boastful chauvinism; Lucas Cross's lechery; and Norman Page's effeminate mother love. In her adulation of Tom's manliness and sexual progressivism, Metalious retreads timeworn stereotypes about black masculinity and reproduces racism in her very attempt to dismantle some of its power.

Like the rape-made-right between Tom and Constance, the scene of Tom's sexual coming of age seems to have escaped especial remark by commentators of *Peyton Place*. In its presumption and assertion of a "boys will be boys" approach to male sexual behavior and its potential violence, it understands Tom's impulses and actions as natural and normal, the way things should be. There are two parts to this kind of status quo: (1) that sex is normal and natural and should be understood and accepted as such; (2) that male sexual aggression is normal and natural and should be understood and accepted as such. Tom's coming of age and Constance's sexual reinitiation are of a piece in their violence and their privileging of Tom's desires over those of his female partners. The episode between Tom and Constance is unique in their relationship, as no other sex scene between them involves Tom's use of force in the service of his sexual satisfaction. While the "brutal," "torturous," "pain"-ridden kisses, the back-handed slaps and demands of silent obedience on Tom's first night of intercourse with Constance mellow dramatically into tender displays of affection in and out of bed, the Sadie story reaffirms his violent potential for more of the same. Tom's sexual initiation reminds us of this tendency and suggests that his assault on Constance may be more the rule than the exception in his approach to sexual relations. Like Metalious's positioning of the rape scene as a flashback within the context of an already established relationship, the strategic placement of the Sadie story in the narrative similarly justifies Tom's use of force. This scene, like Constance's flashback, is presented as part of the dialogue of an affianced couple. Following the flashback as it does, it recalls the violence that brought about Tom and Constance's coupling and indicates that such aggression is condoned by Metalious, not condemned. Indeed, the story is not at all an indictment of Tom and his bedside manner but rather a critique of Constance's own prudish mores and her wishful thinking about adolescent innocence. The novel suggests that Constance has internalized white patriarchal norms. Tom is presented as the cure for what is ailing her.

## Midcentury Masculinity

Male sexual aggression had to some degree been normalized by midcentury. Young women were taught to expect sexual advances from young men and were instructed that it was their job to put a stop to them. If a man "took liberties" with a woman, she was to blame: "either she had not set limits or she was not truly virtuous" (Bailey, 88). This belief system was an outgrowth of what Sabine Sielke has called the "remasculinization" of American national identity after the Civil War (8). This recalibration of male gender identity culminated, according to some social commentators, in a full-blown "crisis of masculinity" by the mid-twentieth century, a term that would appear in the title of Arthur Schlesinger Jr.'s 1958 essay.[2] The nature of modern life at the turn of the century threatened traditional constructions of manhood on several fronts. Commentators raised alarms regarding the threat women posed to men and "decried the 'overcivilization' of the nation by moralizing women and aggressive female reformers who attacked saloons and brothels" (Cuordileone, 525). In an effort to counteract the effects of these threats and the dreaded forces of "overcivilization" (which was of especial concern with the end of westward expansion) that resulted from the excessive influence of women in politics and social reform, white, middle-class American men laid claim to their collectively endangered gender identity by celebrating the very characteristics that had heretofore been considered liabilities: "aggression, passion, combativeness, strength" (525). "Masculinity" itself was a turn-of-the-century coinage and conception. "Manhood" had previously been the yardstick used to determine one's status as a full-fledged male of the species. By the late nineteenth century, one's manhood could no longer be assumed. It needed constant cultivation. One's maleness now needed to be performed and proven in order to be accepted as fact. "Manhood" had signaled the maturation of boys into the gendered adulthood of men. Manhood was a state of being, a kind of achievement of rank that, once accomplished, remained relatively secure because it was most distinctly opposed to "childhood," which was a state of being that one was expected to age out of. "Masculinity," on the other hand, implied a quality of being, something one needed to monitor and perform in order to convince others of its existence. Unlike manhood, the life-stage into which males inexorably aged after adolescence, masculinity was "a set of behavioral traits and attitudes . . . that had to be constantly demonstrated, the attainment of which was forever in question" (Kimmel, *Manhood* 81). Whereas the opposite of manhood was childhood, "masculinity" had to work to define and defend itself against its opposite, "femininity," the performance of those qualities understood to be essentially female and that would confer womanliness upon its actors. These new "-inities" required constant attention, maintenance, and adjustment. What was before considered inherent had been destabilized and was now in need of continuous cultivation, public demonstration, and affirmation.[3]

## Reconstructing Menace: Racial Difference as Sexual Difference

Definitions of masculinity and femininity in American culture came to be heavily dependent on the construction of race. The recalibration of gender identities repositioned the black male body such that the constructed definition of black male sexuality informed the emergent white male gender identity. According to Sielke, this occurred through the conversion of "Southern struggles over political and economic supremacy into emotionally charged narratives of sexuality and gender" (33). She demonstrates how "black masculinity . . . signifies both racial *and* sexual otherness" by tracing the evolution of the relationship between the black male and the white male in antebellum America. Following Walter Benn Michaels, Sielke notes that black male identity was constructed in opposition to white male gender identity by emasculating black men and constructing white masculinity in contrast to it, producing an ideology that "reasserts racial difference by insisting upon black male sexual difference" (36). During Reconstruction, the granting, in theory if not practice, of full status *as* men to black men eradicated the constructed gender differences that had ideologically inhered in the white view of black men, and an effort to define difference based primarily on race dominated. This reworking of difference in order to justify Jim Crow enabled the maintenance and normalization of the continuum that positioned black and white men at its opposite ends. One way white males managed the threat inherent in this view (of the predatory, bestial, savage black man) was through the practice of lynching, which frequently involved the literal castration of its victims as a cautionary tale to others. As a result, the assertion of racial-difference-as-sexual-difference recapitulated the gender differences of the antebellum era with the "paradoxical image of the emasculated black sexual violator" (36). This redirected focus onto black male bodies required reiteration in order to achieve its power. "Just as women had to be instructed into Victorian notions of femininity," Sielke observes, "the reconstruction of masculinity as economic, political, *and* physical dominance did not come naturally" (30).

Unnatural though it may have been, the imaginative reach of this racially renovated masculinity held sway in U.S. efforts to assert white supremacy in the North and South. Furthermore, it helped to normalize male sexual aggression in general and black male sexual rapaciousness in particular, giving rise to what Angela Davis has called "the myth of the black rapist." Like the idea of "masculinity," the widespread view of the sexually threatening black male was largely a postbellum invention, owing to the anxiety attendant on white male gender identity during Reconstruction. Frederick Douglass noted that the postwar belief that black men were sexually dangerous to white women lacked supporting evidence. There were no known charges of black-on-white rape during the war, a time when white male family members were on battlefronts far from home and white women would have been most vulnerable to attack (Davis, 184). Without actual incidents to point to, the imagined sexual menace posed by black men was "not credible for the simple reason that it implied a radical and instantaneous change in the mental and moral character of Black people" (189). Still, the associations between blackness and brutishness and whiteness and virtue have a long history, which enabled late-nineteenth-century sociologists, anthropologists, medical doctors, politicians, and practitioners from a variety of disciplines to shore up and perpetuate the belief in an innate sexual depravity among blacks. Winthrop

Jordan notes that rumors of the African reputation for lasciviousness preceded the Englishman's first encounter with blacks during the Renaissance. It was when English slave traders recognized a need to justify their business that they "found special reason to lay emphasis on the Negro's savagery" (27).[4] Similarly, blackness and whiteness had accrued connotations ahead of English involvement with the slave trade. Following Jordan, Peter Fryer explains, "Blackness, in England, traditionally stood for death, mourning, baseness, evil, sin and danger. . . . White, on the other hand, was the colour of purity, virginity, innocence, good magic, flags of truce, harmless lies, and perfect human beauty" (Fryer, 135). European explorers recorded and circulated tales of Africans engaging in "a beastly copulation or conjuncture" with apes. As a result, in the hierarchy of the eighteenth century's organizing principle of living things, the Great Chain of Being, "the place just above the ape was occupied by the Negro" (Jordan, 229).

The rhetoric of antislavery in the antebellum United States charged slave owners with treating their slaves as if they were beasts. The comparison to animals, Jordan remarks, "was entirely justified if not taken literally. . . . Certain aspects of the revolutionary new racial slavery pushed the colonists toward thinking about their Negroes as primarily and merely physical creatures" (232). Among these were both the manner of transport and the treatment of blacks on slave ships as if they were livestock. Stories of slave revolt or rebellion spread as cautionary tales to plantation owners, signaling blacks' "Barbarous, Wild, and Savage Natures" (qtd. in Jordan, 232).[5] As noted above, in the wake of the Civil War, the image of the black-as-beast was recast as a sexual threat to the safety and chastity of white women and, by extension, the purity of the white race.

The view of Africa as a "land of licentiousness" was long-lived and continued to inform the racist idea that blacks were possessed of barely contained libidos (Fredrickson 276). Anne McClintock notes, "The association of black people and sexuality goes back to the Middle Ages: sexuality itself had long been called, 'the African sin,' and black men on colonial maps were frequently represented with exaggeratedly long penises" (113). Owing partly to the freedoms and rights that had been promised to former slaves, black men were imagined to lust especially after white women. These freedoms, racist propaganda warned, "had led to dreams of 'social equality' and had encouraged blacks to expropriate white women by force. Thus the Negro's overpowering desire for white women was often described as the central fact legitimizing the whole program of legalized segregation and disenfranchisement" (Fredrickson, 282). It was also leveraged as the most effective justification for lynching. Initially, defenders of this brand of white supremacist vigilantism defended the practice first as a deterrent against black uprisings, and then for the sake of maintaining white dominion over blacks (Davis, 185). Neither of these explanations satisfied critics of the practice, who, though sometimes sharing the racist ideological aims of the lynch mobs, held that "lynching tended to be shocking to the kind of 'civilized' sensibilities that were willing to condone milder manifestations of racism" (Fredrickson, 272).

## "The Peril of White Women": Competing Masculinities in *Gone with the Wind*

Enter the figure of the black rapist. In order to justify the brutality of lynching as a fit form of punishment, it was necessary to offer an equally heinous crime as a rationale. Thus arose the "[contention] that many Negroes were literally wild beasts, with uncontrollable sexual passions and criminal natures stamped by heredity" and that these urges tended in the direction of white, female flesh (276). It was in his perceived threat to white womanhood that the black man was most vilified. In defense of the practice, one southern, turn-of-the-century essayist expressed a view echoed by many: "When a desire to indulge in his bad passions comes over him, he seems to be utterly devoid of prudence or of conscience. . . . A bad negro is the most horrible creature upon the earth, the most brutal and merciless" (qtd. in Fredrickson, 278).[6] Though few lynchings actually involved accusations of rape, the specter of black depravity endangering the virtue and chastity of white womanhood remained a compelling one in both the North and South, a threat that cut to the heart of American anxieties about sex, gender, race, and class.

Since its inception after the Civil War, the myth of the black rapist has continued to resonate in the nation's collective consciousness. "When blacks traveled north, the image of the rapist followed them" (D'Emilio and Freedman, 297). The figure of the black rapist was perhaps most spectacularly impressed on the American cultural consciousness through D. W. Griffith's 1915 epic, *The Birth of a Nation*, a film that posits the birth of the Ku Klux Klan as an analogue of the nation's originary moment. Griffith's magnum opus introduced to the masses the "pure black buck," a character whose temperament was "oversexed and savage, violent and frenzied" in his "lust for white flesh" (Bogle, 13). Of Griffith's depiction of black men as brute beasts, film scholar Donald Bogle writes, "the black bucks of [*The Birth of a Nation*] are psychopaths, one always panting and salivating, the other forever stiffening his body as if the mere presence of a white woman in the same room could bring him to a sexual climax" (15). The furor over Griffith's depiction of sexually aggressive black men in *The Birth of a Nation* was so great, according to Bogle, that filmmakers after 1915 effectively backed off of such portrayals and played most black characters for laughs (16).

Just over two decades later, in 1936, Margaret Mitchell's best-selling *Gone with the Wind* reiterated American fears of the libidinous black male and fabulated the widespread predation of black men upon white women. Of all the dangers Mitchell enumerates facing southerners during the tumult of Reconstruction when free blacks "were now the lords of creation" (638), the greatest was "the peril of white women": "It was the large number of outrages on women and the ever-present fear for the safety of their wives and daughters that drove Southern men to cold and trembling fury and caused the Ku Klux Klan to spring up over night" (640). Mitchell capitalizes later in the novel on the fears she has stoked, making Scarlett O'Hara the victim of a robbery perpetrated by two men, one white and one black. The latter boasts "a chest like a gorilla" (770), a comparison in keeping with the catalogue of similes likening blacks to animals wild and domesticated that Mitchell uses throughout. When the black man reaches for Scarlett in order to search her for money, Mitchell refrains from writing a rape; however, the sexual menace is made clear in her description of the assault:

> What happened next was like a nightmare to Scarlett, and it all happened so quickly. . . . As the negro came running to the buggy, his black face twisted in a leering grin, she fired point-blank at him. Whether or not she hit him, she never knew, but the next minute the pistol was wrenched from her hand by a grasp that almost broke her wrist. The negro was beside her, so close that she could smell the rank odour of him as he tried to drag her over the buggy side. With her one free hand she fought madly, clawing at his face, and then she felt his big hand at her throat and, with a ripping noise, her basque was torn open from neck to waist. Then the black hand fumbled between her breasts, and terror and revulsion such as she had never known came over her and she screamed like an insane woman. (771)

Although the robber's sexual intentions are not made explicit, the leering grin coupled with the image of a black hand fumbling between white breasts conveyed a sexual threat to an American readership. The robbery itself is cut short, however, by the well-timed intervention of Big Sam, the foreman of Scarlett's father's plantation. His arrival on the scene allows Scarlett to make her escape.[7] Word of her brush with "outrage" prompts the local KKK to retaliate swiftly, killing both of her assailants.

Though Scarlett escapes the robbery with her honor intact, in a scene that shares quite a bit of the spirit and language with which Constance MacKenzie's forced intimacy with Tom Makris is described, she is later raped by Rhett Butler, at long last her husband, as punishment for her suspected infidelity with Ashley Wilkes, the elusive object of Scarlett's romantic reveries. Rhett, like Tom Makris in *Peyton Place*, is a darkly drawn interloper who is dark-skinned, virile, libidinous, violent:

> He was a tall man and powerfully built. Scarlett thought she had never seen a man with such wide shoulders, so heavy with muscles, almost too heavy for gentility. When her eye caught his, he smiled, showing animal-white teeth below a close-clipped black moustache. He was dark of face, swarthy as a pirate, and his eyes were as bold and black as any pirate's appraising a galleon to be scuttled or a maiden to be ravished. (97)

Scarlett's first impressions are reiterated and ratified elsewhere in the novel. Rhett's body is "powerful and latently dangerous in its lazy grace": "He looked, and was, a man of lusty and unashamed appetites" (177). Rhett's "large and brown and strong" hands cause Melanie Wilkes to shrink from him with fear: "They seemed so predatory, so ruthless" (942).

Rhett's rape of Scarlett is punitive. He believes, as does the rest of Atlanta, that Scarlett and Ashley have been having an affair. He means to teach Scarlett something by forcing her to submit to his sexual will, and indeed he does. Much as Metalious does twenty years later, Mitchell introduces her heroine to a new world of sexual pleasure, occasioned, though it is, by an act of violence. Both Scarlett and Constance are swept up a flight of stairs by their assailants. Like Tom's "bruising, hurtful mouth" (Metalious, 149), Rhett's kisses are marked by "savagery" and "lips too bruising" (Mitchell, 918). Scarlett's initial terror of Rhett's sexual frenzy is quickly transformed into desire and passion:

> Suddenly she had a wild thrill such as she had never known: joy, fear, madness, excitement, surrender to arms that were too strong, lips too bruising, fate that moved too fast. For the first time in her life she had met someone, something stronger than she, someone she could neither bully nor

break, someone who was bullying and breaking her. . . . The man who had carried her up the dark stairs was a stranger of whose existence she had not dreamed. And now, though she tried to make herself hate him, tried to be indignant, she could not. He had humbled her, hurt her, used her brutally through a wild mad night and she had gloried in it. (917–18)

Of course, Scarlett and Rhett come to different ends than Tom and Constance. Scarlett discovers that she loves Rhett; however, she loses him in the end. As feminist film critic Molly Haskell observes, "Afraid that if she yields an inch, she will lose herself completely, she is, contrary to appearances, the least secure of heroines" (132). Insecure though she is to start with, Constance, it turns out, is more readily amenable to Tom's attempts to "destroy completely [her] need for protection" (Metalious, 178). As in the case of Scarlett O'Hara, it is protection in the service of self-preservation. As a result, Constance is rewarded in the end with her marriage to Tom and a life, we are led to believe, of nevermore inhibited sexual pleasure.

Rhett's swarthiness, his virility, his role as *Gone with the Wind*'s romantic hero are presented in contrast to the passé version of masculinity embodied by Ashley Wilkes. Ashley quite literally pales in comparison with Rhett: he is blonde, light-skinned, grey-eyed, slender, and effete. Whereas Rhett unapologetically spends a great deal of his time in brothels, Ashley "was born of a line of men who used their leisure for thinking, not doing, for spinning brightly coloured dreams that had in them no touch of reality. He moved in an inner world that was more beautiful than Georgia and came back to reality with reluctance" (Mitchell, 28). He was raised to assume the role of the Genteel Patriarch (Kimmel, *Gender*, 28–29); however, with the Confederate loss of the Civil War, Ashley finds himself at odds with the world. His incompetence as a farmer is a point of pride for Scarlett: "[He] was bred for better things. . . . He was born to rule, to live in a large house, ride fine horses, read books of poetry and tell negroes what to do. That there were no more mansions and horses and negroes and few books did not alter matters. Ashley wasn't bred to plough and split rails" (Mitchell, 679). His brand of masculinity is obsolete and impractical, no longer viable given the exigencies of the new, increasingly industrialized America.[8] The most incisive assessment of Ashley's obsolescence comes from Rhett, whose mercenary approach to life during and after the war makes him well suited to survival. Rhett corrects Scarlett when she reads his regard for Ashley as contempt. It is pity, he notes, for Ashley's having lost his place in the world:

His breed is of no use or value in an upside-down world like ours. Whenever the world up-ends, his kind is the first to perish. And why not? They don't deserve to survive because they won't fight—don't know how to fight. This isn't the first time the world's been upside down and it won't be the last. It's happened before and it'll happen again. And when it does happen, everyone loses everything and everyone is equal. And then they all start again at taw, with nothing at all. That is, nothing except the cunning of their brains and the strength of their hands. But some people, like Ashley, have neither cunning nor strength or, having them scruple to use them. And so they go under and they should go under. It's a natural law and the world is better off without them. But there are always a hardy few who come through and, given time, they are right back where they were before the world turned over. (756)

In opposing Ashley and Rhett as she does in terms of a dichotomy of light and dark, Mitchell values those attributes associated with her swarthy hero as vital to the survival of the South: virility, cunning, strength, and a thinly veiled brutish nature unleashed when circumstances permit and/or require it. Though Rhett's darkness is clearly meant to enhance his desirability, it is not to be confused with the darkness of the novel's slave and free black population. Rhett Butler is the bad boy of a well-to-do Charleston family whose last name suggests Anglo-Saxon ancestry. It is rumored that he is not received by any of South Carolina's respectable families because of an alleged sexual dalliance with a young girl he then refused to marry. Despite the fact that Rhett is a foreigner to Georgia society at the outset, we can be assured that for all his swarthy skin and animal-white teeth, he is still a free, white, southern male. Dark though he may be in contrast to Ashley Wilkes, Rhett is not the darkest man in town. As if to affirm his white masculinity, he boasts of having "killed a negro for being 'uppity to a lady'" (633).

While Mitchell makes liberal use of the racialized connotations of darkness to draw Rhett as an outsider and to heighten his erotic potential as a romantic partner for Scarlett, their ill-starred union is a safe indulgence and does not threaten miscegenation. This is not to dismiss the ambivalence Mitchell evidences in her portrayal of Rhett. His darkness is clearly sexier to her than Ashley's wan pallor. Still, even though both *Gone with the Wind* and *Peyton Place* both engage with a critique of whiteness that offers a darker alternative as ultimately more viable in its stead, the difference between the two turns on the breadth of their critiques and the matter of ethnicity. In *Gone with the Wind*, Mitchell's critique is essentially limited to a study of competing masculinities: it is the old-guard, effete, ineffectual, and pale style of American manhood that is defunct, and she presents Rhett in its stead as the rugged alternative in the South during Reconstruction. Metalious presents whiteness as defective and dysfunctional for *both* sexes. Both offer a dark hero in place of the defective or defunct alternative but with a significant difference: Rhett Butler is white; Tom Makris is not quite—he is *Peyton Place*'s darkest man in town during the time of the story's telling.

Whatever Mitchell's fascination with tawny, brawny men may be, *Gone with the Wind*'s unself-conscious racism assures us of Rhett's racial whiteness. Metalious's position two decades later is more daring. Tom's Greek extraction distinguishes him not just physically (being the "big, black Greek" that he is), but ethnically from all of the other townspeople.[9] By positioning Tom as the novel's exemplar of sexual health and well-being, the novel comments not only on sexual repression, perversion, and dysfunction on its own terms but suggests that such damage is tied specifically to whiteness.

## The Crisis of White Masculinity

Mid-twentieth-century rhetoric about race held intact many previously established beliefs about black men and their sexuality. Comic books and, in particular, the campaigns against them foregrounded familiar terms in the discourse of race relations in America. Psychiatrist Frederic Wertham's *Seduction of the Innocent* (1954) and Geoffrey Wagner's *Parade of Pleasure: A Study of Popular Iconography in the U.S.A.* (1955) lambasted the violence, eroticism, and race prejudice inherent in comic books, especially those within the so-called jungle comics genre, which "reproduced the master narrative of American racism" in their frequent depictions of bestial black natives in the thrall of white she-goddesses, the objects of their savage desires (Friedman, 212). "The endless circulation of the white-woman-kidnapped-by-an-ape theme," Andrea Friedman observes, "was an iteration of white fears of, and attraction to, black men's alleged sexual prowess" (213). Wertham's attack drew attention to the conflation of sex, race, and aggression and their collective impact on the morality of a predominantly male readership and the implied safety of everyone else, while at the same time reflecting white anxieties about race and class (Friedman, 211–13). In the pre-dawn light of the civil rights era, "heightened attention to the persistence of racial intolerance collided with long-standing fears of African-American difference, especially sexual difference"

(Friedman, 212). In perhaps the most famous 1950s fetishization of any single population, Norman Mailer's "The White Negro" (1957) exalts the physicality and immediacy of his version of the black man's life:

> Knowing in the cells of his existence that life was war, nothing but war, the Negro (all exceptions admitted) could rarely afford the sophisticated inhibitions of civilization, and so he kept for his survival the art of the primitive. He lived in the enormous present, he subsisted for his Saturday night kicks, relinquishing the pleasures of the mind for the more obligatory pleasures of the body, and in his music he gave voice to the character and quality of his existence, to his rage and the infinite variations of joy, lust, languor, growl, cramp, pinch, scream and despair of his orgasm. (214)

If there is meant to be anything at all progressive in Mailer's panegyric, it may be in his suggestion that the characteristics he so admires in black men are the products of a choice, a conscious decision to keep one thing and relinquish another, rather than the emanation of an essence. Despite the admiration Mailer expresses for his artfully primitive, uninhibited, pleasure-seeking subject, his radicalism is racism by another name. Mailer's appreciation of his extraordinary rendition of black masculinity is itself an attempt to critique whiteness by valuing the traits he sees as the dominant characteristics of black men in America and appropriating them into his definition of the 1950s hipster (his "white negro"). The offenses of this essay are many, including his equating of black masculinity with psychopathy. Objectionable though the work is in its execution, it shares with *Peyton Place* an attempt to call attention to the price of white cultural mandates on white folk, offering something more vital, though ideologically problematic, in its place.

Where midcentury social commentators saw normative American masculinity in crisis, so, too, did Grace Metalious. The challenge to the nation's collectively envisioned male gender ideal, which at the turn of the century had inspired the coinage of the term *masculinity*, had reached a fever pitch by the 1950s. Owing to factors ranging from the conformist demands of the corporate workplace to the changing nature of marital and sexual partnerships and fatherhood, demands for racial and sexual equality, and consumerism and the life of leisure it offered, white American masculinity was girding itself from attack in all arenas.[10] What made the midcentury "crisis" new, observes Cuordileone, was that anticommunist America sought to elicit conformity from its citizens. The rugged, muscular individualism embodied by the turn-of-the-century's Rooseveltian "bully manhood" was thwarted by the demands of family and the work-place, the traditional forums for the performance and exercise of male autonomy and authority. Muscles no longer made the man. The problem cut much deeper than that. "At issue now," Cuordileone writes, "was a wholesale *loss of self*," resulting in part from "a 'togetherness' ethos that seemed to reek of collectivism":

> Loss of self was no small concern in the age of the Cold War. The self was the necessary bulwark not simply against the false delicacies and coddled sensibilities that Henry James's hero Basil Ransom ranted about when he declared his generation sadly "womanized" but also against conformity's new mid-twentieth-century corollary: totalitarianism. As such, the postwar expression of a crisis in masculinity, while stemming from a mixture of old and new trends, dislocations and fears, now carried unparalleled weight. (526)

Compounding the strain on the white American male was the fact that he was being asked to behave according to contradictory imperatives. On the one hand, fears of communist infiltration required both the eternal vigilance of the American man and his readiness to engage in militarized violence. At the very same time, while they were being primed for more than just ideological battle with communists within and beyond U.S. bor-ders, the nation's men were being asked to participate in the egalitarian partnership of the companionate marriage in the home, which asked that men not only cede dominion over their families in favor of a democratic partnership with their wives, but that they commit themselves to a "to-getherness" in family life that limited the autonomy central to earlier defi-nitions of masculinity. The discrepancy between these two expectations of male behavior gave rise to the concern that some men would confuse one imperative with the other and misdirect the aggression cultivated on behalf of anticommunism into the heart of the family (Friedman, 219). Alongside these fears of a hypersexualized and violent masculinity run rampant existed worries that loss of male autonomy, resulting from the combined effects of the companionate marriage, too much "togetherness," and "overmothering," would lead boys and men into "gender inversion" or homosexuality.

## The Pale Males of *Peyton Place*

Several of Metalious's male characters exist along a continuum of mas-culinity ranging from inadequate to pathological, and in most cases their whiteness connotes their dysfunction. None of Metalious's white men are particularly ennobled save for the possible exception of Doc Swain, who, interestingly, is said to be possessed of southern qualities. Of the town's power brokers, Seth Buswell, the town's newspaper editor, was long ago bested by Leslie Harrington in the competition for the hand in marriage of Elizabeth Fuller and, ever after, Buswell remains single and committed to his paper and the town. His personal history with Harrington aside, Buswell shies away from using the paper as a platform for exposing Harrington's corruption, opting instead to maintain his long-held position of "tolerant detachment" when he might instead reveal the extent of Harrington's abuses of power (284). Buswell's inoffensiveness and ineffectuality are matched by Harrington's taste for triumphant conquest at any price. It is this obsessive impulse that won him his bride and cost Elizabeth her life. Following eight miscarriages in as many years, and having been told that his wife would not survive childbirth were she able to sustain a pregnancy, Harrington insists that he will have his way (which is to say a son and an heir) and marshals Elizabeth through nine months of bed rest, through childbirth, and, after the first cry from her red-faced newborn son, into her grave (205–6).

With his race and class privilege behind him, Leslie Harrington is in many ways a nightmare version of Ashley Wilkes, had the latter been able to assume the role of Genteel Patriarch that was his antebellum birthright. Having inherited the Cumberland Mills from his father and grandfather before him, Harrington shares with the southern plantation owner the management of a capitalist enterprise on a large scale. His concentration of power in town is nearly absolute and blatantly corrupt. In addition to manipulating and exploiting his labor force, Harrington holds controlling interests in the bank and its mortgage lending practices, runs the local school board, and owns and operates the Labor Day carnival during which he earns back a sum of his workers' wages. Just as Mitchell's dark interloper Rhett Butler makes the sharpest observations about Ashley's shortcomings in *Gone with the Wind*, in *Peyton Place*, Tom Makris sees Harrington's draconian control over his mill for what it is: a way "to hide the mediocre mind and fear of impotency that tortured him" (178). Harrington's lessons to his son, Rodney, (including the misogynistic declaration that there isn't a girl worth over two dollars) pass along his habit of swagger above substance, and in the end his father-to-son teachings secure his impotence in town and effectively signal the sunset of his commercial empire. Rodney is killed in an auto accident while reaching for the bared breast of his date in the passenger seat (314). With Rodney's death,

Harrington loses his only heir, gained cavalierly at the cost of his wife's life. His comeuppance is severe and significantly erodes his power in town. Where he was once feared, he is now pitied.

Harrington's roles, direct and indirect, in the deaths of his wife (in his triumph over her body's reproductive resistance) and son (inculcating in him a value system that prioritizes groping a girl over keeping his hands on the steering wheel) corroborate Richard Dyer's analysis of the relationship between whiteness and death. To be truly white is to transcend the body, claims Dyer, and where this transcendence is meant to be suggestive of a spiritual elevation, to transcend embodiment is to be rid of all that is bodily—functions, desires, fleshiness, fluids. Dyer observes that while "the very struggle for whiteness is a sign of whiteness," the attempt "to recapture whiteness is also to shed life, which can mean nothing else than death" (208). This association is twofold: whiteness is not just the signifier of death; it is also its harbinger. Whiteness is deathly and deadly.[11] Harrington's whiteness is both. He is one of a few characters to whom whiteness is explicitly adjectivally ascribed: it is with "white hands" that he shuffles the cards at the poker game early in the novel. Rodney's death forces Harrington to confront the very fear of impotence Tom Makris suspects daunts him most. It effectively bleeds him of his power in town and his will to wield it.

Leslie Harrington's various abuses of power, socioeconomic as well as sexual, are overcompensations for what he fears he lacks, which is, according to Tom, a belief in his own masculinity. Harrington's deadly compulsion to sire an heir to his mill-yard empire demonstrates one version of the sort of sexual sickliness *Peyton Place* attributes to a white racial identity. In addition to the "emptiness, non-existence and death" connoted by whiteness in the extreme (Dyer, 45), Metalious suggests that an explicitly pale complexion is indicative of a generalized lack of health, a diseased state of physical and/or emotional well-being, often manifest through sexual dysfunction or perversity.[12] Norman Page is another case study in Metalious's catalogue of the toxic effects of white attitudes toward sex. It is through his character that she brings together the sadist and the sissy (to echo Andrea Friedman's pairing) of the midcentury sex panic. Whereas Leslie Harrington's bloodline is cut off with the death of his son, that of Norman, coded as the novel's closeted homosexual, is likely to end with himself.

Norman Page is Allison MacKenzie's sometime boyfriend, the effeminate pretty boy who, after observing an act of oral sex between a husband and his pregnant wife, strangles a cat. Familiar to the townsfolk as "little"

Norman Page (7), he's the easy target of Rodney Harrington's schoolyard bullying. Norman "seemed to be constructed entirely of angles" (7). His face is "pinched-lookin'," "pale lookin'," the color of "dead fish skins" (60), his skin so thinly white that he is "almost translucent" (133):

> Norman was a slight child, built on delicate lines. He had a finely chiseled mouth which trembled easily, and enormous brown eyes which were filled with tears more often than not. Norman's eyes were fringed with long, dark lashes. Just like a girl's, thought Allison. She could see the lines of blue veins plainly beneath the thin skin on his temples. Norman was very good looking, thought Allison, but not in the way that people thought of as handsome. He was pretty the way a girl is pretty, and his voice, too, was like a girl's, soft and high. The boys at school called Norman "sissy," a name with which the boy found no quarrel. He was timid and admitted it, easily frightened and knew it, and he wept at nothing and never tried to stop himself. (62–63)

Norman's effeminacy is tied directly to his mother's unusual affection for and control over him, effected through a combination of emotional manipulation and enemas, the latter a ritual in which Norman takes a "bittersweet sort of pleasure" (62) but one that saps him of energy and requires that he refrain from social interaction and remain in his mother's care.[13] In a particularly unsettling exchange, Evelyn Page extracts from Norman a declaration of his absolute devotion to her by forcing him to imagine her dead. When Norman guardedly admits that he likes Allison MacKenzie, Evelyn falls into a chair and weeps, telling Norman that such weakness and wickedness come from his father's side of the family. At her suggestion that Norman would be happier with her dead, Norman collapses in a heap before her and urgently renounces his affections for anyone but his mother:

> "I love only you, Mother. I don't love anybody else."
> "Are you sure, Norman? There's nobody else you love?"
> "No, no, no. There is no one else, Mother. Just you."
> "Don't you like Miss Thornton and little Allison, dear?"
> "No. No, I hate them! I hate everybody in the whole world except you."
> "Do you love Mother, Norman?"
> Norman's sobs were dry and painful now, and he hiccupped wretchedly.
> "Oh, yes, Mother. I love only you. I love you better than God, even. Say you're not going to leave me."

For a long time Mrs. Page stroked her son's bowed head which rested now on her knees.

"I'll never leave you, Norman," she said at last. "Never. Of course I am not going to die." (72)

Despite his assurances to the contrary, Norman's affections are, in fact, split, and he and Allison do go steady for a summer. It is their belated arrival home from a late summer picnic that sends Constance into the frenzy that unleashes her secret past to Allison in Tom's presence. After their ill-fated date, Norman is forbidden from seeing Allison again, and his formerly tentative approach to satisfying sexual desire (i.e., his seeking permission to kiss Allison) gets repressed and redirected into bursts of sudden and intense violence. When he feels the injustice of his mother's intrusive interrogation of how he and Allison have passed their time together (including his confession of a few shared kisses), and of her ousting of Allison from his life, Norman kills a hapless beetle he had been taunting with a stick (249). Soon afterward, he strangles Miss Hester Goodale's cat, punctuating an episode of sexual voyeurism that Metalious tells us satisfies in Norman an intensity of longing that he will never again know. During a visit with Miss Hester's neighbor, the very pregnant Mrs. Card, Norman hears Miss Hester's tomcat, the eccentric old lady's constant companion, mewing nearby. This, he realizes, means that Miss Hester is looking in unseen on the Card's backyard and inspires in him "a sudden and terrible longing to know *why* Miss Hester watched, and, more important, *what*":

> It was a frantic need to see and to know, and of such proportions that he knew he would never have a moment's peace until he had seen and until he knew. It was fortunate for Norman that he realized the dimensions of his desire, for after this one time, he was never able to do so again. Years later, when he fell prey to vague longings of an indeterminate nature, he brushed them away as foolishness. He never again realized the enormity of a desire the way he did on this hot Friday afternoon in 1939. (251)

Having hastily excused himself from Mrs. Card's company, Norman waits for Miss Hester to take her four o'clock walk and then makes his way to her back porch where he finds her peephole in the hedge and observes nothing more than what he had seen up close in Mrs. Card's backyard— the pregnant woman relaxing on a lounge chair. After Miss Hester's return, however, when Norman seeks cover on his belly in the tall grass surrounding the porch, he witnesses what Miss Hester has no doubt been watching—affectionate sex in broad daylight between Mr. and Mrs. Card, the sight of which makes Norman fiercely queasy.[14] It is Norman's good fortune that this episode between the married couple is too much for the old lady. It kills her, making his escape from her backyard an easy one. Later that evening, on his return from an errand, Norman hears Miss Hester's tomcat struggling to free itself from its lead, which is tied to the rocking chair in which Miss Hester's dead body sits rigidly still. The sound of the struggle and what it signifies to Norman—the trauma of his satisfied curiosity, his deep disgust at the sight of the Cards in a clinch, his violation of his friendship with them through his voyeurism, the secrets he shares with the dead Miss Goodale, and the end (as Metalious has told us) to Norman's awareness of his own desires—are too much for him. Rather than set the cat free, Norman strangles it, oblivious to the pain of the deep scratches he receives in the cat's struggle for its life. Later that night he becomes violently ill at home and when his mother offers him an enema to ease his discomfort, Norman gratefully accepts.

Five years later, Norman returns home from military service in World War II to a hero's welcome, despite having suffered a nervous breakdown. The town remains unaware of Norman's mental unfitness for continued battle, however; Evelyn's scheming has seen to it that his battle fatigue is camouflaged behind fake ribbons and medals and a practiced limp. In addition to experiencing the nightmares of a shell-shocked soldier, he is haunted by a recurring dream that predates his wartime experience:

In his dream, Miss Hester always wore the face of his mother, while the two people whom she watched through the gap in the hedge were no longer Mr. and Mrs. Card, but Allison MacKenzie and Norman. In his dream, when he stroked Allison's abdomen he would feel a tight excitement in his genitals but always, just at the moment of release, Allison's abdomen would first open and spew forth millions of slimy blue worms. The worms were deadly poisonous, and Norman would begin to run. He would run and run, until he could run no longer, while the worms crawled swiftly after him. Sometimes he woke up at this point, covered with sweat and choking with fear, but most of the time he succeeded in reaching the arms of his mother before he awoke. It was always at that moment, when he reached his mother, that Norman reached a climax in the excitement engendered by Allison. At such times, Norman awoke to warmth and wetness and a sense that his mother had saved him from a terrible danger. (309)

While Norman is initially excited by Allison's pregnant belly, the monstrous birth elicited by his touch inspires terror, loathing, fear, and disgust. And though his flight suggests avoidance, it does not quell his sexual response but rather provokes it. Norman's wet dream returns him time and again to his mother whose embrace "save[s] him from a terrible danger," a danger that remains unnamed. It points to a generalized fear of sexuality but more specifically represents Norman's fear of the shape of his desire and calls his heterosexuality into question. In addition to her characterization, however sympathetic, of Norman as a "sissy," and a "momma's boy," Metalious has told us that though he would later "[fall] prey to vague longings of an indeterminate nature . . . [h]e never again realized the enormity of a desire" as he had while waiting to learn what Miss Hester knew about Mr. and Mrs. Card (251). It should be noted that at this time, the term *sissy* referred to the "specific category of deviation" to which homosexuality belonged (Cohan, 86) and the sissy figure was the "exemplary homosexual" in his effeminacy (Cohan, 258). Norman's delicacy, his sensitivity, and the timidity of his sexual overtures to Allison suggest that, by 1950s standards, his masculinity has been compromised. Metalious withholds a direct statement of Norman's desires; however, the "indeterminate nature" of the "vague longings" that haunt him in adulthood point to sexual ambivalence. In his erotic nightmare, having sought sexual shelter in Evelyn, conflating his libidinal response to Allison's fertility with the oedipal oversight of his mother, Norman's release grants him only safety but no sexual satisfaction. Whatever conscious desires he possessed he strangled to death with Miss Hester's tomcat.

Norman Page and Leslie Harrington are among the most extreme examples in Metalious's catalogue of ineffectual men. Just as she surprises with her sympathy for each—the town stands by Harrington as he mourns his son; Norman is an unwitting victim of Evelyn's perverted motherhood—Metalious is unsparing in her critique of Selena's boyfriend, Ted Carter. He is the town's golden boy, its ideal male specimen embodied in an athletic and strapping young lad nearly six feet tall and a healthy 170 pounds, an example of the kind of body that older people look upon with satisfaction. It is to Ted that the town looks for its sense of stability in uncertain times:

> Things can't be so bad, they said, when this country can produce young men like that. In the summer of 1939, when the stage whispers of war in Europe were already audible to the pessimists in America, those who believed that world conflict was inevitable could look at Ted Carter and be comforted.

Things won't be so bad, they said, as long as we have big, healthy boys like that to send to war. Because Ted Carter's body had none of the loose-jointedness, the clumsily put together look of many sixteen-year-olds, his was the envy of every adolescent in Peyton Place. Because of it, and also because of his outstanding talent at sports, other, less fortunate, sixteen-year-olds forgave him his good marks in school, his charm, his easy way of making friends, and the good manners which many mothers flung constantly into the faces of sloppy talking, often discourteous sons. (169)

His "hard and muscular" body, earned through "years of sports and outdoor work," serves as a sign that America is on the right track and will be well served and protected against a belligerent aggressor (169). Ted is the unlikely product of the scandalous union of Harmon and Roberta "Bobbie" Carter, whose exploits culminating in their marriage are still close to the surface of the town's long memory. Together Harmon and Roberta secured their financial future through an arrangement in which Roberta married the old, lonely, and wealthy town doctor, Old Doc Quimby, siphoned his money to Harmon, and stirred up enough rumors in town through her liaisons with each man that Doc Quimby shot himself, clearing the way for the Carter marriage. Because of his good looks, good grades, and good manners, the town forgives Ted the sins of his parents. It also indulges in a bit of *Schadenfreude* when Ted becomes Selena Cross's steady, a matter over which Roberta and Harmon spar with their son. In his relationship with Selena, Ted is as conscientious and respectful as he is in all other aspects of his life. He ignores his parents' prejudice against Selena's lower-class status, one borne of their own origins on the shack-side of town. He plans his future with Selena, he does not press her for sex, and dutifully visits her in the hospital after her "emergency appendectomy."

The town's pride in Ted is misplaced, however. Though Peyton Place looks to him as an exemplar of the good American soldier, Ted, like bad-boy Rodney Harrington, does not go to war. Ironically, Norman Page is Peyton Place's only war hero. Instead of fighting, Ted remains on the home front, protecting not the nation but his ambitions to attend law school and become an attorney, a decision that costs him a fair measure of Selena's respect (291). And though he has calmly defended his association with Selena to his parents by explaining "how little talk matter[s]" in the end (171), Ted is unable to reconcile Selena's reputation as an accused murderess with his aspirations toward practicing law (335). He ends their relationship just before Selena's trial, and, rather than doing so honorably, he does so indirectly, writing to his mother that he's unable to get home from college in time for the proceedings.

Saddened though she is by Ted's lack of backbone, Selena does not fault him for it. She is all too aware of the way talk works in Peyton Place. The extent of Ted's self-interest, however, compromises his integrity. The good-looking, well-muscled, well-mannered, most promising example of young manhood in town lacks a sense of honor and duty. Ted's ruminations on what the town might say against him should he stand by Selena lead him to impugn her character for her ingratitude toward Lucas's sacrifices on her behalf: "There goes the Cross girl. She did in her father. Well, he wasn't really her father. He was more than that. He provided for her all her life, and he didn't have to do it. She wasn't his own. There goes the Cross girl. Married that young lawyer named Carter. Better keep away from him, a feller that'd take up with a murderess" (335).[15] Following Selena's acquittal, Metalious pairs Selena with her defense attorney, Peter Drake, a relative newcomer to town. The last we learn of Selena is that she and Drake were seen "having a very friendly talk" in Constance's dress shop (351). Having sought to protect his future, Ted has inadvertently secured Selena's. She has effectively traded up, landing herself a practicing attorney in place of her aspiring sometime love.

If there is meant to be an exception to the rule of inadequate white masculinity in *Peyton Place*, it is in the figure of the silver-haired, six-foot-tall, widowed, childless sexagenarian Doctor Matthew Swain, who emerges as the heroic white conscience of the town, a role that coincides with his job as the town's healer. A benevolently gruff fellow who is nearly universally beloved by his fellow citizens, Swain is "a good and upright man, and a lover of life and humanity" who "always spoke the truth" (42–43), though sometimes in a manner less than gentlemanly. His only apparent detractor is Marion Partridge, who has never forgiven the Doc for correctly diagnosing her with menopause. His nurses bear his chauvinism good-naturedly, and his housekeeper endures his lewd remarks as a matter of course (41–42). In keeping with her way of complicating the received cultural wisdom of race and gender, Metalious muddles Swain's Yankee goodness by marking his white masculinity with a peculiarly southern flavor. While it sets him apart from the other men in town and elevates his character because of the "gentlemanliness" it accords him, Swain's southernness enhances his entitlement to white class privilege such that he wields the threat of a lynching against Lucas Cross.

While I have discussed the relative racializations of Swain and Lucas and their significance in the context of Metalious's domestic dystopias in chapter 2, here I would like to return to the novel's portrayals of both men, reading Swain's whiteness and its co-construction with masculinity and class. Because of the contingent nature of racialization, Lucas figures in this discussion in that his darkening is catalyzed by Swain's whiteness and the power it confers on him. Though this necessitates some reiteration of the scene I treat in the earlier discussion, my hope is that by reading Swain and Lucas in these separate but related contexts, a fuller understanding of how race functions within *Peyton Place* will result.

It is Swain who is charged with making two of the novel's most difficult moral choices: whether or not to perform an abortion in order to give Selena Cross a chance at living a normal life, and whether or not to very publicly break the silence about Selena's sexual abuse by taking the stand in her defense (as she refuses to do so herself), and thus offer the courtroom the motive for her murder of Lucas. In each case, the good doctor decides in favor of Selena's life and against his own professional best interests. Despite the fact that abortion is illegal and could lose him his medical license, he performs the procedure with the unwitting assistance of the devoutly Catholic nurse Mary Kelley. When Selena refuses to defend herself against the first-degree murder charge to which she initially pleads guilty, a stubborn choice that will certainly send her to the gallows, Swain again values her life over his professional future. Having at the last minute persuaded her to submit a plea of "not guilty" on the day of the trial, Swain's heroic courtroom speech does save Selena's life and reiterates his inherent goodness. Indeed, he is venerated for his risk by the Boston newspaperman Delaney, who remarks, "what a magnificent old gentleman. . . . White suit, white hair and those bright blue eyes. What a gentleman!" (347)

The explicit mention of the various "whitenesses" of the good doctor, his suit, his hair, and the blueness of his eyes, serves to signal the strength of moral character that Swain has publicly demonstrated, elevating him to the level of "magnificence" in Delaney's view because of the figure he strikes. Interestingly, the Doc's whiteness is repeatedly represented throughout the book as being anomalously, but consistently, southern in nature. Indeed, even before Swain himself is introduced, in her travelogue of the well-to-do Chestnut Street, Metalious notes the distinctive architecture of Swain's home, "a white house, fronted with tall, slim pillars. Most of the townspeople defined it as 'southern looking'" (20), a description that is repeated as Selena approaches Swain's house to ask for his help with her pregnancy (141). Swain himself is in the habit of dressing in white suits, something for which Constance holds him in sartorial esteem and that gives the impression that he has been spirited up from the Civil War South. Tom Makris's first impression of "the tall, silver-haired" Swain is that the old doctor "looks like a walking ad for a Planter's Punch. A goddamned Kentucky colonel in this place!" (103). His misapprehension is corrected, however, when Swain greets the other patrons of Hyde's diner with a New Hampshire native's accent. Swain's taste for a racist joke, such as the one he plays on nurse Mary Kelley by persuading her that "niggers fart black" (84), further aligns him with a southern sensibility while at the same time repeating the northern racism that brought Samuel Peyton to New Hampshire in the first place (Watters, par. 4).

Perhaps the most startling link to an especially southern form of white masculinity emerges in Swain's confrontation with Lucas. Having just performed Selena's abortion, Swain pays a call on the Cross shack and surprises Lucas with the news of his stepdaughter's pregnancy. When Lucas refuses to admit his crime, Swain is prompted to intimidate the confession out of him by threatening vigilante justice in the form of a lynch mob:

> I'll raise an alarm all over town. I'll go personally and tell every father in Peyton Place what you did, Lucas. I'll tell them that their daughters aren't safe with you around. The fathers will come after you, Lucas, the same way they'd go after a wild and dangerous animal. But they won't shoot you." He paused and looked at the figure in front of him. "Know how long it's been since we had a lynching in this town, Lucas?"
>
> The eyes of the man in front of him swiveled around frantically, searching for escape from the merciless voice that drummed into his ears.
>
> "It was so long ago, Lucas, that no one remembers, for sure, just when it was. But lynching seems to be something an outraged man always knows how to do. The fathers will know how to do it, Lucas. Not too good, maybe. Not good enough so's you'd die on the first try, maybe. But they'd get the hang of it after a while. (157–58)

Like Allison MacKenzie's earlier comparison of Selena's rape to the dime store book jacket featuring the whipping of a slave girl, Doc Swain's threat calls up a history of racially significant associations that function to ascribe lightness and darkness to characters in Metalious's scene. Swain has already been likened to a "fugitive Kentucky colonel" (103) and his silver-haired, white-suited beneficence is reiterated throughout the novel. He knows he has the room to issue such a threat because of his race and class privilege. Despite his better judgment, he consciously takes advantage of his position, telling Lucas that he has incontrovertible evidence of the latter's paternity, "lying and knowing it, and not caring. . . . [U]sing his superior knowledge now in a way he had never done before. To intimidate the ignorant" (157). By having the southernized Swain perform as Selena's avenging angel and by delivering the threat of a lynching in his voice, Metalious enhances his whiteness, underscoring its power, its destructiveness, and the extremes of its historical privileges.

The postbellum history of lynching in the United States is that of a particularly white mechanism for extralegal retaliation against blacks, most often for alleged "outrages" or sexual violations against white women. Homicide was often the motivation for a lynching; however, rape was the rallying cry. "Although most lynchings were inflicted in response to alleged murder," notes E. L. Ayers, "most of the rhetoric and justification focused intently on the so-called 'one crime,' or 'usual crime': the sexual assault of White women by Blacks. That assault sometimes involved rape, while at other times a mere look or word was enough to justify death" (158). Although whites were sometimes targeted, during Reconstruction lynching was practiced as a particularly virulent instrument of terror directed primarily at black men, one that Judith Stephens has called "a specific and uniquely American form of racial violence that continues to play a fundamental role in constructing an understanding of national identity as well as black and white racial identities in the United States" (656). According to one estimate, more than two and a half times as many blacks as whites were lynched in the United States between the years 1882 and 1968 ("Lynchings by State and Race"). Swain's threat resonates with the racialized history of the practice. Not only is he Kentuckified; he employs the rhetoric of "outrage," the southern euphemism for black-on-white rape. In Swain's usage, it is an adjective characterizing the response of the town's men rather than as an act perpetrated upon its womenfolk. Swain further taunts Lucas by suggesting that the knowledge of how to perform a proper lynching belongs to the realm of (white) male intuition; it is "something an outraged man always knows how to do." Subtly, though significantly, Metalious darkens Lucas at the moment Swain concludes his threat. The reference to the "matted black hair on his forearms" seems designed to signal an embodied difference from Swain's silver-haired whiteness. Moreover, at the moment that Swain invokes the specifically American history of lynching with his threat, Metalious reverses the terms of the associated racializations of Selena and Lucas on that book jacket Allison notices after she's witnessed the rape.

It is hard to encounter a reference to a lynch mob in American literature without reading into it specifically racial connotations, even when the intended victim is not black. In *Peyton Place*, Doc Swain, the avenging would-be hangman is drawn repeatedly as a character type from American Civil War mythology. The crime he seeks retribution for is the "one crime" or "usual crime" used to justify the lynchings of black men. His intended victim, previously described as "white trash," has become darkly hairy and shiny and rank with perspiration (157). The novel's lynching reference pathologically whitens Swain and darkens Lucas. During the scene Allison observes through the window, Metalious reminds us of Selena's "dark, gypsy eyes" and tawny skin (56, 57) but says nothing about Lucas's complexion. His whiteness is affirmed by default and omission: "Lucas Cross was a big man with a chest like a barrel and a disconcertingly square-shaped head. His lank hair lay in strings on his broad skull, and when he smiled his whole forehead moved grotesquely" (55). That and the brief mention of "two grimy hands" and his "terrible, congested purple" face (57) are all Metalious presents in the way of Lucas's physical description in this scene. Allison's comparison of Lucas and Selena to the cover illustration of a white man threatening a slave girl reifies Lucas's racial whiteness and Selena's contrasting darkness for that moment. Yet after having performed the abortion occasioned by the rape, when Swain's fury and disgust lead him to Lucas's door with an agenda of moral retribution, the position of sociocultural power and economic privilege inhabited by Swain negates Lucas's claim to white masculinity, a claim Lucas asserts when he objects to Swain's insulting a man "in his own house" (156), darkening Lucas in turn.

Swain's threat to have Lucas lynched complicates his role as the town's moral backbone. Scholars have pointed out how the ritualized torture that preceded the actual hanging of a lynching victim blurred the line between "civilization" and "savagery" that was supposedly being upheld through the administration of such vigilantism. As Sandra Gunning notes, "Lynching might have a 'desired' effect on black men, but its very bloody execution drew the white avenger too close to the offender" (12).[16] In addition, Gail Bederman points out that in turn-of-the-twentieth-century anti-lynching discourse, a hierarchy of masculinities emerged in which southern white men were characterized as less manly for succumbing to their "savage" impulses to brutalize and kill than northern men, who—racist though they may have been—generally resisted the call to participate in the ritualized public torture and murder of other men (51). More manly still (in their own estimation) were the northern newspapermen whose reports of lynching's atrocities and cheeky commentaries on the occasional botched job elevated them above both the black victim and the southern lynch mobster. An 1893 *New York Times* editorial claimed that if given the chance, its staffers might have been more adept at killing a man than those who were charged with doing so (Bederman, 51–52).

Doc Swain means to affirm and maintain social order by purging Lucas from town. He understands that a man who has neither the cultivated conscience nor the impulse control to know better than to rape his step-daughter is a threat to the greater well-being of the community. However, while Swain works to manage "the sickness and the rage that come to a man when he realizes how thin the layers of civilization on another man can be" (160), he is also drawn inexorably into a sort of collusion with Lucas's experience as he presses Lucas for the details of Selena's rape. Knowing full well that he has enough information to turn Lucas over to the sheriff, Swain instead prompts Lucas into a narrative retelling of his initial rape of Selena, crudely guessing, "She was a virgin when you started, wasn't she, Lucas? . . . You busted your daughter's cherry for her, didn't you, Lucas, you big, brave, virile woodchopper?" (159) Swain's righteousness in the face of Lucas's dreamy confession comes across as somewhat disingenuous, given that he has, in fact, encouraged the disclosure of unnecessary details where Lucas had initially remained silent. What saves and ultimately redeems Swain from his morally tenuous position and from indulging too much in his own depravity is his self-awareness. He knows that he is crossing lines he should not cross; that he has wielded power that is socially, politically, culturally, economically—but not legally—his; that he seeks and receives information he does not need; that he must restrain himself from hurting Lucas in order to hold on to the higher moral ground he claims. Swain's struggle and triumph over his desire to avenge Selena by physically punishing Lucas in fact reiterates and enhances his symbolic whiteness and his role as community conscience, as a "universal signifier for humanity"—a position that Dyer says "encompasses all the possibilities for human existence, the darkness and the light. . . . The really white man's destiny is that he has further to fall (into darkness) but can aspire higher (towards the light)" (28). And it is the potential for this precipitous fall that Swain contemplates late in the novel. He understands how his actions have had consequences he could not have foreseen. Recalling Dyer's assertion that racial whiteness often functions as a "bringer of death," Swain feels keenly the blood of the Cross family on his hands. Drunk and ruminating on the fate of Selena Cross the night before the trial, the Doc assesses the cumulative destruction for which he feels in large part responsible since the evening of Selena's desperate visit to his office. "First the child, he thought, destroyed because it had no choice, and then Mary Kelley destroyed by a knowledge and a guilt which I had no right to press on her. And then Nellie, destroyed because I could control neither my temper nor my tongue and now Lucas, destroyed by Selena because I had not the courage to destroy him myself" (338). On the one hand, his internal monologue smacks of a man suffering from a God-complex; on the other, Swain reckons with the consequences of his uses and abuses of power, realizing how he might have minimized the damage done at each stage of the snowballing tragedy. When he takes the stand, in addition to testifying that Lucas sexually abused Selena, Swain confesses to his own crimes: performing the abortion on Selena and failing to report Lucas to the authorities (347–48). Swain's word is as good as the law, and the presiding judge virtually compels a "not guilty" verdict by corroborating Swain's authority on issues of collective morality, resulting in Selena's acquittal and Swain's exoneration. The doctor's reputed courage in testifying is enhanced by his self-presentation as previously noted—his habitual white suit, his shock of white hair, and the bright-blueness of his eyes, causing the Boston newspaperman Delaney to exclaim his admiration for Swain's "magnificent" whiteness (347). In other words, Swain is the embodiment of a superior morality, which is understood as the dominion of racial whiteness. It is not coincidental that Doc Swain's whiteness would seem striking to both Tom Makris and Delaney. Makris and Delaney are both strangers to town: as the novel's dark interloper, it is not at all surprising that Tom would notice Swain's remarkable likeness (in his Kentucky colonel comparison) to a figure of southern white military authority. And despite his short stint in Peyton Place, Metalious explains where Delaney's particular sensitivity may have come from:

> Delaney was city bred, and did not realize that in very small towns malice
> is more often shown toward an individual than toward a group, a nation or
> a country. He was not unfamiliar with prejudice and intolerance, having
> been called a Mick an extraordinary number of times himself, but name
> calling and viciousness had always seemed, to him, to be directed more at
> his ancestors than at him as an individual. (345)

Delaney understands bigotry, though he is willing to excuse it by redirecting its malevolence despite having himself been the target of ethnic slurs. But Swain's whiteness is not invisible to his fellow citizens—for them it is manifest in a peculiarly southern quality that estranges him from their ranks, notwithstanding his being a Yankee by birth; by his performance of rightness and righteousness in his courtroom testimony; and in the town's attribution of truth to his words, an attribution that becomes most significant during Selena's trial and that is endowed with all of the certainty of the law.

By the end of the novel's treatment of Doc Swain, which is coincident with the end of Selena's trial, Swain emerges as *Peyton Place*'s most nobly heroic male figure, having risked his livelihood by going public with his part in the fate of Lucas Cross. Having done battle with his conscience on the matter of abortion and having triumphed over his visceral desire to destroy Lucas, whatever threat to Swain's heroism or his manhood that might have been posed by his idiosyncratic southernness seems to have been put to rest. Still, as an exemplar of white masculinity, Swain's childlessness points again to *Peyton Place*'s critique of whiteness and sex— if not counterproductive, in this case, it is nonproductive. There is no reason given for Swain's lack of children; the fact is referenced only once in an early chapter of the novel.[17] He has no romantic interests or interludes during the course of the novel; his chauvinistic teasing of his nursing staff is understood by them as benign and nonthreatening. When taken together with the more overtly pathological, passive, and ultimately fruitless manifestations of white male sexuality profiled in *Peyton Place* and addressed above, the novel's portrayal of white masculinity is hardly an encouraging one and necessitates the introduction of an invigorating and promisingly potent alternative into the mix in the form of Tom Makris. Like its disapproval of the American cultural prohibition against female sexual desire and agency for which *Peyton Place* became so quickly famous, the narrative is equally skeptical of those ideological forces at work that pervert, corrupt, and/or thwart white male sexuality. While not arguing a position akin to Teddy Roosevelt's, which accused whites who failed to reproduce bountifully of "race suicide," the novel does seem to be suggesting that there is something inherently dysfunctional about an ideologically white racial identity that forbids sexual pleasure and that, in the world of *Peyton Place*, leads to the end of bloodlines (as in the cases of Seth Buswell, Leslie Harrington, Norman Page, and Matthew Swain), unhealthy repressive regimes, and the re-routing of otherwise normal sexual urges in to abnormal ones (enemas and incest, for instance). Though meant to redress the shortcomings of white masculinity, *Peyton Place*'s answer to this problem—in the form of Tom Makris—is an imperfect solution, relying as it does on sexual pathology (i.e., rape) and racial stereotypes as the antidote to an anemic white manhood. Whether by design or default, Tom Makris and Doc Swain complement one another as dark and light heroes respectively, the former having brought sex to a white woman; the latter removing the evidence of sex from a woman coded as dark. Even so, Makris and Swain remain for later critics of *Peyton Place* problematic exemplars of masculinity for their reiterations of those very stereotypes the novel attempts to dismantle.

# Home Is Where the Haunt Is
## Domestic Space, Race, and the Uncanny

Samuel Peyton's castle is a haunting home. Structured by the racism that forced Peyton to flee Boston, it relocates and reiterates the history of white racial domination in America upon a New Hampshire hilltop. Although the castle has been uninhabited since the deaths of Peyton and his wife and shows the signs of neglect, it remains very much on the minds of those who live nearby. It is a memorial in stone to racial repression, a solidly constructed monument to a national program of disavowal. As such, it is a paradox: a record of erasure. The erasure is, therefore, never complete: Peyton's story can never be fully untold. Part of the reason the town's foundational narrative is so threatening is because it was conditioned by legal noncitizenship and nonidentity, a status that destabilizes the citizenship and identity of those against whom this legal nonexistence is constructed. Writing of Native Americans and the national project of legislating them into civic nonentities, Renée Bergland has remarked, "When America denied the civil existence of the disenfranchised without denying their actual existence, it constructed them as simultaneously there and not there, and it confined them to a spectral role in American politics." Through this denial, these populations are rendered "uncanny figures, made ghostly by their oppression and their repression" (18).

This chapter will explore the uncanny in *Peyton Place* by revisiting the figure of the house, what Anthony Vidler has called "the *locus suspectus* of the uncanny" ("Architecture," 12). Houses, and their affective manifestations, homes, are sometimes spaces of sanctuary and retreat, while at other times they are the keepers and cloisters of secrets. Sometimes they are both at once. The secrets within the private dwellings in the town of Peyton Place are informed by American projects of domestic disavowals, what Bergland calls the "national uncanny."[1] Building on this and Homi Bhabha's work on what he calls "the unhomely," I will look at the ways in which the boundaries of the houses and homes in *Peyton Place* trace and restage national secrets and anxieties about sexuality, race, and the atomic bomb. I contend that in the end, by incorporating Selena Cross into the town's future and by installing Tom Makris as a permanent fixture within Constance MacKenzie's home, *Peyton Place* works against containment culture's attempts to "normalize" the American citizenry by denying difference. Having exploited the fears affiliated with domestic trespasses of both the home and the home front, and in suggesting the limits of the home's ability to keep its secrets contained, the narrative moves toward a model of integration, suggesting that acknowledging and incorporating racial difference—not denying or repressing it—is the route to civic renewal. It is also how to make a home, and a hometown, habitable. Yet despite an apparently upbeat ending that resolves the conflicts of its three female protagonists, by concluding in 1944, the novel remains haunted by an uncertain future, one in which the United States has not yet emerged victorious from World War II. In 1956, atomic anxiety articulated the agitated uncertainty of a national future. This chapter investigates how *Peyton Place* registers these anxieties simultaneously and within the structure of the house and the domestic space of the American home.

## Lost in the Fun House

Late in Book Two, following Nellie's suicide and Constance's abrupt revelation of her past to Tom and Allison, against the blazing backdrop of drought-related wildfires that are encroaching on Peyton Place, Metalious stages a rather grisly scene in an unlikely location: the amputation of a young girl's arm in a carnival fun house. Though it is startling in its grotesquerie, it is not only this: the scene presents us with yet another example of a house with poorly concealed secrets and the high cost of not dealing with them. The Labor Day carnival's fun house is a garden-variety "building of horrors" with all the requisite elements: "evil faces which jumped up in front of the patrons at unexpected moments, distorting mirrors, slanted floors, intricate mazes of dimly lit passages, and a laugh-getting, blush-producing wind machine" (260–61). While playing in front of the mirrors, Allison's friend Kathy Ellsworth notices a hole in the floor through which she can see the fun house machinery. She is drawn to it and mesmerized by "how beautifully all the wheels go around together!" (262). Distracted by the spectacle of the gears, Kathy falls through the gap in the platform. When Kathy's boyfriend, Lewis, reaches for her hand to help her out of the hole, what he retrieves is a hand "on the end of an arm no longer attached to her body" (263). Still fresh from the shock of Nellie's suicide and learning of her own father's true nature, Allison bursts into a fit of maniacal laughter and tells Tom, "Kathy fell and her arm came off, just like a toy doll" (263). The toy doll analogy, the missing limb, the distorting effect of the mirrors, the claustrophobia and disorientation of the structure and the space, and the unintentional exposure of the inner workings of a (fun) house's secrets in an apparently subterranean space all conspire to uncanny effect, rendering the familiar strange, precisely what such structures are meant to do.

The carnival fun house functions as a kind of contained inversion or reversal of the spaces of safety and danger. One enters such a space with the expectation of safely engineered momentary frights and temporary terrors. The journey through the structure's deliberate chaos and crafted distortions returns one back into the outside world, where the security of "normal" is reestablished. In this case, the fun house was not such a place but was instead a space in which its inner-most secrets, in the deep recess of a far corner in a room full of mirrors, were nonetheless not well-hidden enough. Unlike the staged hazards and mechanical horrors of fun houses, residential houses are meant to provide safety and shelter from the chaos and uncertainty of the world beyond their walls. In Peyton Place, they, too, keep secrets, some more hidden than others. Nevertheless, if the proper way of dealing with secrets in a fun house is to conceal them (in order to preserve the illusion of chaos and, in this case, to prevent loss of limb), the proper manner of dealing with secrets within domestic spaces is to do just the opposite: to bring them to light, to acknowledge and reconcile them.

I begin with the figure of the fun house because it is multivalent in its significations and works to suggest the central concerns of this chapter. It is like the town of Peyton Place itself in its failure to protect against the damaging effects of its secrets. The town's collective unwillingness to fully face its black history and the racism that provokes this denial and shame has resulted in profound community-wide dysfunction at the public and private level. By not recognizing and accepting racial difference as part of its identity, the town remains estranged from, which is to say unfamiliar, to itself: it is an uncanny civic space. The town's citizens' attempts to make Peyton Place "home," a space with affective significance, fails because of their collective inability to confront and integrate (I use this term deliberately) the house on the hill, Peyton's Place, into their historical consciousness. In dropping the apostrophe "s" that would otherwise legibly possess the town, the community effects an incomplete erasure of its history, detaching it, ever so slightly, from the castle: there is Samuel Peyton's Place, and there is Peyton Place. Peyton is there and not there in the town's name for itself, a civic uncanny like Bergland's national uncanny noted above. At the private level, this program of denying difference has, for example, dictated the terms of Constance MacKenzie's relationship to her libido, which has effectively become uncanny to her according to one of Sigmund Freud's explanations of the phenomenon: "something that was long familiar to the psyche and was estranged from it only through being repressed" (148). Finally, despite the expectation that it will do so, the Labor Day carnival's fun house does not fully domesticate the dangers within it, as the gap in the floorboards leaves its visitors vulnerable to and unsuspecting of unseen harm. In efforts to manage American fears and anxieties about nuclear war, the Federal Civil Defense Administration (FCDA) sought to "domesticate" the bomb by convincing the public that the family was the first line of defense against attack and the best resource for survival. In doing so, "it sanitized the images and rhetoric [of nuclear warfare] in a desperate attempt to prevent the panic, fatalism and resistance" that experts had suggested would characterize responses to the protracted uncertainties of the nuclear age. "Nothing was as it seemed in civil defense literature: fallout was dust, family fire drills were 'games,' and blast or fallout shelters were 'family,' 'family-type,' or 'home' shelters" (McEnaney, 74). Just as the hole in its floor undermines the sense of safe hazard that is meant to inhere in the Peyton Place fun house, the gap between rhetoric and reality built into government propaganda about domestic durability and survivability in the event of nuclear attack is the space where the truth is not so well hidden from view: that a nuclear attack on home soil would be deadly on a scale never before experienced.

## Of House and Home

In the history of human habitation, houses existed long before homes. The idea and the structural reality of the home and what it has come to stand for—family, privacy, a safe haven from the world at large—is a relatively recent invention, dating back only to the 1600s. The word *home* itself, Witold Rybczynski explains, "brought together the meanings of house and household, of dwelling and of refuge, of ownership and of affection." *Home* connotes the structure that shelters those who live there and the emotional valence of their experiences, the material effects with which it is furnished and that it contains. In addition, Rybczynski suggests, it evokes "the sense of satisfaction and contentment that all these conveyed.

You could walk out of the house, but you always returned home" (62). *Home* has an affective significance missing from the word *house*, which names the structure itself more than it does the experience within it.

The prototype for the child-centered, single-family, bourgeois living space, once clearly demarcated as a privatized sphere against the public world of the street and the marketplace, is said to have taken shape in the Netherlands in the seventeenth century and then migrated to France and England in the eighteenth century (Rybczynski, 51–66). This emergent phenomenon "was closely linked to the new ideals of domesticity and privacy that were associated with the characteristics of the modern family— a family that was child-centered, private, and in which the roles of husband and wife were segregated into public and domestic spheres, respectively" (Hareven, 258). In addition to the activities within the living space that give life to its interior, the design and decor of the house itself—its floor plan, furnishings and finishing touches—function as "a semiotic system that signals status, class, and public display and creates meanings that observers, visitors, and the public may interpret and read" (Mezei and Briganti, 840). Homes, then, contain and tell stories about their residents and the cultures and historical moments in which they are situated.

Houses are capable of such narrative articulations as well. Architectural historian Dolores Hayden explains, "Vernacular house forms are economic diagrams of the reproduction of the human race. They are also aesthetic essays on the meaning of life within a particular culture, its joys and travails, its superstitions and stigmas. House forms cannot be separated from their physical and social contexts" (142). It is perhaps because the house is a cagey metaphor for individual and private experience that many novels; their close cousins, novellas; and short stories often take as their subject houses and the families within them.[2] Marilyn Chandler reads the frequency and foregrounding of houses in American fiction as "a kind of autobiographical enterprise—a visible and concrete means of defining and articulating the self" (3). She goes on to catalogue and explain the tensions created and upheld by, contained and staged within, the figure of the house in the American imagination. The house is at once a landing and a launching pad, marking aspiration and accomplishment while also directing our attention to the quotidian details of upkeep. As such, Chandler continues,

> They are, after all, embodiments—incarnations that threaten to become incarcerations, doubling the stakes of the precarious human condition that entraps the spirit in the corruption of the flesh and bone or wood and stone.

Inseparable from theological or metaphysical issues, houses are also the stage on which the dramas of sexual politics and class warfare are played out. Houses, as much as the wide wilderness and open spaces by which we have defined the reaches of our collective imagination and identity, are the locus of the central conflicts of American life. (6)

Houses in American fiction often serve as evidence of attempts to define the self in the absence of a long national history. The solution for writers, as Chandler sees it, has been to make a paradigmatic shift that dislodges the concerns about which they write from calendrical time and instead "regard[s] both American history and personal history as reiterations of the timeless cycle of salvation history" (11). In addition, the houses written into American fiction are said to be attempts to define the national self within and through a domestic space that actively intervenes in that geopolitical project through what Amy Kaplan calls "imperial domesticity." This imperative "continually projects a map of unregenerate outlying foreign terrain that gives coherence to its boundaries and justifies its domesticating mission" (*Anarchy*, 31). It exercises a simultaneous expansion of female moral influence beyond the home and the retrenchment of domestic space as a fortification against external threats. Though Kaplan's formulation was developed through her readings of nineteenth-century texts, it resonates within twentieth-century contexts such as *Peyton Place* and the sexual and racial anxieties it registers and attempts to resolve. The town's insistent but futile disavowal of Samuel Peyton's history marks its attempt to place itself within a mythologized Anglocentric American narrative, one free from the inconvenience, complications, and contamination of a dark past. Peyton Place's failure to achieve this goal is arguably attributable to the presence of Peyton's castle on a hill overlooking town: the Gothic domicile itself and the stories it houses.

The construction of the house, both the process of erecting it and the materials that constitute its finished product, demarcates private space from public, interiors from exteriors, and in turn creates a sort of world within a world. Until recently, much scholarship has held that women's work in the home and men's work in politics and commerce divided labor and lives along gendered lines into two "separate spheres." The threshold of the home was said to have enacted and held intact a fixed, fortified boundary inside of which the domestic duties of homemaking were undertaken and managed with negligible impact on the world outside. Conversely, commerce and politics were understood to have held their ground outside of the home without infiltrating domestic space or its concerns.

In her study of the imperialist rhetoric of housekeeping manuals and domestic novels, Kaplan demonstrates a consolidation of purpose between domesticity as it applies to homemaking and housekeeping and issues of domestic import defined against those forces that constitute "the foreign." Calling attention to the definition of *domestic* as that which pertains to the house and home space and that which is not "foreign," which is to say contained within and recognized as of "this nation," Kaplan sees domesticity in both senses as a dynamic, ongoing process that constantly manages the boundaries constitutive of definitions of the home and the world, "conquering and taming the wild, the natural, and the alien." This aspect of domesticity, she observes, marks its sociopolitical valence through its civilizing imperative, "and the conditions of domesticity often become markers that distinguish civilization from savagery. . . . Domesticity monitors the borders between the civilized and the savage as it regulates the traces of savagery within its purview" (*Anarchy*, 25–26). The domestic space of the household, then, is not opposed to but rather of a piece with the domestic territory founded by the establishment of national borders. This merger of the two unites middle-class women and men in a vigilant maintenance of boundaries against infiltration by the "foreign." In this way, "the domestic," understood and undertaken as both home space and homeland, suggests the common commitment of public and private domestic discourses to the project of containing and controlling those wily forces that threaten the peace and stability of the bounded terrain of the home, both ideological and actual.

Kaplan posits the relationship between race and domesticity "as structural to the institutional and discursive processes of national expansion and empire building" ("Manifest," 583). Rather than understanding domestic space as a static home base for masculine nation building, Kaplan writes that women's home-work extends its influence beyond the household through the moral influence of the mother and through the production of viable citizens. In addition, this energy reifies the borders of the home and country by continually redefining the parameters of foreign versus domestic: "narratives of domesticity and female subjectivity [are] inseparable from narratives of empire and nation building" (583–84). Women, then, become critical participants in the project of nation building. In this, their sphere of influence is not limited to hearth and home but is coextensive with a geopolitical masculine expansionist project. At the same time, the fear of foreign contamination is managed through the administration of women's domestic practices. As we shall see, *Peyton Place*'s home spaces bear the traces of these concerns. The foreign does infiltrate the domestic, and Peyton Place's homes articulate the failure of domestic practice to keep these issues at bay.

## Home Front as Battle Front

In an era famous for its fertile families, early Cold War America extolled the virtues of house and home both as a safe place in an uncertain world and as the beating heart of capitalist democracy, the seat of the ideological duel with communism. The period has come to be known for its "new Victorianism" with good reason. The middle classes experienced a retrenchment of gendered work as men, husbands, and fathers labored for wages outside the home while women, wives, and mothers were discouraged from doing so; instead, they were charged with oversight of a domestic economy replete with all the latest mechanical wonders of the modern home, including automatic washing machines, dishwashers, two-speed blenders, and television sets (Strasser, 280). In a surprising bit of statecraft, one of the era's most famous ideological battles took place in an American home erected on Muscovite soil: the 1959 "kitchen debate" between then Vice President Richard Nixon and Soviet Prime Minister Nikita Khrushchev. This war of words serves as an apt example of Kaplan's assertion that the "domestic" signifies the character of the work that takes place within the home while simultaneously aligning men and women together in the work of fending off the danger that infiltration by the "foreign" poses to the domestic and its relation to national security. A forty-two-day exhibit of the "American way of life" displayed an array of consumer products from appliances to automobiles to stereos to "convenience foods," many of which were curated in a model of a suburban ranch house as testimony to the level of comfort the typical middle-class home could now offer its resident family in a thriving capitalist society (Hellman, par. 6–7). The American suburban homestead was presented as a bastion of comfort and ease against the hostile outside world, providing a sense (if not a guarantee) of security. According to Elaine Tyler May, the roiling cultural changes of the postwar era were transformed from threats and liabilities to adaptive elements of domestic existence. In the Cold War suburban homestead, "Sex would enhance marriage, emancipated women would professionalize homemaking, and affluence would put an end to material deprivation" (14). Significantly in this historical context, suburban life's democratization of the American dream would prevent communism from gaining a foothold by ameliorating class conflict. Though May points out that Nixon overstated the access to suburbia, "he described a type of domestic life that had become a reality for many white working-class and middle-class Americans—and a powerful aspiration for many others" (14). Suburban domesticity and its material comforts and enhancements would help defeat the Red Menace.

In the face of the new nuclear age, the desire for both a comfortable and safe place is understandable. The rhetoric and practice of World War II and the immediate postwar era brought the war home through advanced military technologies. Air raids, firebombing campaigns, and, finally, the dropping of atomic bombs on Hiroshima and Nagasaki caused mass civilian casualties in addition to those suffered on battle fronts by soldiers (Zarlengo 925). Though the United States was spared these devastations, the threat of their deployment hovered over the citizenry. Even when the technologies were refined such that damage could be effectively limited to "tactical" military and industrial targets, the value of what euphemistically came to be called "making a psychological impression on a population" was not lost on wartime strategists on both sides of the conflict (926). Significantly, the targeting of civilian populations became the calling card of the atomic age and brought the war home to the United States. In the new era of military deterrence (also famously known as mutually assured destruction, with its apropos acronym "MAD") the threat of nuclear annihilation hung like a sword of Damocles not just over military targets, but over every last civilian, home, and family in the country.

As a result, all American citizens were effectively transformed into cold warriors. The Federal Civil Defense Administration crafted a message that "[regarded] civilians as soldiers—as targets of powerful bombs with the double capacity of horrifying people and destroying vast areas and populations" (928). As an antidote to the anxieties attendant upon nuclear annihilation, the federal government encouraged the American citizenry to think of themselves as the first line of defense against atomic anarchy. The greatest threat to national stability following a nuclear attack, claimed Federal Civil Defense Administration Chief Val Peterson, would be a population run amok with panic. Foremost among his list of "panic stoppers" published in a *Collier's* magazine article, was "faith": "It may be faith in yourself, in your neighbors, in your leader, in your cause, your country or in God. In the best sense, real faith is all of them working together. But whether it is faith in yourself or in a purpose or power exceeding your own limitations, it is the ultimate solution to the ultimate weapon" (qtd. in Zarlengo, 931). In this arrangement, this application of faith(s), Peterson's call to devotion, Zarlengo argues, is arranged "like a set of nesting dolls" in which "family, city and nation [are figured] as parallel structures" sharing in common "safety, earned with technical strength and defensive capability; sovereignty, based on individuality and inventiveness amidst fierce competition; fortification in the name of freedom; and domestic security" (931). In this "nested arrangement," she explains, "urban planning, community planning, and household activity were figured in public information rhetoric as downsized deterrence efforts in concert with war-preventive militarism" (932). Zarlengo is careful to point out that this civil defense rhetoric did not stand in the way of "families,' individuals,' and institutions' capacities to intelligently question, defy, or complicate national policy" (931). She goes on to say, however, that the result of the civil defense campaigns was a recasting of the ideological role of the 1950s female—in particular, the 1950s homemaker and housewife—from the keeper of the home fires to a defender of the home front through an ideological militarization of domestic space:

> Civil defense rhetoric explained that the American household, run by housewives, had become an agency of the nation, patriotism a domestic duty, and housework a civic obligation with grave consequences. While the common civil defense claim that "dangerous fallout is like dust and can be removed like dust" trivialized fallout, it also glorified a mundane household duty. A housewife's ability to maintain a dust-free environment could be interpreted as her potential to protect her family from harm. (941)

Home front merged with battle front in the nuclear age. As potential targets in an atomic attack, women and children became "a new class of soldiers—deterrence soldiers beckoned to peacetime behavior that was in concert with war prevention" (940). For FCDA Chief Peterson, the American living room was a key zone of preparedness, and domestic delinquency in this civic duty, he charged, was tantamount to a "fifth column action which undermines our national defense" (qtd. in Zarlengo, 940). While women were expected to tidy up after the big mess made by an atomic attack, it would fall to men to secure the subterranean perimeter by preventing infiltration by one's radioactive friends and neighbors or anyone else unfortunate enough to have lacked either funds or foresight to construct a fallout shelter for themselves (939).[3]

## Urban Dispersal and Suburban Sanctuary

The recasting of women's roles as new militants in a large-scale defensive national security maneuver was made possible in conjunction with the process of suburbanization. The single-family suburban dwelling with its landscaped yards reproduced on a small scale some of the strategic elements of newly conceived plans for municipal land use, which included wide buffer zones (called "life belts" or "safety zones" in designs by MIT cyberneticist Norbert Wiener) between central or downtown areas and residential settings (Zarlengo, 934, 939). The design of the home itself reconfigured space internally through the miracle of climate control and by relocating the kitchen from formerly private quarters to a centrally located public space. Externally, the home was reshaped into the popular single-story, ranch-style model, the 1950s' vernacular house form par excellence. The ranch home was said to reflect a "unity with nature" in its unimposing silhouette (Clark, 179). It also offered a living space on the same plane as the land upon which it was built. Its single story enabled freedom of movement within the home, unhindered by intrusive staircases, as well as unobstructed passage into and out of the house itself (May, 153). Architectural historian Clifford Clark Jr., notes that the purported "unity with nature" to which such a design scheme aspired was heavily qualified by a vision of nature "as a tamed and open environment. Like the technological re-creation of the temperate California climate, the 1950s designs conceived of the natural world in a simplified and controlled way that eliminated anything that was wild or irregular" (179).

The vision of nature espoused by the new suburbanites in the postwar era is congruent with the containment culture ethos that established itself within the home space by stationing white, middle-class American women in the role of militarized housewives. At the same time, the structure and situation of the bumper crop of single-family suburban homes on formerly pastoral or agricultural landscapes also spoke to the white, middle-class desire to manage the perceived threats to a newly attained standard of living. The vigilance necessary to maintain the normative white, middle-class civic sanctity and security of the suburban American home bespeaks an ongoing uncertainty about the ability to successfully keep the wily and "untamed" forces that endanger such hegemonic dominance at bay. This is a point to which I will return in a slightly different form in a moment. For now, however, an interesting additional aspect of suburban ranch house design bears mentioning. While one-story homes were sold as affordable and attractive opportunities through which potential homebuyers could enter the real estate market and realize the American dream of homeownership, a sinister reality undergirded the marketing of single-story homes in newly hatched communities located at a commutable distance from urban settings: the exigencies of survivability in the nuclear age. In short, single-story homes showed less damage from atomic blasts than two-story structures in FCDA tests in Nevada (Tobin, 25).[4]

It is important to acknowledge at this point that the 1950s ranch house was certainly not the only home design on the market for the aspiring suburbanite. The most successful developer of the early postwar era, Bill Levitt, built his business on the Cape Cod–style home (sold with television and washing machine included), and a decade after he began, in 1956, he added the "expanded" ranch and two-story colonial home (Halberstam, 135, 142). The example of the ranch-style home is meant to demonstrate the ways in which civil defense not only infiltrated the home, as Zarlengo has skillfully illustrated, but also influenced the shape and situation of civilian existence in the early postwar era, from the design and dimensions of the single-family suburban dwelling, to its location, situated at a "safe" remove from city centers. Suburbanization, Kathleen Tobin asserts, was not only or simply a consumer-driven phenomenon; rather, it was enabled and subsidized through federally sponsored programs, many of which were informed by civil defense initiatives.[5] Whether it was Bill Levitt's original Cape Cod tract house, the ranch-style house, or a two-story structure, the new American home was redesigned (and in the case of the ranch home, reshaped altogether) in an attempt to give American citizens "shelter from the elements," architectural historian David Monteyne's double-entendre for the project with which architects who worked to advance civil defense objectives were charged: to design safe housing from the radioactive elements of atomic and nuclear fallout (190).

Suburbanization, then, was itself part of a larger national project, encouraging and enabling the dispersal of large numbers of the people away from urban centers (the presumed prime targets of an atomic attack) so as to reduce the temptation to bomb them in the first place. Fewer people concentrated in the nation's metropolitan downtowns would mean fewer casualties. Tobin's work reveals how the federal government helped to direct decentralization efforts by founding agencies and underwriting several programs that served to make it easier for real estate developers and homeowners alike to lay claim to a small plot of land and the shelter of a single-family home well outside of the big city's limits. As a corrective to the conventional wisdom that the postwar suburban housing boom was strictly an answer to a teeming market's demand for it, Tobin argues that the mass dispersal of populations from American cities in the decade after the end of World War II was instead guided by a government-sponsored push to diminish the economic and human impact on the nation in the event of an atomic attack on American soil.

New Deal era legislation had shifted some of the burden of the nation's Depression era housing problems from city governments to the national level. This led to the establishment of offices and agencies such as the Federal Housing Administration (FHA), Housing and Home Finance Authority (HHFA), Federal Savings and Loan Insurance Corporation (FSLIC), Homeowner's Loan Corporation (HOLC), and the Reconstruction Finance Corporation (RFC) (Tobin, 3). At the dawn of the nuclear age, in addition to enacting laws that helped finance construction for builders and provided affordable mortgages to new homeowners in a burgeoning suburbia, Congress approved the Housing Act of 1954, which fed the housing boom by, among other things, expanding FHA assistance through longer-term mortgages and targeting the construction of single-family homes. Additionally, the bill mandated that the HHFA fall in line with civil peacetime preparedness by requiring that it and all other "departments or agencies" under its purview or involved in housing issues (including the Veterans' Administration) "shall exercise such powers, functions or duties in such manner as consistent with the requirements thereof, will facilitate progress in the reduction of the vulnerability of congested urban areas to enemy attack" (qtd. in Tobin, 24). There now stood a federal imperative to abide by whatever design specifications were deemed most likely to withstand the shock of an atomic blast.

The war-gaming and fear-mongering that produced attack scenarios often assumed that if a bomb were dropped, it would land at city center in order to produce the greatest number of civilian casualties as well as do damage to industry and infrastructure. In a 1946 *Bulletin of Atomic Scientists* article titled "Dispersal of Cities and Industries," hydrogen-bomb pioneer Edward Teller, along with economist Jacob Marshak and social scientist Lawrence Klein, warned, "In an atomic war, congested cities would become deathtraps. . . . Dispersal is costly and it means great changes in our way of life. However, it is a form of defense" (qtd. in Tobin, 7). Teller, Marshak, and Klein recommended both "cluster" and "linear" cities in their theorizing of a new urban America. Though the ideal solution was an even distribution of the nation's population throughout the country, they conceded the impossibility of such a plan and, even with viable urban dispersal plans at the ready, they concluded, "Nothing that we can now plan as a defense for the next generation is likely to be satisfactory; that is, nothing but world union" (qtd. in Kargon and Molella, 766). Atomic age city planning thus sought to decentralize by developing new municipal land-use plans. These included physicist and Manhattan Project alumnus Ralph Lapp's "doughnut" shaped model, which would position industry, residences, and road networks at a safe radial remove from an essentially empty center. Alternatively, in a similarly "circumferential" configuration, planners would work with existing metropolitan areas in order to channel large segments of the city-dwelling population into outlying areas beyond a buffer zone that would increase one's chances of survival and, ideally, reduce vulnerability to attack in the first place. The "Wiener Civil Defense Plan," as it was called, reimagined the landscape as a series of concentric circles of land-use arranged to maximize survival in a worst-case scenario (Zarlengo, 934).

## Citizen-Subjects and Sitting Ducks: Suburban Survivability and Urban Annihilation

Popular media and culture also envisioned and represented the nation's cities as the most vulnerable to attack, producing what David Monteyne has called "a textual explosion of apocalyptic nuclear disaster narratives" that tended to resolve in one of two ways: either with the complete decimation of the city and its people or with the triumphant rising from the ashes of a few fortunates in whose hands the future of the nation lay (183). Monteyne has shown how the architectural profession conspired with civil defense "imagineers" (his term) in this latter nation-as-phoenix fabulation, remarking that they "help[ed] construct the myth that nuclear war, like natural disaster, was survivable through preparation and properly designed shelter" (183). The professional discourse yoked nuclear war to meteorological metaphors, treating it as a "purely technical problem, like keeping out the weather" (180).[6] More significant, the survival fictions imagined the continued existence of a certain kind of American: a white, middle-class, idealized citizen-subject who had the economic means, and the blessing of the federal government (e.g., free from FHA redlining policies), to relocate beyond the projected periphery of a city-center ground zero. In reducing urban vulnerability, plans for dispersal "contained" within a city's limits ethnic and racial minority populations as well as whites without the economic means to relocate. They would become "'sitting ducks' whose existence challenged the myth of a unified American identity. The unified America, the one to be preserved by civil defense, was clearly a nonurban place, where research and design envisioned a white, male, universal subject as the ideal citizen" (191).

Visual models of attack and survival scenarios staged a white, middle-class citizenry rising from the radioactive rubble. The aforementioned home designs tested in Nevada's Operation Doorstep (in which ranch-style homes with venetian blinds fared best) contained within them mannequin models of nattily dressed white nuclear families oblivious (as one might expect) to the imminent explosion. Fallout shelter literature and media presented images of white, often male, bodies as the central, and sometimes the exclusive participants in all stages of readiness for atomic attack, from preparation to survival to rebuilding. "This narrow demographic recurs in the texts of civil defense," writes Monteyne, thus "reinforcing the whiteness and patriarchy of the nuclear family and its key component, the ideal citizen. Here the architectural discourse forms a microcosm of national discourse: the 'restricted profession' parallels restricted citizenship." Furthermore, and what he deems "more sinister" in its implications, "the white male is imagined as the most necessary survivor" (193–94). More sinister still was the possibility that if all were to go according to plan and should the combined efforts of architectural ingenuity and civil defense planning have the effect of enabling the survival of a fortunate and chosen few, an atomic attack would go a long way toward ridding America of those "others" whose continued existence threatened white, middle-class American identity. The bright side of the atom bomb, the mushroom cloud's silver lining, was that it might serve as an expedient form of slum clearance (198–99).

Interestingly, the meteorological metaphor with which architects managed the threats of an atomic bomb blast cannily morphed into meteorological matter when radioactive rain showers pelted Troy, New York, in 1953 and Chicago in 1955. While the federal government pressed its urban dispersal initiatives, fallout from nuclear testing in the Nevada desert was being dispersed into the atmosphere and, consequently, all over the country. At a press conference following the startlingly successful detonation of a hydrogen bomb in the Bikini Atoll in March 1954 (it was three times more powerful than scientists had anticipated), Atomic Energy Commission Chairman Lewis Strauss was asked whether an H-bomb could destroy a metropolitan area the size of New York City, to which Strauss replied in the affirmative. The magnitude of the blast was a frightening 750 times greater than that of the bomb that was dropped on Hiroshima, and the far reach of its fallout raised the stakes in the nuclear arms race. By 1955, the Soviet Union had developed its own "Hell bomb," as it was called by the prescient author William Laurence in his 1950 book on the subject. The advent of the hydrogen bomb considerably lessened the likelihood that an all-out thermonuclear war was survivable (Gaddis,

64).[7] With the ushering in of the thermonuclear age, Kargon and Molella observe, "the day of dispersal for defense was over" (777). In effect, nuclear fallout *had* been naturalized. It wasn't simply "like" the weather; on occasion it *was* the weather (and, consequently, in the nation's food, milk, and water supply). As such, it could not be contained. City, suburb, small town, and rural farmland were all living "under the cloud" of thermonuclear fallout. For all of the nation's forethought regarding community planning for a post-apocalyptic America, the radioactive realities of the pre-apocalypse challenged the supposed safety one could secure for oneself at the recommended circumferential remove from any of the projected urban ground zeroes in the nation. The act of militarizing the "suburban citadel" and the fact that postwar suburbanization was made part of a federal program of civilian preparedness for nuclear war undermined the very sense of security many of its residents sought in their move away from the nation's urban centers. Though the suburbs initially provided solace by virtue of their theoretical remove from the epicenter of nuclear attack, they were also imagined to serve as post-atomic safe havens for city-dwelling survivors. That they were understood as such was indicative of the pervasive anxiety of the era (Henriksen, 96).

Suburbia drew millions of the white middle-class and assimilated ethnic and upwardly mobile working-class Americans away from urban centers with a promise of peace and security, safety and abundance. In doing so, the resettlement of middle America worked to consolidate a national identity in enclaves of nearly identical (and sometimes exactly identical) houses inhabited by similarly configured male-headed, female-managed families. In the thermonuclear age, however, suburbia guaranteed nothing in the face of an H-bomb exchange with the Soviets. Furthermore, the threats experienced from within were articulated not just in anticommunist and atomic terms. With the early stirrings of the civil rights movement afoot by the mid-1950s, America's segregationist policies were being openly challenged, and in the case of *Brown v. Board of Education*, overturned, in the nation's courts. The sanctuary and security that was sold as part of the dream of single-family homeownership in America was belied by the sense that it was ever and always in danger of infiltration or annihilation by undesirable elements—human or radioactively chemical. The militarization of the home front in the national struggle to contain the spread of communism and keep other so-called un-American ideologies, practices, and people at bay suggested that the American home, then, had the potential to be a very unhomely place.

## New England Gothic: *Peyton Place* and the Uncanny

Peyton Place is, of course, a well-established New England small town dating back to just before the Civil War, not a newly founded suburban development. Even so, similarities exist between the two kinds of American residential communities. The first Levittown homes were all Cape Cods, though "awkwardly proportioned" (Hayden, 8), that echoed the New England village aesthetic without the same logic of community land use. Early in *Peyton Place*, Allison MacKenzie regards the town from high up on a hill and sees a cluster of identical white clapboard Cape Cod–style homes and, despite being a longtime resident, is unable to distinguish her home from the rest. The visual sameness that obscures Allison's sense of home recalls the aerial photographs of Levittown, which reveal row upon row of tract housing. Their racial homogeneity is similar: Bill Levitt had a strict policy of not selling to blacks, claiming that he was a businessman first and foremost, not a social crusader. In Peyton Place, there are no blacks living in town during the time in which the narrative takes place. And the apprehension expressed by the town's middle-class residents upon learning that there will soon be a Greek in their midst indicates a collective wish to maintain a dominant white identity.[8]

Allison attempts to distinguish her home from those of her neighbors in order to divert her attention from the "gray stone pile of Samuel Peyton's castle," the story of which causes her to "[shiver] a little in the warm sun" and then recast her gaze from the town's abandoned founding fortress to its present day residential section (12). Peyton's castle is not at all like the white clapboard Capes that Allison looks out on, at least not materially. At the same time that *Peyton Place* tells the story of a town and the secrets its residents struggle to keep, it is also the story of a house, "the Peyton place," the dwelling for which the town is named, a story that the novel holds in abeyance until very nearly its end. The dwelling, a castle in which "every stick and stone, every doorknob and pane of glass" has been imported from England, was built by an escaped slave named Samuel Peyton (331). Having secured his freedom, or perhaps to prevent recapture, Peyton moved overseas, became a shipping industry magnate and married a white Frenchwoman named Violette. Expecting to take up residence in Boston among the city's moneyed elite, he was kept out of the housing market despite his considerable wealth and sought refuge in the remote woods of New Hampshire. Once construction of his veritable fortification was complete, he swore never to emerge from its high-walled perimeter again. In addition to the castle's scandalous reputation on account of race and miscegenation, rumors of treason attach to its history. The depths of Peyton's anger at his northern reception are said to have prompted him to supply arms and munitions to the Confederate cause during the Civil War. Lacking next of kin, Peyton deeded the castle and his land to the state, stipulating only that trespassers be kept out. It is in the shadow of the castle that the town comes into being.

Although the townspeople work with varying degrees of success to prevent their private secrets from being made public, they are in silent agreement that the black ancestry of the town itself should remain unspoken. The only exception to the rule of collective repression is the gossipy Clayton Frazier, who seems to delight in the provocation he anticipates will accompany the revelation of Peyton's blackness. Frazier notwithstanding, the collective repression of the town's history is a forgetting doomed to failure, memorialized as it is in the architecture of the castle that sits high on a hill above the town proper. It is apparently Peyton Place's greatest shame that its founding father is black, that the castle remains an ever-present reminder of miscegenation, and that its foundational moment is one of racial protest, anger, and resentment. And though the castle is the town's originary home space, it bespeaks difference on all fronts: in its Gothic architecture, the foreign materials with which it was constructed and furnished, and the racial difference with which it was inhabited. Though Allison MacKenzie later tells Norman Page that Peyton's castle is haunted, it may be more true to suggest that the Peyton place is a home that haunts.

This haunting, which takes the form of an English castle, lends itself to a consideration of select gothic elements in the text as well as the function of the uncanny within the narrative. The chiaroscuro characteristic of gothic literature's representations of physical spaces (e.g., its dimly lit, claustrophobic interiors) and attributions of character (e.g., fair heroines and dark villains) are constitutive of American gothic in significant ways. Puritanical rhetoric, the early discourse of the nation, organized experience according to a rigid binary of good and evil categorically associated with light and dark, respectively. The institutionalized presence of abject black bodies on national soil through slavery informed the American imaginary and the generic evolution of the American gothic (Lloyd-Smith, 110).

The castle is perhaps the quintessential element of gothic fiction (Punter and Byron, 259). The uncanny, "a peculiar commingling of the familiar and unfamiliar" (Royle, 1), is perhaps the quintessential gothic effect. Anomalous though it seems perched atop a New Hampshire hill, the Peyton place is a castle indeed, boasting towers, turrets, and high stone walls. Just as Peyton's castle might have served the dual purpose of haven and fortification in its original English context, its purpose stateside was both residential and defensive against a society inhospitable to racial integration. The structure has a "sinister, dark look, sinister and secretive looking even in the hot open-faced sunlight" (Metalious, 328). For those townsfolk vulnerable to its intrigues, the sight of it can chill even on a warm Indian summer's day, as it does for Allison. Its mere mention can stop a conversation cold, as Tom Makris discovers almost immediately and twice in rapid succession just after he arrives in town (100, 102).

The castle in gothic fiction "is a sign of antiquity, of a life that has preceded our own but appears never to have gone away, and as such it refers as much to a condition of the unconscious as to a historical moment of feudalism" (Punter and Byron, 262).[9] In American literature, the site for the exploration of the persistence of the past-in-the-present is seldom a castle, as the nation lacks a feudal past, but more often the American family home. Marilyn Chandler has argued that the houses of American fiction are not simply the discursive spaces in which both familial and cultural conflicts are articulated. American literary architecture, she suggests, actively structures the stories it tells: Its houses are "powerful, value-laden, animated agents of fate looming in the foreground, not the background, of human action; our novels are about houses and homes as much as they are about the people who inhabit them" (4). As noted above, literary domestic spaces are themselves the subjects of the narratives in which they appear. As much as the frontier has figured in the American imaginary, so too, Chandler holds, have the settlement, the homestead, and the private dwelling figured as the "locus of the central conflicts of American life" (6). Houses in American fiction mark aspiration and arrival as well as the more gothic conditions of "entrapment" and entombment. As "incarnations that threaten to become incarcerations," American literary architecture becomes "the stage on which the dramas of sexual politics and class warfare are played out" (6). Ideological tensions are contested at least as much as they are contained in the houses of American narrative.

While the house, for Chandler, serves as the "locus of the central conflicts of American life" (6), as architectural historian Anthony Vidler has observed, it also provides "an especially favored locus for uncanny disturbances: its apparent domesticity, its residue of family history and nostalgia, its role as the last and most intimate shelter of private comfort sharpened by contrast the terror of invasion by alien spirits" ("Architecture," 7).

This is not coincidence but rather a definitive attribute of the uncanny, given its etymological roots in the German term *das Unheimlich*, which literally translates into English as "unhomely." In his famous essay on the subject, Freud defines the uncanny as "everything that was intended to remain secret, hidden away, and has come into the open" (132). Later, he states that the uncanny "is actually nothing new or strange, but something that was long familiar to the psyche and was estranged from it only though being repressed" (148). The estrangement produces the effect or illusion of difference between an object/experience and its uncanny incarnation or reiteration in refashioned form. As Maria Tatar explains, however, what is uncanny isn't frightening because of its difference from that which is familiar, but because of its likeness to it (169). This intimacy between the strange and the familiar is reflected in the relationship recognized by Freud of *unheimlich* to its apparent opposite *heimlich* ("homely" as in "of the home"), which can mean either "what is familiar and comfortable" or alternatively, "what is concealed and kept hidden" (Freud, 132). The affiliation of concealment with what is "of the home" makes sense, Tatar says, when we consider how the home can be made to function as a space for the safekeeping of secrets:

> A house contains the familiar and congenial, but at the same time it screens what is familiar and congenial from view, making a mystery of it. Thus it comes as no surprise that the German word for a secret (*Geheimnis*) derives from the word for home (*Heim*) and originally designated that which belongs to the house. What takes place within the four walls of a house remains a mystery to those shut out from it. A secret, for the Germans in any case, literally ex-cludes others from knowledge. (169)

The prefix *un-* in *unheimlich* does not function antonymically here, as it most often does. Instead of signifying opposition, Freud calls it a "token of repression." Through the defamiliarizing of the known that is effected through the process of repression, the known is alienated but is not fully eradicated from awareness to such an extent that it becomes no longer known.[10] It would be more correct to say that the familiar, now repressed, goes unrecognized, obscured from recognition, and is thus experienced as strange in subsequent encounters. It is this lack of recognition that transforms the *heimlich* into the *unheimlich*. The *un-* is a sign of the familiar made strange, a signifier of misrecognition rather than disavowal.[11]

A notoriously slippery concept to pin down, the uncanny is not simply an eerie sense or instance of haunting but rather, according to Vidler, a "revisit[ation] by a power that was thought long dead" (*Architectural*, 27). The uncanny can transform safety into danger, security into uncertainty. Nicholas Royle helpfully distills a definition of the uncanny in the introduction to his book-length study of the phenomenon, where he isolates what I would argue is one of the signature effects of the uncanny: the blurring of boundaries. This is evident, appropriately enough, in the merger of the apparent opposites *heimlich/unheimlich* and *canny/uncanny*. This intrusion of the strange into the space of the familiar, the slipping of the familiar into the place of the strange, or the breaching of secrets are all evidence of the disorientation and breakdown characteristic of the uncanny. Royle explains:

> [The uncanny] disturbs any straightforward sense of what is inside and
> what is outside. The uncanny has to do with a strangeness of framing and
> borders, an experience of liminality. It may be that the uncanny is a feeling
> that happens only to oneself, within oneself, but is never one's "own": its
> meaning or significance may have to do, most of all, with what is not oneself,
> with others, with the world "itself." It may thus be construed as a foreign
> body within oneself, even the experience of oneself *as* a foreign body, the
> very estrangement of inner silence and solitude. It would appear to be
> indissociably bound up with a sense of repetition or "coming back"—the
> return of the repressed, the constant or eternal recurrence of the same thing,
> a compulsion to repeat. (2)[12]

The "strangeness of framing and borders," the "experience of liminality" refer at once to the spaces of the body, the home, and the nation. Though Royle's use of "foreign" here is figurative, it may also be usefully extended to connote the "not-of-this-nation."

Homi Bhabha has applied the uncanny to his elaborations on the postcolonial condition in which he capitalizes on the connotations of the "unhomely" to develop a theory of the colonized body, in which the traditional boundaries of space and time are blurred, breached, collapsed, stilled, rent. The unhomely addresses the obliteration from history of populations and peoples whose subjugation, disenfranchisement, and dislocation have relegated their histories, stories, and voices outside of the master narrative of cultural progress to a liminal elsewhere and "else-when" such that the potential disruption arising from their individual and collective differences is stanched. The recovery of these repressed voices requires a reach into the repository of the "beyond" where they have been held, locked up in time as a result of having been written over by formal history:

"Beyond" signifies spatial distance, marks progress, promises the future; but our intimations of exceeding the barrier or boundary—the very act of going *beyond*—are unknowable, unrepresentable, without a return to the "present" which, in the process of repetition, becomes disjunct and displaced. The imaginary of spatial distance—to live somehow beyond the border of our times—throws into relief the temporal, social differences that interrupt our collusive sense of cultural contemporaneity. The present can no longer be simply envisaged as a break or a bonding with the past and the future, no longer a synchronic presence: our proximate self-presence, our public image, comes to be revealed for its discontinuities, its inequalities, its minorities. (5–6)

The return to the present after a reach into the beyond (future or past) necessarily destabilizes or untethers the present from its present, insofar as it creates a "disjunct[ure]" between the moment of the reach and the moment of the return. The "present" is then repeated in this reach and return; however, it is a repetition-with-a-difference. The return cleaves to the moment of the reach but is now constituted by the memory or trace of the extension into the beyond, marking its difference from the site/ moment from which the reach began and, in turn, displacing it from the time of its initiation. Bhabha's "beyond" raises questions of where and when one belongs in that "it captures something of the estranging sense of the relocation of the home and the world, the unhomeliness, that is the condition of extra-territorial and cross-cultural initiation":

> To be unhomed is not to be homeless, nor can the "unhomely" be easily accommodated in that familiar division of social life into private and public spheres. . . . The recesses of the domestic space become sites for history's most intricate invasions. In that displacement, the borders between home and world become confused; and, uncannily, the private and the public become part of each other, forcing upon us a vision that is as divided as it is disorienting. (13)

Peyton's castle serves as an example of the beyond brought to bear on cultural identity and difference. "To dwell 'in the beyond,'" Bhabha writes, "is . . . to be part of a revisionary time, a return to the present to redescribe our cultural contemporaneity; to reinscribe our human, historic commonality; *to touch the future on its hither side*. In that sense, then, the intervening space 'beyond,' becomes a space of intervention in the here and now" (10, emphasis his). Samuel Peyton's beyond-ness in

*Peyton Place* is signified by his black skin and his quest for a home in the world. Resident gossip and unofficial castle historian Clayton Frazier takes note of Peyton's unusual relationship to history, remarking that he "musta lived before his time, or out of his element, or whatever you want to call it. Anyhow, he lived a long time before anybody ever heard of a feller called Abraham Lincoln. The reason I say he lived out of his time was that Samuel had funny ideas. He wanted to be free, and this was at a time when most folks looked on niggers as work horses, or mules" (329). Where Bhabha explores what it is to "dwell 'in the beyond,'" in *Peyton Place*, "the beyond" is manifest in a dwelling, Peyton's castle, which stands as a relic of several moments of traumatic "extra-territorial and cross-cultural initiation" (Bhabha, 13). The structure speaks to Peyton's having been brought, bought, or born into slavery; his flight to freedom and his escape from the South to France, first, then England; his return from overseas during the middle of the Civil War and his subsequent rejection on the basis of race by Boston society; and his move "far enough away from Boston that he'd never set eyes on a white man again as long as he lived" (330). Frazier surmises that Peyton was prevented from taking up residence among Boston's well-to-do because he effectively was not "black enough" despite being "big and strappin' and black as the ace of spades":

> Reckon Samuel musta thought that with all his money, and everybody lovin' the niggers, that he was gonna be able to move right onto Beacon Hill and start in entertainin' the Lowells and the Cabots. Well, the upshot of it was that Samuel couldn't find any kind of a house anyplace in Boston. If he'd of been in rags with welts all over his back, and if Vi'let had been black and had looked like she was all pooped from bein' chased by bloodhounds, maybe they'd of had an easier time of it. I dunno. I reckon Boston wa'nt too used to seein' a nigger wearin' a starched frill and a hand-embroidered waistcoat, and boots that cost forty dollars a pair. (330)

Peyton fails to conform to the image of abjection espoused by northerners. He is too much like them in his manner of dress, his choice of wife, his belief in personal liberty, and full subjectivity. Peyton is out of place in the nation both as a captive, colonized body, and as a freeman seeking a home of his own.

While Peyton himself signifies the "imaginary spatial distance" of "liv[ing] somehow beyond the border of [one's] times" (Bhabha,6), the reconstruction on American soil of the English castle that comes to bear his name marks a concretized spatial presence of foreignness, articulating temporal and spatial distance and difference. Of the Gothic castle, Punter and Byron ask, "Does [it] belong to the present or to the past, and with what suppressed denizens of our own pasts does it menace us as we try to 'read' its ambiguous signs?" (261). The castle belongs, of course, to both present and past. In *Peyton Place*, it belongs to more than one past, further imbuing it with the unhomeliness of which Bhabha speaks. In the narrative's present, its presence haunts the town from its highest hill. It has stood empty since Peyton's death and has therefore ceased to be a human habitation and has instead become a sort of mausoleum. Peyton's wife, Violette, is rumored to have died either from tuberculosis or from having "just faded away from bein' cooped up in the castle," a living entombment (331). Her grave is marked by a tall headstone of white Vermont marble and his by a black marble headstone imported from overseas, visually marking their racial difference, memorializing it with foreign materials. The interior of the castle is in ruins, the expensive fabrics and furnishings that make up its decor moldering from three-quarters of a century's worth of neglect.

Peyton's last request, that the state "look after [the] place 'til it falls apart" by keeping the gates locked and trespassers out, suggests an attempt from beyond the grave to keep the world out of his home. Like the town's futile effort to disown and disavow its origins, cast as they are in stone, and in the marble at Samuel and Violette's gravesites, Peyton's wish was doomed to failure: the world was already there. The racism that excluded Peyton from Boston structured his response to it. Peyton builds his home in the world defensively. Despite the isolation of his high-walled fortress and Peyton's desire to never see a white man again and because of the circumstances under which it came into being, the castle is always fated to be inhabited by the exigencies of the nation's and the world's history. Its revenge is that in its turn, the castle stands as a reminder of the racism that structured it. It stands as a monument to repression, individual and collective, personal and civic, straining to speak the story the town will not tell about itself.

## The World in Her Home: The MacKenzie Unhomely

The MacKenzie household is among the most unhomely domestic spaces in *Peyton Place*. Within it, the threat of miscegenation, which imbues Peyton's story with no small measure of its scandal, is restaged and updated as Constance's white clapboard Cape Cod becomes home to Tom Makris by novel's end through his marriage to the town's fairest female. The house frames Constance's story; the home furnishes her legitimacy. Though pristine, kept so through the housekeeping labor of Nellie Cross, and well appointed with a "magazine rack filled with copies of *The American Home* and *The Ladies' Home Journal*" (40) and a prominently displayed portrait of Allison MacKenzie Sr. enshrined on the fireplace mantle, Constance's home is not what it seems. It is not the home of a widow and her daughter; it is that of a thirty-something never-married mother and her illegitimate child. The photograph of Constance's dead lover maintains the masquerade of respectability for Constance, her daughter (as yet unaware that her parents never married), and all houseguests: "No one ever questioned the fact that Constance was the widow of a man named Allison MacKenzie. She kept a large, framed photograph of him on the mantelpiece in her living room, and the town sympathized with her" (17). At the same time that it secures Constance's social standing, it also marks her transgression, hiding it in plain sight. Allison MacKenzie's portrait serves the same function as the portrait of Clifford Pyncheon in Nathaniel Hawthorne's *The House of the Seven Gables*, a work that depicts one of the quintessentially uncanny home spaces of American literature.

The portraits in *The House of the Seven Gables* and *Peyton Place* are the keepers of the family secrets, and in each case, the repressed past threatens to erupt into the present day of the narrative. In Hawthorne's gothic romance, "[t]he secret that serves as the matrix for the uncanny events in *The House of the Seven Gables* is concealed by a portrait of the family's progenitor" (Tatar, 175). In Hawthorne, the figurative weight that the Pyncheon portrait bears as a result of concealing the secret is so great that legend has it that its absence would cause "the whole edifice [to] come thundering down, in a heap of dusty ruin" (Hawthorne, 170). Were Constance to prematurely remove the portrait of her supposed husband or, alternatively, to never have installed it on the mantle in the first place, the "edifice" of her plausible fiction might similarly follow suit and collapse into the dust of domestic disintegration. The framed image of Allison MacKenzie guards the secret of Constance's past and her daughter Allison's origins, effectively keeping order by suggesting that Constance has held to socially acceptable modes of behavior, the most important being that she was well wed when she became a mother. The necessity of its place and position in a public room of her house attests to the power the portrait asserts in the lives of the dwelling's two inhabitants and its significance to the surrounding community, speaking to and ensuring the town's need for domestic (i.e., civic) order. The portrait neutralizes the threat Constance would otherwise pose to the social order if it were known that she had willingly entered into an adulterous affair with a family man *and* brought forth a child by him. It speaks to the presence of the world in her home that Constance must present in her own living room satisfactory evidence of her propriety in order to avoid "getting herself talked about."

Just as the portrait obscures the truth of Constance's past by enabling her to perpetuate and inhabit a fiction, it also obscures her relationship to herself. As discussed earlier, Constance buys into her manufactured persona to the degree that she begins to imagine herself to be utterly uninterested in sex. She has consolidated her "official story" with her private knowledge and convinced herself that her affair with the married Allison MacKenzie was a matter of loneliness above all else. In doing so, Constance has estranged herself so completely from her sexual desires that she insistently mistakes them for indigestion.[13] Her conversion of her sex drive into an unsettled stomach (until Tom's reconversion through rape) has made her sexuality uncanny to her, "a secret once familiar but made alien by the process of forgetting" (Tatar, 176). In her sexual estrangement from herself, Constance might be said to "experience [her]self *as* a foreign body" (Royle, 2, emphasis his). Having fully disavowed her libido, she is unable to account for her restlessness in the months following Tom Makris's arrival in town, nor is she able to abolish the anxiety and fear that Tom's presence in town inspires. She is initially apprehensive upon hearing that he, like her dead lover, is from New York and thus might be the harbinger of her past, yet the fact that there's no glimmer of recognition in his eyes at their introduction does nothing to calm her. Instead,

> Constance began to be plagued with restless nights and frequent attacks of indigestion. Twice she had glimpsed Tomas Makris on the street, and both times she had run rather than face him, but afterward she could not think of a reasonable explanation for her action. Perhaps she had been more apprehensive than she had first thought when Allison had told her of the new headmaster who was coming to town from New York, and she was suffering now from the after effects of a terrible anxiety. (106)

Her anxiety, while initially stoked by Tom's New York connection, has not yet passed. What Constance reads as "after effects" are instead evidence of her unacknowledged and continued sense of insecurity, a visceral, primal fear associated with Tom whenever he draws near, diminishing only slightly in his absence. His proximity haunts her, causing her sleepless nights and considerable irritability during the daylight hours. Following the hasty arrival of a belated spring season, the final settling of the weather marks the contrast of Constance's continued frustration; "it was only [she] who was left disquieted":

> Even with the turbulent days of April gone, and with her calendar showing her that it was May and a time of sunshine and silent growth, Constance was as unstill as the river in floodtime. She did not recognize the symptoms in herself as akin to the painful restlessness of adolescence, nor did she admit that the dissatisfied yearning within her could be a sexual one. She blamed the externals of her life; her daughter, the heavier responsibilities of an enlarged business, and the constant effort she had to make toward both. (110)

Her disquiet rises quickly and consistently into fear at the mere sight of Tom, and whenever possible she retreats from his approach so as to avoid contact. When he enters the shop on a blustery May day, the sight of Tom's shoulders in a trench coat "gave him a look of strength and power that left Constance terror stricken" (111) and sends her into the store-room for sanctuary. Though she can recognize and articulate his sexual threat, remarking, "*Anyone*, she declared to herself, would be impressed with a man that size, with his almost revolting good looks and that smile that belongs in a bedroom" (106), she fails to understand what it might mean for her. His presence in her boutique reminds her of a "bull in a china shop, but it did not amuse her in that moment. She could only imagine too clearly the smashing havoc of such a situation" (111). Though Constance misreads the reason for her responses to Tom in public and private, she is, in fact, accurate in her assessment that he presents a threat to her. The night of the eighth-grade formal dance, Tom waits on the corner in front of Constance's house until Allison has left with her date. When she answers the doorbell's summons and discovers Tom on her front stoop, Constance is seized by "a feeling of unreality" that leaves her speechless as he explains himself. Tom tells her that he worried that she would never invite him to call on her so he decided to thwart convention and call upon her uninvited. Following his opening gambit, throughout which he "push[ed] gently at the outside of the door," Constance admits him into the hallway, where he addresses her fear openly and at close range, "close enough to her so that she had to raise her head to look up at him, and when she had done so, he smiled down at her gently. 'Don't be afraid,' he said. 'I'm not going to hurt you. I'm going to be around for a long time. There's no hurry'" (120).

Despite Tom's assurances, Constance's fear is justified. He does hurt her, sexually assaulting her later that summer in her own home. Constance's fear of the familiar in Tom, that he brings with him to Peyton Place the knowledge of her secret, that her reputation precedes her, that he knows her already, is in its own way on target. Though he does not know the particulars, Tom intuitively senses her fear and, to some degree, her disguise and designates Constance as someone in need of a radical erotic renovation, taking it upon himself to transform her from the "ice maiden" she enacts into the "passionate, love-demanding woman" he knows her to be (178). Tom's nearness reawakens Constance's repressed libido even though she remains committed to her masterful revirginization—what Madonne Miner has appropriately termed her "second adolescence" for its anticipation of a second coming of age (66). Constance's season of indigestion may also be attributed to Tom's resemblance to the deceased Allison MacKenzie (both are dark men who hail from New York), the man whose practical desire to avoid the "unearthly stink" of divorcing his wife in order to be with Constance helped to shoehorn her into her current existence (15).

The portrait of Allison the elder is significant not only for serving as the cornerstone of what Tom refers to, even before he knows the truth, as Constance's "false existence." It has also been the basis for the bogus identity of the younger Allison MacKenzie. She is neither who she thinks she is (she is not a legitimate MacKenzie) nor how old (she is actually a year older that her birth certificate indicates). The photograph on the mantle has also been the source of Allison's storybook dreams of a handsome prince. Indeed, thinking of the portrait one night as she is drifting off to sleep, she calls her father "my prince," at which moment "the image in her mind seemed to take on life, to breathe, and to smile kindly at her" (20).[14] Allison's fairy-tale wishfulness in this direction, that her father was just such a man and that she too may find hers someday, leads her to follow unwittingly in her mother's footsteps and fall into bed with a New York family man. Though she avoids the wrinkle of illegitimate pregnancy, Allison returns to Peyton Place for Selena Cross's murder trial with the knowledge of sexual experience and a new empathy for the difficult choices her mother has made. During a conversation with Tom on the Peyton castle grounds, Allison admits, "I understand how it could happen. Mother was just unluckier than most, that's all" (369). That this conversation takes place on Peyton's property is significant for the difference it points to in Allison's relationship to the castle. Prior to her sexual initiation, she had regarded the estate with shivery terror. Of all the characters in the novel, Allison is the one most notably and consistently un-settled by the story of the Peyton place. For her, the castle is as an example of the quintessentially haunted house. Metalious introduces the dwelling into the narrative through Allison's point of view, sending a chill down her spine that signals the sway it holds over her imagination. When Allison confesses her fear of the castle grounds to Selena and asks if her friend is similarly scared by the structure and its history, Selena's matter-of-fact reply is steeped in the hard wisdom of her own life: "Dead folks can't hurt you none. It's the ones that are alive, you have to watch out for" (35). When Norman Page confides to Allison that he finds the spinster cat lady Miss Hester Goodale's house frightening, he uses the Peyton place as the yardstick by which to measure his fear of her. He would sooner spend time at the castle than spy on Miss Hester. Though Allison chides him for this, when she stops to regard the Goodale house, she corroborates his fears and "musingly" deems it "sinister looking." Norman's fears are redoubled by Allison's declaration. The house transforms in his imagination so that its "windows stared back at him like half-lidded eyes" and the dwelling "looked suddenly to him as if it were about to sprout arms, ready to en-gulf children and sweep them through the front door of the brown shingled cottage" (63). With the help of Allison's imaginative assessment of Miss Hester's home, Norman's terror is transferred from its occupant to the house itself. Despite the house's sinister aspect, Allison dismisses Norman's apprehensions. "There's nothing spooky about Miss Hester Goodale," she tells him. "The castle's full of spooks, though. It's haunted" (64).[15]

Allison's assertion that the castle is "full of spooks" speaks to the as-sumption that a structure such as Peyton's castle is haunted. Hers is the only claim of its kind, however, and it is only mentioned once in her ex-change with Norman. There is nothing supernaturally inexplicable about the castle. There are no tales of ghoulishness, or ghostliness, visitations or specters, nor any reports of eerie and unattributed shrieks, howls, cries, or wails. As with Poe's famously fractured family home, the House of Usher, "any sentiments of doom were more easily attributed to the fantasies of the narrator than to any striking detail in the house itself" (Vidler, "Architecture," 7). The fact that most of the details of Peyton's story are withheld until the end of the novel suggests this as well. It is Al-lison's projection of her inarticulate fears upon the castle and the town's collective reluctance to discuss the matter that conveys the sense of a haunt-ing. However, in the absence of such evidence (anecdotal or otherwise) pertaining to the structure itself, the suggestion, then, is that the house itself is the agent of the haunting and the town is the haunted space.

Whether haunted, as Allison believes, or haunting, as is my contention, there remains something essentially and collectively unspeakable about Peyton's place for the town's residents. That something is, of course, the tangle of anxieties that attend upon an originary home space erected defensively against northern bigotry and inhabited by a wealthy black man and his foreign white wife. Despite a lack of evidence presented before or after her remark in support of her claim that the Peyton place is "full of spooks," Allison's assertion at once misunderstands her own psychological entanglement with the castle's story (it is she who is haunted, not the castle) and, though her use of "spooks" seems to mean "ghosts," it may also serve as a derogatory double-entendre that anticipates the later revelation that Samuel Peyton was black.

In her eager, adolescent attempt to write Miss Hester's story, one of her earliest authorial endeavors, Allison soon discovers that she does not really know her subject and concludes to herself, "I can't write about Miss Hester because I don't know her. . . . I'll have to make up a story about somebody I know about" (66). Despite having articulated at the start of her literary career the wisdom of the writer's mantra "write what you know," Allison forgets this in her ambitious novelization of Samuel Peyton's story as a young writer living in New York City. The attempt is a professional failure that she soon afterward attributes to her essential unfamiliarity with her subject. In a conversation with Tom on her first walk to the site of the castle itself, she admits, "I've never been there. . . . Perhaps that's why I couldn't write about it successfully. A long time ago I realized that it was a waste of time to try to write about something one does not know about" (369). Though Allison recognizes the source material for a good story when she sees it, she lacks the proper knowledge to transform it into a compelling and marketable book. Interestingly, Allison learns of her failure almost immediately after she has gained the knowledge that might have served her in her efforts to write Sam Peyton's story in the first place. She has just lost her virginity to the bearer of her unfortunate professional tidings, her agent, a father surrogate who, like her mother's lover before her (which is to say, her own father), is a philandering family man from New York.[16] Allison returns to Peyton Place in the wake of this double disappointment and in time for Selena Cross's murder trial, and she finds that neither the town nor the castle threatens her peace of mind as they had in her past. Her inability to translate Peyton's story successfully into a novel, by her own admission, stems from incomplete knowledge. Though she attributes this to having not seen the castle up close, it seems equally a matter of a lack of self- (i.e., sexual) knowledge. Having returned home with the latter, she finds she is no longer afraid of either the castle or the town. This follows the same pattern as the relationship between the acquisition of knowledge and the diminution of the uncanny according to Tatar:

> In *The House of the Seven Gables*, disenchantment comes through knowledge. The supernatural draws its strength from the absence or repression of knowledge, for what is shut out from consciousness can return with a vengeance as a physical presence. Once knowledge comes to light, this external power is revealed to be no more than a psychic reality. The mysterious and eerie give way to the familiar and well known. Knowledge lifts the sign of repression from what is *unheimlich* and renders is *heimlich* or *heimisch*. (178)

The "psychic reality" that Allison inhabited and to which she was subject by a homely haunting prior to her sexual initiation has been displaced by the experience of her hometown as no more intimidating than a "toy village" (371). Because her coming of age so nearly repeats her mother's, though without the illegitimate pregnancy, Allison gains not only sexual knowledge but uncanny insight into her mother's predicament. Possessed now of the true story of her father and of her own origins, sexual awareness, and a sexual encounter with a father surrogate that reiterates her mother's sexual history, Allison is fully disenchanted of the castle's mystery and, in turn, the town's hold on her unhappiness. As a result, the portrait of her father loses its potency in her imagination and is retired from its guardianship of the MacKenzie household.[17] Though Tom Makris's self-appointed task had been to destroy the "tedious, expensive shell" within which Constance has been living for so many years (177), it is not he who removes the picture of Allison MacKenzie Sr. from its place of semipublic prominence in Constance's living room. It is Allison who does so. With the "token of repression" unseated from its throne on the mantle and thus its reign in the lives of the MacKenzie household as silent witness to the home's secrets, "what was formerly *unheimlich* becomes *heimlich*: the once hostile world becomes habitable again. Knowledge can either exorcise the real ghosts of the marvelous tale or disenchant the imaginary specters of the strange story. In either case, it expels them from the fictional world" (Tatar, 182). Allison is no longer afraid of Peyton Place. In fact, she has reconciled her fears so completely that she embraces the town in a private declaration to herself, extolling its "beauty" and "cruelty," its "kindness" and "ugliness." "[N]ow I know you," Allison exults, "and you no longer frighten me. Perhaps you will again, tomorrow or the next day, but right now I love you and I am not afraid of you. Today you are just a place" (371). Having expelled the "imaginary specters of the strange story" of Peyton's castle from her psyche, Allison is no longer haunted by the house on the hill, and her home (and her hometown), following Tatar above, "becomes habitable again."

## Intricate Invasions in Intimate Spaces: The Cross Family and the Domestication of Difference

Secrets alone do not necessarily confer uncanniness onto a home space, and for this reason I resist framing a discussion about the uncanny and the Cross family specifically in terms of their home and what it hides. To be sure, the Cross family's secrets are so highly charged that they erupt into the full consciousness of the town when Selena is brought to trial for Lucas's murder. However, what is more useful in this case is a discussion of Selena as the embodiment of the town's uncanny other and of the Cross home as the site where this uncanny identity is reified. It is worth mentioning again what Bhabha has to say about the intrusion of history into the family home and the vertiginous blurring of boundaries effected by such trespasses: "The recesses of the domestic space become sites for history's most intricate invasions. In that displacement, the borders between home and world become confused; and, uncannily, the private and the public become part of each other, forcing upon us a vision that is as divided as it is disorienting" (13). The Cross home is ritually, purgatively turned inside-out when Selena is brought to trial for the murder of Lucas. It is also the site that enables Selena to recast and, in the end, be freed from her domestic difference, refashioning its interior with an eye to the MacKenzie household. The renovation of the Cross shack into a respectable dwelling in conjunction with the very public presentation of her and her family's most intimate secrets during her murder trial transforms Selena from the town's dark other into one of its own. The mark of her difference is lost, and Selena is incorporated into the future of Peyton Place.

Prior to the arrival of Tom Makris in town, Selena Cross is the duskiest resident in Peyton Place. Metalious offers no explanation to account for Selena's skin tone: her mother Nellie's appearance suggests the effects of a lifetime of poverty and hardship, but there's nothing to suggest that her skin color is in any way remarkable, as it in fact bears no remark. Selena's biological father, Curtis Chamberlain, is mentioned but not described (130), which is indicative of the American writer's default position of indicating whiteness (were he otherwise, it would be made explicit) (Dyer, 2). Selena's body bears an unexplained, indeterminate darkness that distinguishes her both from her mother and from the overwhelming majority of the town's residents (Tom Makris joins Selena in her racialized minority when he arrives in Peyton Place). Her gypsylike beauty emphasizes not only her tawny skin but also confers a sense of foreignness upon her—that she is from somewhere else, an elsewhere similarly marked by a racialized, ethnic otherness of a sort that in its southern and eastern European likeness affiliates her with Tom Makris's Greekness.

Selena, like Samuel Peyton long before her, embodies the lived reality of what it is to be unhomely (not-at-home) in the world. She is out of place in Peyton Place despite having been born and raised there, and she is out of sync with the time that has been measured by her chronological age. Selena is wise beyond her years "with the wisdom learned of poverty and wretchedness" (31). The home itself lags behind modernity. It has no running water, no sewerage, a single bare light bulb for illumination, and no privacy. Selena defensively works to keep the world out of her home as best as she can by greeting Allison at the door whenever the two girls are to spend a day together and by discouraging Doc Swain from intervening on the night he hears Lucas and Nellie in a pitched row.

The rehabilitation of the Cross house from a single-room shack into a cottagelike home serves to elevate Selena above her lower-class status and has the apparent effect of effacing the darkness that has distinguished her from her fellow citizens. The process of mainstreaming Selena is well under way by the time she is finally able to remodel her home. Her relationship with Ted Carter and her employment as a clerk and then manager in Constance's boutique have forced the town to partially reconsider its preconceptions of shack dwellers. Charles Partridge, one of the denizens of Chestnut Street and the county attorney, tells Ted Carter that the aspiring lawyer "couldn't do better than Selena Cross. . . . Not for looks and not for brains" (170). The Carters themselves, formerly high up on the list of Selena's detractors, even recant their earlier misgivings, admitting "it took a real smart girl to manage a business all by herself with no help at all from the owner. . . . Selena did it alone, and a girl had to be real smart to be able to do that at the age of eighteen" (291). Following Nellie's suicide and Lucas Cross's exile at the behest of Doc Swain, the Cross shack is transformed into a home with the help of Selena's older half-brother Paul and his wife Gladys, who declares upon seeing it for the first time, "Christ, what a shit house this is!" (269). It is radically remodeled such that it is transformed from a shack into a home with running water and separate bedrooms, a renovation that meets with the town's consensus on what a house should look like, at least as far as they are able to discern from its exterior.

For Selena, however, the single most important upgrade was the "needless extravagance" of a fireplace, a finishing touch that for her transforms the house into a home and realizes for her the dream of living like the MacKenzies. To Selena, "everything about the MacKenzie house seemed luxurious—and beautiful, something to dream about" (35). When her brother Paul teases her for coveting such a "dirty and old fashioned" amenity as a fireplace, she confesses that it was the time she spent on Constance's hearth that led her to her idealized vision of domesticity—and feminine beauty. She recalls, "I used to sit in front of hers, with Allison, and think about the day when I'd have one of my own. . . . I used to wish that I had blond hair so that when I had my fireplace I could sit in front of it and let the fire make highlights in my hair, like it does in Connie's. I would have given anything to look like her, to be that beautiful" (292).[18] Selena is, of course, beautiful by all accounts, and having gained a measure of legitimacy through the rehabilitation of the tar-paper shack into a cozy home complete with warm hearth, she has lost a measure of her darkness. Her anomalous complexion ceases to be explicitly noteworthy from this point forward in the novel, and her eyes, though full of "unshared secrets," are no longer characterized as "dark" (293). Likewise, when Selena is brought to trial for Lucas's murder, it is specifically what she is wearing that earns notice from the suspicious mind of Marion Partridge, for whom Selena poses an imagined sexual threat.[19] Her tan skin, her dark hair and eyes, her full red lips have become less significant than her sense of domesticity and fashion.

Selena's affiliation with darkness, though less descriptively explicit, is still in play, however. It is her murder trial, the town's latest scandal, that occasions the full telling of the story of Samuel Peyton. Peyton Place's most shameful secret about itself is disclosed to, of all people, a newspaper reporter who, even before the start of the trial, imagines beginning his first article with, "In the tragic shadow of Samuel Peyton's castle . . . another tragedy has taken place." (332). Selena's story becomes a public spectacle at the center of which are the abuses of her body. All of the sordid details of her family and the mortifications and humiliations of her body are revealed to the public. Peyton Place's "three sources of scandal: suicide, murder and the impregnation of an unmarried girl" are all visited upon the Cross household with the added sordidness of rape and incest (241). In Selena's defense, Doc Swain must reveal all that she has endured in order to make the best case for her acquittal: repeated rape and incest, pregnancy and abortion. Her body is the site upon which all of the worst sins of the town are inscribed; her home is the site in which these sins are made to take place.

Doc Swain's testimony convinces the jury and the courtroom full of Peyton Place's citizens that in killing Lucas, Selena acted in self-defense, and she is acquitted and exonerated and surrounded by her fellow towns-folk outside the courthouse (350). Instead of being purged from the future of the town, Selena is incorporated into it. When Allison expresses doubts that Selena could remain in Peyton Place the wake of such public exposure, Kathy Ellsworth reports that Selena has been observed in "very friendly" conversation with her defense attorney, Peter Drake, himself a transplant from an undisclosed elsewhere and therefore perhaps less responsive or beholden than Ted Carter to the town's residual wagging tongues. Whereas initially Selena had been spatially and geographically marginalized in "the village" of tar-paper shacks, following her acquittal she has become part of Peyton Place's social fabric, belonging, at last, in town. Illustrating Kaplan's assertion that "[domesticity] travels in contradictory circuits both to expand and contract the boundaries of home and nation and to pro-duce shifting conceptions of the foreign" ("Manifest," 583), Selena has effectively been integrated, despite living in precisely the same location as she had before. Her civic acceptance in its way suggests that her prior "otherness" has been dispelled and her uncanniness in relation to the town has been demystified in a slight variant Tatar's "disenchantment through knowledge." Everything about Selena Cross that was meant to remain hidden has come to light through her trial. As a result, the wrongs that enabled such a tragedy to occur have been redressed by drawing atten-tion to the town's collective responsibility for the plight of an individual household (Cameron, xii). In addition to having lost her uncanniness, Selena has also shed her embodied darkness through narrative omission. Although the correlation between the timing of the revelation of the truth behind the Peyton place and the eve of Selena's trial does reiterate her initial racialization by Metalious, Selena's increasing affiliation with white, middle-class domesticity, dress, and aspiration eradicate her early difference to the extent that by novel's end, her former darkness has been effaced.

## Dis-ordering Difference

Selena Cross, Tom Makris, and Samuel Peyton are affiliated by virtue of their shared darkness and difference from the majority of Peyton Place's citizens. The collective anxiety attached to the story of Peyton's castle might be understood as a result of the ordering of the terms of difference itself. As Samuel Peyton is the founding father of the town, the white settlers who come after his originating blackness are in fact the bearers of difference, a difference that their descendants cannot seem to bear. This reversal of terms, darkness as precedent, whiteness as difference, exposes the truth of the history not only of Peyton Place, but of the United States. A black founding father married to a white foreigner is apparently no source or cause for civic pride and dis-orders the national fiction of white primacy and dark alterity. Peyton's difference marks the town's difference; however, this difference, the scandal of its origins, is in fact a part of the nation's history, revealing whiteness as a second term to darkness's priority. Minor character Miss Hester Goodale's house provides another example of the confounded relationship between precedents and successors and their uncanny effects. Miss Hester's brown-shingled Cape Cod–style house is visibly "different" from those nearby: according to Allison, it "looks out of place . . . because it sits right next to a lovely little white and green Cape Cod" (65). It does not occur to Allison that perhaps the white Cape is out-of-place, inhabited as it is by a married couple (the Cards) who have recently moved to town and are expecting their first child. Despite the fact that Miss Hester's house has been in her family for generations (as has Allison's own, a house she also faults for its familial difference of fatherlessness), for Allison, the Goodale home is the anomaly. What is interesting about this perspective—this assessment of difference— is that it connects Miss Hester's home to Peyton's castle, not only through its gothic signifiers (e.g., the tomblike home, the disrupted generational line, a haunting house) but also in the manner through which "difference" is defined and prioritized. Just as Miss Hester's family precedes her neighbors in Peyton Place by many years (perhaps two generations—hers and her father's at the very least), Peyton and his wife were the first settlers to build a permanent residence in the area. This is important in that, in each case, the true difference is not inherent in the first term (because it is the originating one) but rather in the second, the one that comes after. In other words, just as Allison confuses the order of things by remarking that it is the Goodale house that is out of place (and that her point of comparison is limited to only one other house might also be said to render her judgment suspect), the difference with which the castle is imbued—racial, architectural, temporal—is incorrectly assessed by the town. Those who settled in the shadow of the castle bear the mark of the town's difference—

not Peyton's. Peyton Place's historical shame, then, is also the nation's shame. Town and country both repress and suppress elements that cannot be readily reconciled with the project of producing and circumscribing a dominant white civic identity and citizenry. The castle and its story embody and expose an American habit of misconstruing and disordering the terms of difference in the service of white hegemony.

## Assimilating Selena, Integrating Tom

Peyton Place's welcome embrace of Selena following her acquittal comes as a surprise. It is expected that, like shamed heroines of sentimental novels, she will be forced to leave for having become such a public symbol of the town's shortcomings (Gault, 996). Delaney, the newspaperman who now knows the whole of the town's dark history, asks Selena's lawyer, "Has she any plans? Where will she go?" (350), assuming that she will not be able to make a life for herself within the same space where she has been so public a lightning rod for so many of its scandals. And prior to her own private reconciliation with the town, Allison condescendingly declares Selena "a fool" for staying and tells Kathy Ellsworth, "In the end, Selena will have to leave" (351), citing the court of public opinion as the reason. However, Selena's post-trial life in Peyton Place is the culmination of an ongoing project of assimilation that is conflated with her class mobility. In other words, Selena has, by novel's end, been whitened to the degree that she not only remains a resident in town without disturbing its equanimity, but she achieves a middle-class existence. Her presence is no longer at odds with the town's mainstream; instead it is congruent with it. The danger here is that such an assertion threatens to deny the significance of her former difference from the town's vision of its future self. And the fact that Selena remains in Peyton Place after having been the means of such a public purging of the community's sins subverts generic expectation. Many a literary heroine has been made to suffer not simply the indignity and subsequent public humiliation of sexual assault, but has been purged from the community either through exile or death. Thomas Hardy's Tess of the d'Urbervilles comes to mind, as do Charlotte Temple and Clarissa Harlowe. My intention is not to minimize the impact of Metalious's choice to keep Selena in town but rather to note the terms under which she does so. On the one hand, the incorporation of Selena into the town's future that is suggested by the encircling courthouse crowd and her continued residence in Peyton Place is a hopeful gesture enabled through the ritual exposure of the town's shortcomings during the murder trial. On the other, it must be noted that having narratively lost the mark of her difference by being less discursively dark by novel's end, Selena is less of a threat and may therefore be more readily, less dangerously, incorporated into the community.

The question then arises: can the same be said of Tom Makris, the novel's dark stranger whose arrival in town occasions the first explicit mention of Samuel Peyton's race? This issue came up for discussion at an academic conference where I presented some of this work. The moderator for my panel, a professor of whiteness studies, asked whether I thought Tom had been whitened by novel's end. I considered it at the time without answering definitively, and have since concluded that while I believe that Selena is, Tom is not. The query was useful in helping me to crystallize my thinking about how the novel resolves issues of whiteness, darkness, difference, and diversity. It also pointed out a possible pitfall of such endeavors, that is, the potentially assimilationist impulse of readings that presume that all nonwhite characters are necessarily whitened by contact with whiteness. To presume so seems to me to reenact the habit of white hegemony that the field of whiteness studies seeks to critique. I would argue, then, that because Tom Makris does not undergo a transformation as radical as Selena's, he is not whitened in order to enable his continued existence in town but instead is integrated into the community on his own terms. He is, in fact, the agent of Constance's transformation, recuperating her libido for her in order to bring her back into sexual wholeness. Rather than whitening Tom, Metalious in effect darkens Constance. As part of her critique of whiteness's dysfunction, the full flowering of Constance's sexuality as the result of Tom's influence leads her into an apparently stable and sexually fulfilling marriage. In the end, it is Constance's Anglo identity (Standish/MacKenzie) that is effaced socially and legally when she takes Tom's Greek surname after their marriage. Unlike Selena's, Tom's class status does not change while he is in Peyton Place. Though he was born and raised in New York's Lower East Side and has spent part of his adult life working as a laborer, he is fully matriculated within the ranks of the white-collar world when he comes to town. In addition, he arrives there to fill an influential position and remains securely within that stratum throughout the rest of the novel. As the principal of the Peyton Place schools, he exerts considerable influence over many of the town's residents by managing the educational curricula of their children, helping to mold the young minds that will be charged with carrying the nation forward into the future. Furthermore, with his marriage to Constance, Tom becomes the head of the MacKenzie—now Makris—household. The boundaries of Constance's home have been ideologically redrawn to accommodate Tom's permanent presence there such that Metalious implies that it is where he belongs. By positioning Tom in such a manner, without requiring of him some measure of sacrifice for the privilege of living among middle-class whites, and by emphasizing the bliss and sexual health he and Constance enjoy within their marriage, Metalious offers a vision of domestic harmony that values—perhaps even insists on—racial and ethnic integration for the health of domestic spaces writ large and small.

## At Home at the End of the World

*Peyton Place*'s three main storylines conclude on overtly optimistic notes. Selena's life is saved, her home is more comfortable and secure than ever, and she may be on the road to romance with a good man. Constance has settled into married life and sexual fulfillment with Tom. Allison has resolved the fears and sorrows of her youth and has made peace with Peyton's castle and the town. The novel's final image presents Allison running toward home to reunite with a man her own age who promises a right kind of romance (as opposed to her oedipally motivated obsession with her agent). Allison has finally let go of her father fantasy, and her fantasy father, in favor of a potential relationship with a male friend and confidante who is patient, trustworthy, and understanding.[20] This trio of happy endings is belied by a fundamental lack of resolution undergirding the text. The novel ends in the fall of 1944, when the United States is still at war, and despite the personal victories of Metalious's three heroines, the future of the nation remains at stake. World War II has not yet been won, and the world hangs in the balance. The war itself is said to have had little measurable effect on the town and its people; it "had not made the soil of northern New England less rocky, more yielding, or the weather more predictable. The wresting of life from the land had always been difficult, and the war made no difference one way or another" (289–90). Though many of Peyton Place's young men are soldiering overseas, victory is a foregone conclusion, at least for the gossips at Tuttle's general store:

> The idea of an alien foot, whether German or Japanese, trodding the acres first settled by the grandfathers of the old men in Tuttle's was one so far-fetched, so impossible to visualize, that it was spoken of—and listened to—with the hushed attitude in which the men might have held a discussion

on extrasensory perception. It was all right to talk and to listen, but one simply did not believe it. A stranger, coming to Peyton Place for the first time from a place where the war had passed, might well have been dumbfounded by the lack of concern in evidence in the town. . . . To the old men in Tuttle's, the war was almost like a game, a conversational game, to be played when other subjects were exhausted. A stranger to Peyton Place might have easily mistaken disbelief of danger for courage, or faith for indifference. (290)

War is more parlor game than reality for these men, and its large-scale implications are eclipsed the following summer by the local sensation of Selena's murder trial. Foreign infiltration seems outlandish to the point of being nearly altogether inconceivable, but here Metalious seems to be critiquing the town's provincialism by indicating that the possibilities do exist despite a collective failure of imagination. By leaving the novel in the midst of a war, however faraway it may seem to the town, Metalious subtly connects the novel's continued uncertainties with national insecurities contemporary with *Peyton Place*'s publication in 1956. The Cold War creeps into the text once again in surprising ways. In the scene in which Allison exuberantly comes to terms with her hometown, Peyton Place looks to her like no more than a "toy village" from her lookout at Road's End (371). Metalious uses this same image to much different effect in an earlier scene signifying not a site of harmlessness but rather a depopulated residential wasteland. On this particular hot, midsummer's day in 1939, Allison's search for solitude leads her up the hill to Road's End, where she experiences "a feeling of being the only inhabitant in a dry, burnt-out world" (133). When she encounters Norman Page similarly seeking sanctuary from human interaction, their small talk begins with the stillness of the town and the river nearby. Allison observes, "It looks like a toy village, with everything made out of cardboard," to which Norman responds, "That's what I was thinking just before you came. I was thinking that everybody else in the world was dead, and I was the only one left" (133).

Such an image of sole survivorship in the wake of a global disaster and human decimation, though placed in the novel in the year 1939, would have resonated with the daunting possibilities of thermonuclear war to an American readership in 1956. On the one hand, it might be argued that the second "toy village" reference is meant to be a corrective to the first, occurring as it does in an optimistic moment of a protagonist's reconciliation with her past, a coming-to-terms that enables the possibility of her romantic renewal in the form of a proper partner. I maintain, however, that the second reference is instead haunted by the first, given the still-precarious nature of the future of the nation within a novel that concludes in the heat of a world war and that is released and circulated in an age of pervasive and looming uncertainty—not simply for the future of an American small town, but for America overall.

# Conclusion

The frenzy and the furor that greeted *Peyton Place*'s arrival in stores in September 1956 had been deliberately stoked by a great deal of advance publicity about the naughty novel by the New England mother of three. Owing in part to a clever marketing campaign alleging that *Peyton Place* had put George Metalious's job in jeopardy, the novel became the fourth-best-selling book in the country a full week before its publication (Toth, *Inside*, 130). Within its first ten days on the market, sixty thousand copies had vanished from booksellers' shelves and into the paper bags and hidden coat pockets that such spicy reads were said to have required at the time (135). By the end of October, *Peyton Place* had sold more than 104,000 copies (131), and by late November, the novel had reached number one on the *New York Times* best-seller list and remained there for over a year (Cameron, viii). After having been in print for only three months, *Peyton Place* became the third-best-selling book of 1956, and sales throughout 1957 bumped it up to that year's second-best top seller according to *Publisher's Weekly* (Hackett, 203). It soon outsold *Gone with the Wind*, which had reigned as America's best-selling fiction title for nearly two decades (Toth, *Inside*, 207). Beginning in 1958, *Peyton Place* settled in for nearly ten years as the nation's all-time best seller. By 1990, Metalious's "Small Town Peep Show," the catchy title for the *New York Times*'s review of the novel, had sold more than 20 million copies (Dodson, 94).

*Peyton Place*'s extraordinary popularity was met with alarm by America's moral guardians. The same month that the novel reached number one on the *New York Times* best-seller list, *Catholic World* decried *Peyton Place* as "one of the cheapest, most blatant attempts in years to present the most noxiously commonplace in ideas and behavior in the loose and ill-worn guise of realistic art" (qtd. in James and Brown, 640). Some viewed its brisk sales as a harbinger of the American apocalypse. *Manchester Union-Leader* publisher William Loeb vituperated that the popularity of *Peyton Place* heralded no less than "the collapse of a civilization": "for there to be enough people to place this book at the top of the best-seller list in the nation is not only shocking, but most revealing of the state of culture and ethics in our day" (par. 4). Syndicated columnist Margaret Latrobe took Metalious to task for violating gender norms by giving voice to such "dirty words" and "dirty themes." Having reasoned that a certain roughness to male-authored texts seems intended to affirm the masculinity of those writers, Latrobe concludes that "Mrs. Metalious, apparently, wants to prove that women writers aren't effeminate, either; that at least one can be just as ugly-spoken as any man writing" (par. 6).[1] Other commentators lacked the righteousness of *Catholic World*, Loeb, and Latrobe, opting instead for a straightforward dismissal of the novel's value. The editors of the *Franklin Journal-Transcript*, for instance, claimed that the novel had no greater "merit of authority than the stuff which keeps so many janitors busy in public rest rooms, painting over and erasing, endlessly. It is not a bad book because of the bad words, but because it doesn't say anything worth saying" (par. 6). In the face of such criticism, and perhaps resulting in no small part from it, the novel's sales figures continued to soar.

While newspaper editors and columnists tended to be unsparing in their criticism of *Peyton Place*, book reviewers offered more even-handed assessments of Metalious's work, recognizing the skill and realism with which the novel presents its social commentary on life in a small American town. The novel's sexual content still dominated the discussions, as critics characterized the prose as "over-ripe" (*Chicago Sunday Tribune*), "offensively crude" (*New York Herald Tribune*), "earthy" and "lurid" (*New York Times*). Even so, many found that Metalious's writing did have its merits. Both the *Chicago Sunday Tribune* and *New Yorker* commended the novel's pace, the former attributing it to Metalious's "great narrative skill." Though *Time* magazine remarked that Metalious's "love scenes are as explicit as love scenes can get without the use of diagrams and tape recorder," the same review observed that "when Authoress Metalious is not all flustered by sex, she captures a real sense of the tempo, texture, and tensions in the social anatomy of a small town" (all qtd. in James and Brown, 640). *New York Times* critic Carlos Baker called her "a pretty fair writer for a first novelist," granting that "[i]f Mrs. Metalious can turn her emancipated talents to less lurid purposes, her future as novelist is a good bet" (par. 5). Despite these positive notices in respected publications by notable critics, *Peyton Place* troubled America because it aroused America. It sold in large part on the basis of its smuttiness and, for many like William Loeb, it signaled the decline of American culture.

Evan Brier's work contradicts the conventional wisdom that the *Peyton Place* phenomenon presaged a new era in American publishing and that it was single-handedly responsible for a precipitous plummeting in the quality and character of the nation's cultural output. Brier takes issue with Ardis Cameron's contention that the novel was the book trade's first "blockbuster" and that it "transformed the publishing industry" (Cameron, viii). He notes that Cameron leaves the term *blockbuster* undefined and undertakes one himself. Following Thomas Whiteside, the author of *The Blockbuster Complex*, Brier notes that blockbusters are conceived and produced with "mass commercial success" in mind, and the possibility of lucrative film and television adaptations may figure into a publisher's original decision to go forward with the book. "To call a novel a blockbuster in Whiteside's sense of the term," Brier remarks, "is both to make a negative literary judgment—the badness of the work a fait accompli given the circumstances of its production—and to observe a new set of institutional relationships between publishers, Hollywood studios, and television networks" (*Novel*, 116).

*Peyton Place*, Brier asserts, does not meet these standards: "There is little evidence to suggest," he writes, "that *Peyton Place* was published with mass success in mind" ("Accidental," 55).[2] Instead Brier argues that the transformation of the book-selling industry had been under way for some time and that *Peyton Place* was a product of this ongoing process. Of particular interest is the evidence he presents to defend the book against charges of the debasement of the American novel. What Brier discovers is that *Peyton Place* was not published and marketed "in a sphere of culture separate and apart from the sphere that produced 'high culture'—on the other side, as it were, of a cultural divide" ("Accidental," 56). Rather, it shares genealogical links with James Joyce's *Ulysses*, a modernist masterpiece that sold very well on the basis of sex and scandal. Aaron Sussman, the person in charge of marketing *Peyton Place* for Julian Messner, Inc., in 1956, had been a key player in the publicity campaign for *Ulysses* at Random House in 1934.[3] Like *Peyton Place*, *Ulysses* had been censored because of sexual content. The difference, Brier notes, is that in the case of *Ulysses*, the controversy arose organically out of a legal challenge to the book's merits. In *Peyton Place*'s case, Sussman capitalized on the serendipitous timing of George Metalious's job woes relative to the novel's release. Although the local school board maintained that there was no causal link between the potboiler's publication and their decision not to renew George's teaching contract, the coincidental timing of the two events was promoted to enormously profitable effect.[4] The controversy in the latter case was, Brier writes, "a contrivance"—an application of the wisdom gained while watching *Ulysses* become a best seller (*Novel*, 124). Because of this relationship,

> no great institutional divide and, just as important, no cultural-historical rupture separate *Ulysses* from *Peyton Place*; they are products of the same book trade. Both novels were commodities marketed to great success by some of the same people, using the same strategies. Though typically viewed as a lamentable sign of things to come, when viewed in its institutional context *Peyton Place* has more to tell us about the marketing of literary novels that preceded it—that they were marketed with great savvy, their dual status as both works of art and commodities—and about the impressive growth and modernization of America's publishing industry and the growth of the audience of educated consumers in the first half of the twentieth century than it does about postwar cultural decline, the consolidation of the book trade, and the literary value (or lack thereof) of the blockbusters that followed. (*Novel*, 125)

*Peyton Place*'s reception, then, was in part the result of preemptive provocation, a well-placed lit match intended to set American culture ablaze. Although Brier emphasizes that "[t]he links between *Ulysses* and *Peyton Place* are institutional rather than literary" (*Novel*, 125), he is not interested in regarding the latter strictly as a commodity. Rather, he notes that reviewers of Metalious's first novel focused on her "possibility and potential; her career is considered a literary one and it is on those grounds that she succeeds or fails" (*Novel*, 112). In the wake of the outcry against its content, however, *Peyton Place* was demoted from "novel" to "sensation," its literariness effaced in part by commercial success and sexual content (ibid.). It has not fully recovered from this attempt to dissociate it from the ranks of literature; however, Brier has suggested that this dislocation may be redressed in part by looking at the novel not only as a cultural product of 1950s America but as part of the evolution of the nation's book trade during the first half of the twentieth century.

## Banned and Contraband, Dog-Eared and Dirty: The Return of *Peyton Place*

In the fifty years since *Peyton Place* first scandalized American readers, the novel has remained renowned for its sex and its sales figures. When its name is applied to current events, as it was during the President Clinton–

Monica Lewinsky debacle, it is often intended as an epithet of derision as well as moral censure.[5] Gilmanton residents still hold a grudge against the novel; memory for the unsolicited attention that *Peyton Place* drew to the town lingers long and runs deep. Neither the State of New Hampshire nor the Town of Gilmanton commemorated the fiftieth anniversary of *Peyton Place*'s publication in September 2006. Gilmanton Selectman Donald Guarino explained, "Some people felt they would just as soon let it go. They said 'Let it rest; there's no need to revisit it'" (qtd. in Schweitzer, par. 6). Mores have changed, and sex itself has become more promiscuous and less shocking, but *Peyton Place* still courts controversy a half-century later.

Owing in large measure to the cumulative efforts of Emily Toth and, more recently, Ardis Cameron to bring some respect to a much-maligned novel, *Peyton Place* has emerged from the shadows of ignominy and is being taken seriously by a still small but growing number of scholars. Toth's literary biography of Metalious remains the only one of its kind. Her commitment to her subject embroiled her in the early 1980s in a tenure and promotion battle over to the "trash[y]" material to which she had devoted her scholarship (*Inside*, 380). Ardis Cameron, a professor at the University of Southern Maine, spearheaded efforts to reissue *Peyton Place* in paperback (at the time, it was only available in a pricey library edition) and shared the burden of blame for its reappearance with Northeastern University Press, which published the new edition (Fialkoff, par. 1). As it did when it first emerged on the American scene, *Peyton Place* still courts controversy and elicits smug dismissals by the gatekeepers of good taste. *Library Journal* called Northeastern's 1999 reissue "ridiculous" in its headline announcing the print run and expressed disbelief that the mid-century "potboiler" should find itself within the purview of academia (Fialkoff, par. 2).[6] In its review of the Northeastern imprint, *Kirkus Reviews* took issue with Cameron's reading of *Peyton Place* as social commentary, asserting, "Peyton Place [*sic*] is, on its own terms, both a perfectly decent popular novel and an honest one. But it never was an important one, and no amount of retroactive puffery can make it so" (qtd. in Filosa, par. 63). Despite the disbelief and the dismissals, Northeastern had already sold four thousand copies (half of its run) prior to the book's release (Fialkoff, par. 2). Though these figures pale in comparison to the tens of thousands in initial sales in 1956, for a university press whose average print run is a mere one thousand copies, the figures were (and are) impressive (Ayoub, par. 4). They are also consistent with the novel's historical track record of brisk sales.

In addition to the publicity following *Peyton Place*'s return to bookstores in 1999, the celebration in 2006 of the fiftieth anniversary of the book's publication occasioned a flurry of articles in both popular and scholarly journals that explored the novel's relevance to millennial readers and its value to American culture. Millennial responses to *Peyton Place* "[tell] us how sex roles have changed" (Toth, "How to Teach," par. 37). As the godmother of *Peyton Place* scholarship, she has found in recent years that her female students no longer swoon and sigh as she reports they once did at the line, "Untie the top of your bathing suit. I want to feel your breasts against me when I kiss you" (Metalious, 149). Instead, they tend to react with disgust, calling Tom a "domineering pig" and naming his presumption in terms unknown in the 1950s: "[b]ordering on date rape" (Toth, par. 36).[7] Writing in *Vanity Fair*, Michael Callahan calls the novel "a hybrid of the literary and the sordid" that is "a manifesto, a blistering indictment of small-town values, classism, and racism" (360). In colorful language of which Metalious herself might have approved, one writer energetically declared that *Peyton Place* served as "a melodramatic bitch-slap to the duplicitous nature of propriety in Eisenhower's America. While Joseph McCarthy was busy rounding up putative enemies to the American way of life, Metalious exposed the rot within—the racism, sexism, class snobbery and lies—that undermine a civil democracy" (Kingston, par. 2). Even conservative *New York Times* columnist David Brooks finds something redeeming in *Peyton Place*, that it is essentially about the need to "engage in the high-risk search for unpleasant truths," to face them, and to reckon with them (par. 10). For Brooks, though, these truths are personal and idiosyncratic—in his estimation (he calls it "fact"), "the first striking fact about the book is that in its pages the personal is not political" (par. 4). He sees no relationship between the "unpleasant truths" and the social system in which they reside and out of which they arise, and concludes that, in the end, Metalious "only wrote soap operas" (par. 13).

I disagree, of course. My work throughout this book has been motivated by a reading of *Peyton Place* that sees the novel as decidedly political. This investigation is in its own way a response to dismissals such as Brooks's and that of the *Kirkus* reviewer that *Peyton Place* "never was an important book." It strikes me as irresponsible to disregard a work that resonated so thoroughly within American cultural consciousness that it was a success in each of its manifestations: novel, film, and prime-time television drama. I also find it interesting that none of the millennial reconsiderations of the novel directly contend with the town's (and apparently the narrative's) big secret, its black ancestry. I am not sure why that is. A few of the newspaper and magazine clippings mention racism and ethnic hatred in passing in their short lists of the narrative's tensions. My feeling is that this issue needs to be brought into the foreground of discussions of the book, not relegated to a brief note within a discussion of the sexual scandal for which the novel is more famous. This study stands as a start toward this goal.

Dark pasts are still the stuff of danger and deception. My mother, ever watchful for material that might assist my work, called me very excitedly one Saturday while I was working on this project to tell me about an episode of the Boston-based crime drama, *Crossing Jordan*, that she thought I might find interesting. The plot involved death of a white man from a prominent family who was killed along with a black woman in a drunk driving accident. The patriarch of the white man's family attempts to derail the police investigation by issuing a court order sealing the autopsy results in order to keep silent what the official episode summary calls "a shocking secret" ("Someone to Watch over Me"). The reason for the secrecy? The medical examiner discovered that the dead son had sickle-cell anemia. The family's patronymic? Payton. Whether this naming is intentional or coincidental, I do not know. I do wonder whether the invoking of a homonymic "Payton" is meant to call up a cultural memory for the scandal caused by Metalious's *Peyton Place*. I also wonder if the episode's writers were aware of the specific scandal of Metalious's Samuel Peyton and his place. In either case, whatever the reason and however cannily or coincidentally the "Payton" patriarch in *Crossing Jordan* was named, white anxiety about racial identity remains the stuff of drama and American cultural production into the twenty-first century and will arguably remain so for some time. Grace Metalious knew this, and her "dirty book" about secrets in a small town may have been keeping its own secret by default: that the sexual scandal it produced was a red herring, or at least not the whole of the scandal. Rather, *Peyton Place*'s intervention in the history of American race relations and its critique of midcentury sexual mores through a critique of whiteness's dysfunction may well have been the lit fuse that set off the novel's cultural explosion.

# Notes

## Introduction

1. Hilfer points to Mark Twain's story "The Man That Corrupted Hadleyburg" as one such early critique of the inherent, unassailable goodness of small-town life. Other literary assessments of the American village include works by Mary E. Wilkins Freeman, Sarah Orne Jewett, E. A. Robinson, and Edith Wharton.

2. I have been asked about the origins of Samuel Peyton and his castle in the novel. Mark Sammons and Valerie Cunningham have said that Peyton was in part based on Richard Potter (1783–1835), a black magician who settled in Andover, New Hampshire, after whom the village of Potter Place was named (109). In keeping with *Peyton Place*'s repression of Samuel Peyton's black identity, the roadside historical marker for Potter Place in Andover does not indicate that Potter was black. Metalious said that she chose "Peyton Place" for her town's name "because a two-word name with balance was desired and there is no town or hamlet of that name in the United States" (Smith, par. 23). The source for the castle remains more of a mystery, as there is no published information indicating how the idea for it came about. A very good but perhaps forever unverifiable possibility is the Kimball Castle that overlooks Lake Winnipesaukee from a hilltop in Gilford, New Hampshire. Commissioned by a wealthy railroad baron, it was built between 1897 and 1899. The design is said to have been modeled after a German castle, and the building was constructed in part from imported materials and surrounded by stone walls ("Castle History," par. 1–2). The only additional clue that potentially links the Kimball Castle to Peyton's is that until 1812, Gilford was part of Gilmanton, the town reputed to be the basis for *Peyton Place* ("About Gilford," par. 1).

## 1. Dark Past, White Lies

1. In this way, the term is etymologically related to *Indian giver* and *Indian corn* in their associations with falsehood and misrepresentation (*OED Online*).

2. Using Metalious's characterization as an example, Adam Sweeting also notes that the season's "evocative power to deceive" may have contributed to its naming, as its mild temper "offered Indians the best opportunity to stage surprise

attacks" on whites. "An interlude remarkable for its beauty," writes Sweeting, "Indian summer also contains no small amount of cultural mistrust" (6).

3. Kennan's containment thesis, the basis for American foreign policy throughout the Cold War, was heavily informed by anti-Asian sentiment. Pejorative characterizations of the Soviet Union based on its "Asian-ness" underwrite a great deal of Kennan's thinking on the matter. Borstelmann explains,

[Kennan] located a major—if not the major—root of Soviet despotism and tyranny in the Soviet Union's partly Asian identity. He considered the suspiciousness and inscrutability of Soviet diplomats and leaders "the results of century-long contact with Asiatic hordes." The "Long Telegram" that he sent to the State Department from the U.S. embassy in Moscow in February 1946, which first put him on the upward path from obscure diplomat to major policymaker, attributed much of the Soviet government's behavior to its "attitude of Oriental secretiveness and conspiracy." The Bolshevik Revolution of 1917 had stripped away "the westernized upper crust" of the old czarist elite, revealing Russians in their true form as "a 17th-century semi-Asiatic people." It was Asia and "Asian-ness" that had done so much to corrupt the healthier "European" elements of Russian life and character, according to Kennan, and that now made it imperative to contain the USSR within its own boundaries. (Borstelmann, 50)

The racialization of the nation's archenemy in the discourse of international diplomacy suggests that May's application of the "containment" metaphor, though not identical to Kennan's use of the term, is appropriate to discussions of domestic politics at a time when race prejudice was moving to the fore of domestic and international conversations about the meaning of democracy.

4. Despite their best efforts to reveal a considerably more complicated view of the time, however, Foreman also notes that little has changed about the way Americans (and their popular culture) imagine the decade (2).

5. In a 1947 petition titled, "An Appeal to the World," the NAACP urged the United Nations to take notice of the injustice of race prejudice in America. The statement declared, "The disenfranchisement of the American Negro makes the functioning of all democracy in the nation difficult; and as democracy fails to function in the leading democracy in the world, it fails the world" (qtd. in Dudziak, 44). One Harlem resident's response to a question by newspaper columnist Walter Winchell is particularly illustrative of the need for reform. When she was asked what punishment would fit Hitler's war crimes, the woman responded, "Paint him black and send him over here" (qtd. in Miller and Nowak, 183).

6. In 1943, one of the acid tests for patriotism was struck from civil service loyalty investigations—the question asking whether an individual had ever belonged to organizations whose meetings were racially integrated (Borstelmann, 44). Even though this suggested that "[p]atriotism no longer required segregationism" (44), Truman's federal loyalty program, established in 1947, considered interracial friendships evidence of radicalism (Borstelmann, 65). W. E. B. DuBois

was rebuked for airing the nation's dirty laundry before an international audience through the NAACP's petition to the UN, "An Appeal to the World," and later lost his U.S. passport as a result of his civil rights activism (67).

7. Writing on the side of Metalious's detractors, syndicated columnist Margaret Latrobe condemned Metalious's vulgarity, especially repugnant in her view for having been penned by a woman (Toth, *Inside*, 145). *New York Times* book reviewer Carlos Baker, on the other hand, located Metalious squarely within an American literary tradition of small-town social critics: "Sinclair Lewis would no doubt have hailed Grace Metalious as a sister-in-arms against the false fronts and bourgeois pretensions of allegedly respectable communities" (par. 3).

8. Interestingly, though not entirely surprisingly, the film and TV show both whitewashed the seamier elements of the novel. Though *Peyton Place* was a highly successful and subversive commodity as a book, once it was developed for sale as a known quantity in different media (film and TV), the scandals were toned down or just plain eradicated from the text. Despite these emendations by film director Jerry Wald and television producer Paul Monash, *Peyton Place* met with similar commercial success on the big and small screens.

9. See Breines, *Young, White, and Miserable*; Miner, *Insatiable Appetites*; Hendler, *Best-Sellers and Their Film Adaptations*, and Brier, *A Novel Marketplace*.

10. In "Fatherless and Dispossessed," Emily Toth very nearly dismisses the importance of ethnic and racial difference in the novel, claiming, "Grace Metalious's best and most memorable writing is her angriest, the writing that comes from a childhood of poverty and oppression. The strongest episodes—both the most lurid and most moving—involve sex and class, but not ethnicity" (30). I maintain that the most significant episodes in *Peyton Place* absolutely involve ethnicity and race. The fair-skinned Constance's rape by the "big black Greek" Tom Makris is a turning point in her character development, a moment that begins her reconciliation with her past and culminates in a sexually fulfilling marriage with her assailant.

11. Garner makes this distinction in the conclusion of *Whiteness: An Introduction*. Regarding this coinage, he clarifies that it is intended "to cover the way of problematising social relations so that the racialisation process is at the heart of them, and that 'white' marks a powerful spot." The difference here, one that he urges us to be mindful of, is between "whiteness as an analytical framework used by researchers" and "whiteness as a set of social relationships" (174).

12. In fact, the editors of *Off White* have recanted, or at least reconsidered, their position. Having stated in that volume that no subsequent editions of their collection would be published, having been "so bold as to suggest that books on whiteness should stop being published," they have since issued a revised edition in 2004 with a new subtitle ("Readings on Power, Privilege, and Resistance") that no longer aspires to having the final say on the matter of whiteness. Acknowledging the "rippling effect" of whiteness studies across multiple disciplines, the second edition's editors grant that interest in the field has grown but not to its detriment. The "profitable works" that have come about since 1997, "have not 'ended'

whiteness studies; more accurately, they have demonstrated the power and impact of excavating and highlighting that which had previously been unnamed" (ix).

13. See, for example, bell hooks, *Black Looks: Race and Representation* and *Where We Stand: Class Matters*; McClintock, *Imperial Leather: Race, Gender and Sexuality in the Colonial Contest*; Gayle Wald, *Crossing the Line: Racial Passing in Twentieth-Century Literature and Culture*; and Ware, *Beyond the Pale: White Women, Racism and History*.

14. At the outset of her study of racial passing in American literature and culture, Gayle Wald also resists the race/class duality and its partitioning from gender, asserting "that racial, class, and gender discourses are mutually reinforcing and inextricably linked" (9). Vron Ware also calls attention to the connotative power of gender and race in combination, noting, "To be white and female is to occupy a social category that is inescapably racialized as well as gendered. It is not about *being* a white woman, it is about *being thought of* as a white woman" (xii, her emphasis).

15. As further evidence of the manufacturing and manipulation of racial categories, Borstelmann observes, "So few blacks lived in Hawaii in the early twentieth century that the census classified them as 'Puerto Ricans,' while Puerto Ricans were in turn defined as 'Caucasians' and thus—unlike Indians—as whites. In other words, along Waikiki Beach, blacks were white" (8). For an in-depth treatment of *United States v. Thind*, the 1923 Supreme Court case to which Borstelmann refers, see Ian F. Haney-López, *White by Law: The Legal Construction of Race*, 56–77.

## 2. The Color of Incest

1. Skolnick notes that the belief that women's employment and the need for day care were Soviet-style approaches to American public policy extended into the 1970s with President Richard Nixon's veto of the Comprehensive Child Development Act of 1971 (69). Among his stated objections to the initiative were that the bill would "commit the vast moral authority of the National Government to the side of communal approaches to child rearing over against the family-centered approach" (Nixon, par. 36).

2. Truman's loyalty program looked into the backgrounds and activities of applicants to and employees of the federal government in order to prevent infiltration by "disloyal" or subversive persons (Miller and Nowak, 26, 35). Nearly seven thousand Civil Service Commission workers resigned or were fired because of investigations into their daily activities by federal officials (Coontz, 33). Millions of citizens were investigated and lost their jobs as a result, though there were apparently no cases of treason turned up by any of the inquiries (Miller and Nowak, 26).

3. The cookie-cutter image of the American household was formed in part through the television industry's application of the rule of "least objectionable

programming," which normalized the look of the 1950s family in order to encourage the broadest possible audience. This meant that prime-time families were white, middle-class, suburban, with a stay-at-home wife and mother, a commuter dad, and a claque of kids embarking on relatively harmless misadventures. The whiteness imperative meant that the Hispanic gardener on *Father Knows Best* (played by actor Natividad Vacio) had the improbably Anglo name of "Frank Smith" (Coontz, 30). In *Cold War, Cool Medium,* Thomas Doherty offers that the homogenous vision of the American family at midcentury is a misremembering caused in part by a technological fluke: whereas domestic sitcoms like *Leave It to Beaver* and *Father Knows Best* were recorded on kinescope and thus preserved for posterity, many variety shows and dramas featuring black actors and performers were not. The live feeds that carried such programs meant that images of black and white performers together on the same program or sharing the same stage were broadcast in the Jim Crow South. Although reruns of 1950s television programming re-present a starkly "monochromatic" view of the decade, it was not, in fact, the only vision of America projected into the nation's living rooms; rather, Doherty argues, television was not necessarily the conservative medium that it is often credited with (or faulted for) being: "The nationwide transmission of the ethos of equality was television's most important contribution to the ongoing civil rights revolution. . . . [T]elevision in the 1950s ran far ahead of the tolerance curve" (73).

4. Coontz compares the high rate of teen births in the mid-1950s (97 out of 1,000 for girls fifteen to nineteen in 1957) to the so-called "epidemic" numbers of the early 1980s (52 out of 1,000 for the same age group in 1983). Though illegitimacy was an issue in many of these cases, and many young women were pregnant as they exchanged their vows, the young marriage age helped to keep sex contained within the parameters of family life.

5. There are those who contest the idea that the Cold War brought about as reactionary a sea change within American society and culture as that with which it has often been credited. Peter Filene writes, "The baby boom and domesticity— and more generally, the craving for security—began before the Cold War and would have continued without it. Cold War policies nudged attitudes and behavior, but gender dynamics were shaped far less by national leaders than by what the public had experienced long before containment" (163). Domestic containment, then, was more coincidental to than it was a consequence of Cold War foreign policy. Similarly, Jane Sherron DeHart questions the suitability of the containment metaphor altogether as shorthand for the American way of life in the postwar era. Containment abroad was different from the containment policy exercised at home; the difference, she suggests, is that between "peaceful coexistence" intended (if not effected) between the United States and its rivals and stateside "repression and rollback" (128). In the end, though, DeHart decides that it is in the twin concerns of international and domestic "boundary maintenance" that containment-as-metaphor finds its most useful expression.

6. On the issue of birth control, May notes that given its availability to married couples, the fact that the baby boom happened as it did was the result of a concerted effort on the part of its participants (14).

7. Weiss's work takes the long view of the 1950s family and finds that the snapshot of the Cleaver/Nelson prototype ignores the evolution of gender roles (expectations and performance) over the course of a marriage. The young families of the 1950s were in the first stages of their domestic life and in many cases, once childrearing responsibilities eased, so too did the adherence to the traditional division of labor.

8. While Selena's case is the most dire, the less extreme dysfunctions Anderson addresses are those of Allison's "unnatural affection for her deceased father" and Evelyn Page's "abnormally intimate attachment to her son" (par. 9). Incest is the common denominator in all three examples.

9. Nellie's belief echoes the perverse conventional wisdom that blames the victim of domestic violence while at the same time reading the assaults as a sign of affection. Of her brutalization by Lucas, Nellie tells Allison, "Why, honey, beatin's don't mean nothin'" (130) and later that "a man didn't go around beatin' a woman he didn't give a damn about" (228–29).

10. Although I have found Hellman's comments interesting and useful, I would like to address her assertion that Metalious presents Nellie "as an other through a combination of her dark skin and poverty" (par. 38). My argument here rests on a reading of poverty as racialized, and in this I am in agreement with Hellman. However, Metalious does not offer any descriptions of Nellie that explicitly state she has dark skin. She may be "not too clean" and "grimy" (31), but she is not literally dark in the way that, for instance, Selena Cross and Tom Makris are, two characters for whom darkness is explicit. In fact, it is in some ways because of Nellie's lack of darkness that Selena's is all the more mysterious, or at the very least, unaccounted for.

11. Cameron does not list a source for this claim; however, this may be a reference to S. K. Weinberg's *Incest Behavior* (1955). Dorothy Willner cites Weinberg, writing that "fathers, father surrogates and older brothers impose[d] themselves on girls with a frequency which was documented as 1.9 in a million in the 1950s" (Willner, 139). It is also repeated by Stephanie Coontz in *The Way We Never Were* (35) who attributes it to Elizabeth Pleck in *Domestic Tyranny* (156–57).

12. In which case, in Peyton Place, the incidence is at least 3 in 3,675—the census figure on the town's welcome sign when Tom Makris arrives (98).

13. This variability results from the fact that Russell took information about both the subjects' (i.e., incest survivors') own class backgrounds and education. She learned that

> [f]ewer of the incest victims came from low-income backgrounds, and more of them came from high-income backgrounds than was the case for women who had never been incestuously abused. Similarly, the incest victims were slightly better educated than women with no incest history. However, when

the respondents' fathers' education and occupation were used as the measures of social class, there was no relationship between incest victimization and social class background. (qtd. in Wilson, 40–41, her emphasis)

14. In her work on literary representations of incest, Minrose Gwin investigates the complicated interplay of race, class, and gender within scenes of intrafamilial sexual violence. In works such as Alice Walker's *The Color Purple* and Toni Morrison's *The Bluest Eye*, "'fathers' . . . do exert physical and psychological power over their 'daughters.' This is not to say that their power is not complicated and caused by historical and material contravention. Their own disempowerment, however, does not render them powerless over their daughters but rather complicates the limits of their empowerment in other areas" (65). Writing on the rape of Pecola Breedlove by her father Cholly in Toni Morrison's *The Bluest Eye*, Gwin asserts, "It cannot be overlooked that, however disempowered he is and has been in other spaces, in the house, specifically in the kitchen, Cholly feels empowered enough to rape his daughter" (75). This same matrix of public sociopolitical disempowerment and private entitlement informs Lucas's abuse of power within the Cross home.

15. Tom is also described as "dark-skinned, black-haired, obviously sexual" (100), "*real* dark, and big" (103), and "a big, black drunk" (263).

16. The certainty of this dictum is illustrated appropriately enough in a scene in which a shack dweller's son presents evidence of foul play in the Cross case to Sheriff Buck McCracken. When he asks for a reward and McCracken "savagely" dismisses him, the boy's mother calls from the waiting room, "'I tole you, sonny,' she whined. 'I tole you 'n' your Pa both, that it wa'nt no good at all, gettin' mixed up with what's none of our business'" (325). Interference in the law never favors the shack dweller, even when it is the shack dweller who is offering assistance.

## 3. Domestic Disturbances

1. Doc Swain ventriloquizes this opinion in the film adaptation of *Peyton Place* when he advises Constance to do right by Allison and give her a sibling, warning her that only children receive all the energy of the parents, good and bad. When Constance defends herself, telling Swain that Allison seems to have turned out all right, he counters that she's still a work in progress: Allison has not fully "turned out" and that time will tell.

2. Bailey's survey of women's advice literature of the 1940s and 1950s turns up several frank and blatant examples of the marketplace metaphor in the language used to convince women of the benefits of chastity. They include terms and turns of phrase such as "cheap and valueless," "low price tag," "collector's item" vs. "bargain-counter article," "marked-down," "easy to afford," and a direct appeal to teenage girls to "Reprice your line. Limit the supply of yourself, your time and interest. Make yourself scarce and watch your value go up" (Bailey, 94–5).

3. One of the articles that Bailey references cautions, "[I]n a permissive culture, a girl becomes easy prey to any male strong enough to take her" (qtd. in Bailey, 96).

4. In a footnote, Cameron notes that the term *sex panic* derived from attempts in the 1990s to police the sex trade "and public arenas of sexual exchange." She explains, "It has since come to mean the social and cultural fears of sexual agency and the kinds of antisex crusades that such fears spawn" (xxviii–xxix).

5. The era's most well-known vituperation against motherhood and "megaloid momworship" is Wylie's *Generation of Vipers*, a misogynist jeremiad first published in 1942, which the American Library Association named on its list of significant nonfiction titles of the first half of the twentieth century (xii). There are many quotable passages in the chapter "Common Women," in which Wylie makes the case against American motherhood. Arguing that the comforts and conveniences of modern life have extended "Mom's" life span while "depriv[ing] her of her social usefulness" and turning men into overworked patsies for the sake of satisfying her "caprices" he continues:

These caprices are of a menopausal nature at best—hot flashes, rage, infantilism, weeping, sentimentality, peculiar appetite, and all the ragged reticule of tricks, wooings, wiles, suborned fornications, slobby onanisms, indulgences, crotchets, superstitions, phlegm, debilities, vapors, butterflies-in-the-belly, plaints, connivings, cries, malingerings, deceptions, visions, hallucinations, needlings and wheedlings, which pop out of every personality in the act of abandoning itself and humanity. At worst—i.e., the finis—this salaginous mess tapers off into senility, which is man's caricature of himself by reversed ontogeny. But behind this vast aurora of pitiable weakness is mom, the brass-breasted Baal, or mom, the thin and enfeebled martyr whose very urine, nevertheless, will etch glass. (186–87)

6. Ferdinand Lundberg and Marynia Farnham's widely read analysis of American womanhood drew heavily on psychoanalysis. The phrase "the malicious orgasm" originated with psychoanalyst Helene Deutsch's work on women's psychology.

7. See the essay "Shunned" in Meredith Hall's memoir *Without a Map*, which testifies to the prejudicial attitudes toward female sexuality that adhered and persisted in the American small town a decade after *Peyton Place* reckoned with them in the 1950s.

8. The long history of the marital rape exemption in English common law and in the United States judiciary lasted until 1976, the last year in which the marital rape exemption stood in all fifty states. And while marital rape has since been recognized as a punishable crime, to date, only twenty states and the District of Columbia see no distinction between marital rape and stranger rape (Bergen, 2).

9. See Ian Watt, *The Rise of the Novel: Studies in Defoe, Richardson and Fielding*; Michael McKeon, *The Origins of the English Novel, 1600–1740*; and Peter Brooks, *Body Work: Objects of Desire in Modern Narrative*.

10. Sielke's argument writes against those feminists whom she sees as having reiterated the internal logic of rape discourse in their *anti*-rape discourse through the reinscription of victimization. In so doing, she follows Mieke Bal's lead in her understanding of the deliberate omissions of explicit content from (many, though not all) rape scenes in literature. Bal holds that rape

> cannot be visualized not only because "decent" culture would not tolerate such representations of the "act" but because rape makes the victim invisible. It does that literally first—the perpetrator "covers" her—and then figuratively—the rape destroys her self-image, her subjectivity, which is temporarily narcotized, definitely changed and often destroyed. Finally, rape cannot be visualized because the experience is, physically, as well as psychologically, *inner*. Rape takes place inside. In this sense, rape is by definition imagined; it can exist only as experience and as memory, as *image* translated into signs, never adequately "objectifiable." (142)

This shares much in common with Ferguson's argument establishing consent, intention, and mental states, though perhaps is more deliberately provocative in its assertion of rape as "imagined." This idea does not seem intended to suggest that it's all in the victim's head; rather the trouble arises in the rendering of rape into discourse (here, specifically, as text). Both Ferguson and Bal (and Sielke, for that matter) seem to be in agreement that there is a dual violation of interiority (physical, emotional) in acts of sexual aggression, and that language is always already inadequate to the task of representation.

11. Sielke explains: "In metonymy such substitution is based on relation, association, or contiguity that forms syntactical connections along horizontal, temporal lines and has therefore been associated with realism. Metaphor, by contrast, substitutes on the basis of resemblance or analogy, and creates semantic, spatial links along a paradigmatic, vertical line, often suggesting (poetic) truth-value" (5).

12. The language used to describe it is quite liberal—Constance's dalliance was the result of loneliness, not love; and in a move suggesting a great deal of self-determination, Metalious indicates that it was Constance who had "taken a lover," rather than having been taken by one (140).

13. There is still a veiled threat of danger that recalls their first night together. In the sex scene that follows, Tom places "a hand gently on her throat so that she could feel her pulse against his finger tips" (278). Having struck her forcefully across the mouth with his hand during their first encounter, Tom's hands convey a frisson of violence even in their gentleness, and especially on Constance's throat.

14. Metalious announces their marriage in a rather unceremonious manner very early in Book Three: "Constance Makris closed the oven door of her stove and straightened up with a startled squeak. Her husband had come up quietly behind her and encircled her with his arms" (270). Her sexual renaissance occurs in a scene framed as a flashback four pages following this wedded domestic nuzzle.

### 4. The Good Rapist, the Bad Rapist, and the Abortionist

1. That is, if Tom's reputation was endangered to begin with. This may be more of a modern-day peril than one experienced by *Peyton Place*'s first-generation audience.

2. Where Michael Kimmel applies the "crisis of masculinity" label to the ongoing evolution of white male gender identity beginning at the turn of the twentieth century, K. A. Cuordileone shies away from that generalization, instead reserving the term for the midcentury culmination of male anxiety. "If not a crisis in masculinity," she concedes, "at least a preoccupation with male regeneration was well underway by the turn of the century" (525). Gail Bederman hedges as well, offering that while middle-class men at the turn of the century were "unusually interested in—even obsessed with—manhood" (10), their search for and demonstrations of manly prowess did not result in a mass male exodus from domestic life. She holds that to call the renegotiation of male gender identity a "crisis" is going too far. Gender, Bederman reminds us, is a fluid, flexible, dynamic "ongoing ideological process. . . . Thus, change in the gender system—even extensive change—doesn't necessarily imply a 'crisis'" (11). Bederman's point is well taken; however, where the challenge to midcentury postwar gender roles is concerned, I think applying the term *crisis* is appropriate. Given the *Oxford English Dictionary*'s third definition of the word as "a vitally important or decisive stage in the progress of anything; a turning-point; also, a state of affairs in which a decisive change for better or worse is imminent; now applied *esp.* to times of difficulty, insecurity, and suspense in politics or commerce" (OED Online), it seems sufficient and not overstated.

3. "Masculinity required proof," writes Kimmel, "and proof required serious effort, whether at the baseball park, the gymnasium, or sitting down to read *Tarzan* or a good western novel. Suddenly, books about the urban 'jungle' or 'wilderness' appeared, which allowed men to experience manly risk and excitement without ever leaving the city. . . . Or they could flip through *National Geographic* (1888 on) to encounter the primitive 'other'" (*Manhood*, 82).

4. Jordan notes also that initially, Englishmen emphasized the savagery of Native Americans in order to emphasize differences in custom where differences in appearance were more difficult to draw. The blackness of the African encountered by English explorers embodied difference more definitively. As above, when the slave trade required justification, however, black savagery was foregrounded. Southerners took a similar approach in justifying lynching.

5. In fact, Jordan notes, such rebellions underscored the humanity of those involved: "The urge to rebellion . . . was an undeniably human attribute; cattle did not ordinarily conspire to kill their owners and fire the town" (232–33).

6. Arkansan Clifton R. Breckenridge concurred in his address to the Montgomery Race Conference: "When [the black race] produces a brute, he is the worst and most insatiate brute that exists in human form" (qtd. in Fredrickson, 278).

And Dr. William Lee Howard lent his name and professional expertise to the assertion that "the large size of the negro's penis" was to blame for the "sexual madness and excess" of black men (qtd. in Fredrickson, 279).

7. Interestingly, Big Sam is described as a "black buck" earlier in the novel. As he and a corps of other slaves make their way through the streets of Atlanta en route to dig trenches for the Confederate soldiers nearby, Scarlett notices

> a singing black buck in the front rank. He stood nearly six and a half feet tall, a giant of a man, ebony black, stepping along with the lithe grace of a powerful animal, his white teeth flashing as he led the gang in 'Go Down, Moses.' Surely there wasn't a negro on earth as tall and loud-voiced as this one except Big Sam, the foreman of Tara. (299)

Instead of posing a threat, Sam is a gentle giant (his "huge black paws" envelop Scarlett's "small white hand") who brings deliverance to his white mistress at the moment when we are led to believe she is in the greatest danger.

8. "The Genteel Patriarch," according to Kimmel, "derived his identity from landownership. Supervising his estate, he was refined, elegant, and given to casual sensuousness. He was a doting and devoted father, who spent much of his time supervising the estate with his family" (*Gender*, 28). With the acceleration of the capitalist economy in the latter half of the nineteenth century, the Genteel Patriarch was "[cast] aside . . . as an anachronistic feminized dandy—sweet, but ineffective and outmoded" (ibid., 29).

9. We know he is the town's only Greek-American resident because Corey Hyde, owner of the local diner, expresses relief that there's not another with whom Tom might join forces and open a restaurant (95).

10. Midcentury misogyny turned a blind eye on what was happening in a traditionally male corner that critics have since suggested was responsible, at least in part, for men's increased anxieties: the military-industrial complex. Following Michael S. Sherry, Cuordileone writes, "Militarization exacts its own conformity; the assertion of United States global superiority its own burdens and frustrations; the threat of nuclear war its own sense of dread, powerlessness or impotence" (527).

11. Dyer points out that "white death" was synonymous with tuberculosis and that Victorian representations of death by consumption portrayed such ends as reverently beautiful. He also elaborates on bell hooks's remark that whiteness "wounds, hurts, tortures" blacks, calling up the chilling image of the white-robed Ku Klux Klan, "an image of the bringing of death," not the salvation that *The Birth of a Nation*'s narrative sympathies suggest. "When we see the Klan riding to the rescue of the beleaguered whites in *The Birth of a Nation*," writes Dyer, "it is undoubtedly intended that we should see them as bringing salvation, but it is now hard to see in these great splashes, streaks and swirls of white on a white screen anything but the bringing of death to African-Americans" (209).

12. This holds true for several of her female characters as well as many of her men: the otherwise "honey-tan" Selena becomes notably pale from morning

sickness and fear (138, 139); Elizabeth Fuller Harrington is said to have been "a rather pale and thin-looking character" (196) and "a tall, slim girl who had the aristocratic look which sometimes comes after generations of inbreeding" (205). The town's witchy spinster, Hester Goodale, is more wraithlike than real, with "skin [that] seemed hardly to cover her angular bones, and her eyes gleamed like coal set into a sheet of white paper. Her hands were no longer slim fingered, but clawlike, and even her hair thinned to a sparseness that barely covered her bony skull" (67). Goodale's particular peccadillo is playing peeping Tom on her neighbors. And, then there is, of course, Constance, who has internalized cultural prohibitions against women's sexuality, self-punitively denying her desires, and who has worked to imbue her daughter with a similar distaste for and ignorance of sex and men.

13. Metalious's Norman anticipates and invites comparison with two other men who share unusual relationships with their mothers in the postwar era: another Norman (surname "Bates") in Alfred Hitchcock's horror film *Psycho* (1960), and Raymond Shaw, the pawn in his mother's communist plot in John Frankenheimer's adaptation of Richard Condon's political thriller *The Manchurian Candidate* (1964). Evelyn Page's scheme to pass Norman off as a war hero is repeated in Frankenheimer's film by Raymond Shaw's mother with chilling (and unintended) consequences for herself and her son. For a discussion of *Peyton Place* as a likely source for *Psycho*, see McDermott, "'Do You Love Mother, Norman?': Faulkner's 'A Rose for Emily' and Metalious's *Peyton Place* as Sources for Robert Bloch's *Psycho*."

14. While Metalious makes it clear that Norman finds this encounter between husband and wife more off-putting than exciting, she suggests equally clearly that this is a passionate and loving couple engaged in (unintentionally public) oral sex:

Mr. Card had unbuttoned the straight, full jacket of Mrs. Card's dress, and now he was loosening her skirt. In the next instant, Norman could see the huge, blue-veined growth which was Mrs. Card's abdomen, and he thought he would throw up. But Mr. Card was running his hand lovingly over the growth; he caressed it gently and even bent his head and kissed it. He held Mrs. Card in the circle of his dark, black-haired arms, and Mrs. Card's body looked very, very white. . . . Mr. Card's big hands were cupping Mrs. Card's breasts now, and Norman saw that these, too, were swollen and blue veined. . . . Norman glanced through the gap in the hedge. Mr. Card was on his knees on the ground, his face hidden in Mrs. Card's flesh, and Mrs. Card was lying very still, with her legs spread a little, and a smile on her face that showed her teeth. (253–54)

15. Ted repeats some of the same ideas Lucas uses to justify his abuses of Selena—that as step-relations, they are not actually related, that Selena should be grateful to Lucas for providing for children who are not biologically his (296).

16. Indeed, addressing his fellow statesmen in 1907, South Carolina Senator Ben Tillman declared without irony that due process was not to be borne in the case of the black rapist:

Shall men coldbloodedly stand up and demand for him the right to have a fair trial and be punished in the regular course of justice? So far as I am concerned, he has put himself outside the pale of the law, human and divine . . . Civilization peels off us, any and all of us who are men, and we revert to the original savage type whose impulses under any and all circumstances has always been to "kill! kill! kill!" (qtd. in Gunning, 5)

17. In chapter 5, the residents of Peyton Place's wealthiest avenue, Chestnut Street, are introduced, among them Swain and Harrington. In its unified voice, the town muses over Swain's living situation:

The doctor's wife had been dead for many years, and the town wondered why The Doc, as he was informally known, insisted on keeping his big house.

"Too big for a man alone," said Peyton Place. "I'll bet The Doc rattles around in there like a marble in a tin cup."

"The Doc's place ain't as big as Leslie Harrington's."

"No, but it's different with Harrington. He's got a boy that's going to get married someday. That's why he keeps that big house since his wife died. It's for the boy."

"I guess that's so. Too bad The Doc never had kids. Must be lonely for a man with no kids, after his wife goes." (20)

## 5. Home Is Where the Haunt Is

1. Bergland argues, "Phantasmic descriptions of African Americans, women, aliens, and the poor point out the strength of the ghost metaphor and its strong association with white American men's anxiety and guilt over their complicity in American hierarchies of race, class, and gender" (19).

2. Noting that the emergence of the novel is contemporaneous with the privatization of the family and its living space, Mezei and Briganti find the metaphor of the house well suited to exploration within the novel—a genre predicated on interiority—asserting that the house, too, is an articulate text that, like the novel, has interior and exterior features both aesthetic and affective. The novel's house-like characteristics include "its layout and style, its use of symbols, and its exterior facade—book cover, design, and blurbs. Thus, our responses to houses and texts can be seen as comparable, perhaps even interchangeable, interpretive acts" (840).

3. A *Time* magazine article in August 1961 illustrated the "deadly serious" nature of this possibility. Titled "Gun Thy Neighbor?" it quoted one homeowner in the process of building his underground retreat as saying, "When I get my shelter finished, I'm going to mount a machine gun at the hatch to keep the neighbors out if the bomb falls. I'm deadly serious about this. If the stupid American public will not do what they have to to save themselves, I'm not going to run the risk of not being able to use the shelter I've taken the trouble to provide to save my own family" (qtd. in Henriksen, 204).

4. Houses were built at distances of one and two miles from ground zero and were intended to measure the damage from both the explosion itself and the heat generated by it. In a curious but unexplained finding, Tobin notes that in addition to the advantage afforded by a low-lying shelter, "the interiors of those furnished with Venetian blinds stood up better to heat tests" (25).

5. Although she acknowledges Clifford Clark's analysis of American home design, which credits consumer desire with influencing elements of home design, Tobin's work builds on sociologist Leo F. Schnore's assertion in 1957 that "[t]he choices of building sites are made be [sic] contractors, real estate operators, and others, notably those involved in the initial capitalization of new developments. Families and individuals are not decisive agents in the process of land-use conversion" (qtd. in Tobin, 24).

6. For more on this, see Monteyne, 187–91. He includes as an example a July 1954 *Architectural Forum* advertisement for Fenestra Metal Building Panels that asks potential buyers, "Can your building resist earthquakes, great winds, and bomb shock?"

7. "The critical event," writes Gaddis, "was BRAVO, an American test conducted in the Pacific on March 1, 1954, that got out of control." He explains:

The yield turned out to be fifteen megatons, three times the expected five, or 750 times the size of the Hiroshima atomic bomb. The blast spread radioactive fallout hundreds of miles downwind, contaminating a Japanese fishing boat and killing a member of its crew. Less dangerous debris set off radiation detectors around the world. The question posed for nuclear warfighting was a stark one: if a single thermonuclear blast could have global ecological consequences, what would be the effects of using tens, hundreds, or even thousands of nuclear weapons?" (64)

8. Tom Makris joins the town's only Pole (Theodore Jankowski), Jew (Mr. Shapiro), and Italian (Enrico Antonelli) in diversifying the southern and eastern European ethnic makeup of Peyton Place.

9. Punter and Byron usefully enumerate the several ways in which the castle figures in gothic literature:

The castle is a labyrinth, a maze, a site of secrets. It is also, paradoxically, a site of domesticity, where ordinary life carries on even while accompanied by the most extraordinary and inexplicable of events. It can be a place of womb-like security, a refuge from the complex exigencies of the outer world; it can also—at the same time, and according to a difference of perception— be a place of incarceration, a place where heroines and others can be locked away from the fickle memory of 'ordinary life.' The castle has to do with the map, and with the failure of the map; it figures loss of direction, the impossibility of imposing one's own sense of place on an alien world. (261–62)

10. I hesitate to use *unknown* here, given the unstable connotations of the prefix *un-*. To say *unknown* suggests no prior relationship to the knowledge in

question. Here knowledge once possessed has become estranged, not erased or eradicated.

11. Like the German *heimlich*, the word *canny* repeats this etymological transmogrification into its opposite, an intriguing evolution that Tatar traces and is worth quoting at length:

The word "canny," as the *Oxford English Dictionary* tells us, evidently derives either from the verb "can" (in the sense of "to know how, to be able") or from the Scottish noun "can" (signifying "knowledge, skill") and was, in its earliest usage, nearly synonymous with the adjective "cunning." . . . For the Scots . . . the most general meaning of "canny" is: "careful or cautious in motion or action; *hence*, quiet, gentle . . . ; free from commotion, disturbance, or noise." From this definition, it is easy to see how the words also came to mean "quiet, easy, snug, comfortable, pleasant, cozy"—definitions that build a bridge to the German *heimlich*. "Canny," a word that originally pertained to a bridge to special knowledge, was also used to describe domestic comfort, while *heimlich*, a word that concerns the home, came to signify secret knowledge. Furthermore, "canny," like *heimlich*, shares one meaning with its antonym. The "canny" was once associated with occult or magical power, and in this sense the word coincides perfectly with the primary dictionary definition of "uncanny": "partaking of a supernatural character; mysterious, weird, uncomfortably strange or unfamiliar." What is canny can thus easily become uncanny. The uncanny, like *das Unheimliche*, does not necessarily represent something entirely strange or unfamiliar—*pace* the compilers of the *OED*—but also something strangely familiar. The prefix *un-* in both words can figure as a token of repression. (170–71)

12. The uncanny is notorious for its multiplicity and has provided both a playground and an enduring thought problem for literary critics since Freud. The most common manifestations of the uncanny include instances of repetition, haunting (a form of repetition), coincidence, fate, déjà vu, the doppelganger, animism, and the macabre. For Royle's rather glorious introductory catalogue of effects, see *The Uncanny: An Introduction* (1–2). Punter and Byron's brief explanation of the uncanny in *The Gothic* is also useful.

13. Metalious writes,

The truth of the matter was that Constance enjoyed her life alone. She told herself that she had never been highly sexed to begin with, that her affair with Allison had been a thing born of loneliness. She repeated silently, over and over, that life with her daughter Allison was entirely satisfactory and all she wanted. Men were not necessary, for they were unreliable at best, and nothing but creators of trouble. As for love, she knew well the tragic results of not loving a man. What more terrible consequence might come from allowing herself to love another? No, Constance often told herself, she was better off as she was, doing the best she knew how, and waiting for Allison to grow up. If at times she felt a vague restlessness within herself, she told herself sharply that this was *not* sex, but perhaps a touch of indigestion. (17)

14. Madonne Miner has addressed the oedipal nature of Allison's longings, noting that just before she imaginatively transforms her father in to her "prince," she had indulged in the guilt-ridden thought of an alternative life in which her father was the surviving parent, not Constance. The desire to be the only female in her father's life is illustrated also in the animation of the photograph when Allison utters the words "my prince" to herself—a title that Miner notes "obscures familial relations" and, as Allison's last thought before falling asleep, enables her to fall "asleep *with* her father" (64). Furthermore, Miner suggests that the extent of Allison's shock at the discovery of Nellie Cross's body in her closet is informed by Allison's repressed wish to see her own mother dead for destroying her idealized vision of her father and for having gone to bed with him in the first place: "Nellie, the woman who replaces Constance—cooking, cleaning, ironing in the MacKenzie home while Constance works in her dress shop—serves as the perfect stand-in" for Constance (65). While convalescing in the hospital, Allison tells Doc Swain that she believes that she is responsible for Nellie's death because of a nasty squabble the two had engaged in on the morning of the suicide. Miner explains, "Allison realizes that her wish has come true; a 'mother' (that mother who has served as focus for anger Allison cannot express openly to Constance) is dead" (65).

15. Despite her initial dismissal of Norman's fears, after seeing him to his doorstep, Allison retraces her steps past the Goodale property, confirms its sinister character and compares it specifically to "The Fall of the House of Usher" in the moment that she is inspired to attempt a literary treatment of Miss Hester's story. The similarities between the Usher estate and the Goodale residence are, on the one hand, superficial. There is a "spooky story" to be told in each case, although neither Norman nor Allison know what that story might be. It is Norman who eventually understands most clearly that what makes Miss Hester strange is her taste for watching her neighbors have sex. Also like the House of Usher, the houses themselves seem sentient in some way, possessed as they are of "eye-like" windows, and the domestic architecture of each family suggests the psychological states of the houses' inhabitants. Allison's excited characterization of Miss Hester as a witch has no evident connection to Poe's story at all aside from Allison's broadly conceived understanding of the gothic genre. Nevertheless, as with the House of Usher, "the family itself was almost extinct, doomed by a history that lent the air of the tomb, the family vault, to this once living abode" (Vidler, "Architecture," 8). Miss Hester is the last of the Goodale line, and her death will punctuate the family's history in town. In this way, the Goodale house is implicitly connected with Peyton's castle, a structure left vacant following the death of its childless inhabitants. The space itself suggests repression instead of generation, an effect that has infiltrated the repressive, underfertile families in Peyton Place.

16. There is something irresistible in the homonymic correlation between Allison's agent's name, "Bradley Holmes," and the thematic persistence of Allison's

search for a comfortable home. Fortunately for Allison's sake, she does not find her home with Holmes just for the sake of the pun. Madonne Miner has enumerated the several similarities she sees between the novel's most influential male characters: the elder Allison MacKenzie, Tom Makris, Bradley Holmes, and Lucas Cross. I find her inclusion of Lucas in this list a bit of a stretch (at least for my purposes), arguing as she does that he, like the others, is described as "dark" (70). I agree that he is dark*ened* by the novel, as I have previously argued occurs when Doc Swain confronts him about his rapes of Selena; however, Lucas himself is never explicitly described as such. Likewise, Holmes is not dark; he is simply "dark-haired." Holmes is, however, linked to Tom in his build and his age (he is forty; Tom is forty-one) and in the nature of his quick, sharp temper and tongue, which might suggest a sort of kinship that darkens Holmes by default. Allison MacKenzie Sr. is dark-haired, and Allison (the younger) reads a bit of mischief into the devilish air conferred on his picture by his widow's peak.

17. Tatar remarks in her analysis of *Oliver Twist* that it is only when the identity of the portrait of his mother is revealed to Oliver that it is dispossessed of its uncanniness (179). Though Allison knew the photograph on the mantle to represent her biological father, it loses its uncanny sway only after she learns his true identity (husband and father to another family) and hers (illegitimate daughter of a never-wed mother) and gains the same brand of sexual knowledge (illicit sex with a married family man) through which Allison herself came to be in the first place.

18. Hepworth notes that fireplaces were not only functional but held symbolic value in the Victorian era. "The hearth," he writes, "as the place where heat is generated before the invention of central heating, is closely associated with the heart as the organ which gives life and is traditionally regarded as the source of human emotion. To be welcomed at the hearth is to anticipate a closer and more intimate form of human relationship" (25). The installation of the "needless extravagance" of the fireplace invests Selena's updated home with a source of real and figurative warmth, both of which had been lacking in its past life as a tarpaper shack.

19. "The girl was wearing a dress of lavender linen, which Marion was willing to bet cost at least twenty-five dollars, and a pair of sheer stockings which Marion immediately classified as black market nylon. Selena's shoes were new, and Marion wondered if the girl had used a wartime ration coupon to buy them, or whether Constance Makris had got them from a friendly salesman" (344).

20. Her co-worker David Noyes has provided an open ear and soft shoulder throughout Allison's crush on and subsequent heartbreak over Bradley Holmes, following her discovery on their long weekend together that he has a wife and kids. As Allison is energetically running down the hill from Road's End—her favorite hideaway—on an Indian summer day just like that with which the novel began, Constance calls out from her shop that David has arrived from New York on a surprise visit to see Allison.

# Conclusion

1. Curiously, Latrobe seems compelled to try her hand at evoking the obscene by posing the question, "If sex with sodomy sauce is found in literary art, is that not what made it art?" (par. 6). This query is, however unintentionally, as frankly pornographic as anything contained within the pages of *Peyton Place*.

2. That it experienced enormous success and that it led to a big-budget Hollywood film, a sequel, and a television series (the first of its kind, which Jack Paar called TV's "first situation orgy" [Toth, *Inside*, 359]) seems to have given impetus to savvy industry insiders, who saw a goldmine in the franchising of future novels. It is also credited with enabling the careers of Harold Robbins, Jacqueline Susann, and Jackie Collins by clearing a path for them on best-seller lists (Korda, 103).

3. Sussman penned an ad with the headline "How to Enjoy James Joyce's Great Novel *Ulysses*," which continues to be regarded "as a landmark in the marketing of modernism to the general reading public" (Brier, *Novel*, 123–24).

4. Brier observes, "Sussman has the unique distinction of helping to sell both the most celebrated literary novel published in English in the twentieth century, the acknowledged high point of high modernism and high culture, and one of the most reviled, the purported symbol of that culture's decline" (*Novel*, 124).

5. When South Carolina Republican Congressman Lindsey Graham asked, "Is this Watergate or Peyton Place?" on the first day of impeachment hearings against then-President Bill Clinton, he was making a value judgment. Is this a matter of significant import, or is it simply tawdry and inconsequential, "a gross Beltway bodice-ripper that deserves only a sorry rebuke for its relentless domination of the nation and its political leaders"? (Clines, par. 3).

6. *Library Journal* reported that the executive director of the Association of American University Presses responded to the news of Northeastern University Press's undertaking with "a whoop of laughter." He then reasoned that it is the survival instinct of the academic publishing industry that might account for the selection of such a surprising title for a press's catalogue, musing "How far do you go to be lucrative and how far do you dilute programs of scholarly publishing? I don't think there is any clear answer" (Fialkoff, par. 3).

7. I find it interesting that Toth herself still does not refer to the encounter as a rape scene, and I am left to wonder why. At the lake, the action may be skirting the edges of rape, as Toth's student observes. In Constance's house, the rape is fully realized, and this fact remains absent from Toth's commentary, as it did in her original reading of the scene in *Inside Peyton Place*. Instead, Toth reiterates a point she advanced in 1981. A quarter-century later, she once again remarks that Metalious's "best female characters are businesswomen, teachers, and would-be novelists—who protect, cherish, and mentor each other" ("How to Teach," par. 20). This is where I find myself in the odd position of agreeing with conservative *New York Times* columnist David Brooks and respectfully disagreeing with a scholar

to whom I am deeply indebted for legitimating *Peyton Place* as the subject of study. Brooks grants "that much of the action in the novel is initiated by strong women." Nevertheless, he goes on to clarify that "Metalious treats their strength and sexuality as obvious features of human society, and clearly rejects the notion that to be a woman is to be a member of a cause or the sisterhood collective" (par. 3). Much as it pains me to admit it, I find Brooks's reading here the more insightful. The women may be interested parties in each other's fates, but generally speaking, they are not banded together as a unified group. Their battles are fought individually, on distinct and disparate terrains.

# Works Cited

"About Gilford." Town of Gilford, New Hampshire. http://gilfordnh.org.

Alcoff, Linda, and Laura Gray. "Survivor Discourse: Transgression or Recuperation?" *Signs* 18, no. 2 (1993): 260–90. JSTOR. http://www.jstor.org/stable/3174976.

"Amid Scandals, Much Good Work Continues." Editorial. *Concord Monitor*, 4 Sept. 2007.

Anderson, Benedict. *Imagined Communities: Reflections on the Origin and Spread of Nationalism*. London: Verso, 1991.

Anderson, David D. "Sherwood Anderson and the Critics." In *Critical Essays on Sherwood Anderson*, ed. David D. Anderson, 1–17. Boston: G. K. Hall, 1981.

Anderson, Sherwood. *Winesburg, Ohio*. 1919. Introduction by Jeffrey Meyers. Reprint, New York: Bantam, 1995.

Anderson, Stacey Stanfield. "Toxic Togetherness in a Postwar 'Potboiler': Grace Metalious's *Peyton Place*." *Americana: The Journal of American Popular Culture, 1900 to Present* 5, no. 2 (2006): http://www.americanpopularculture.com/journal/articles/fall_2006/anderson.htm.

"Another Prominent Citizen with Feet of Clay." Editorial. *Concord Monitor*, 2 Sept. 2007. Concord Monitor and New Hampshire Patriot. http://www.concordmonitor.com/article/another-prominent-citizen-with-feet-of-clay.

Ayers, Edward L. *The Promise of the New South: Life after Reconstruction*. New York: Oxford UP, 2007.

Ayoub, Nina. "Hot Type." *Chronicle of Higher Education*, 9 Apr. 1999. Academic Search Premier. http://o-web.ebscohost.com.lib.rivier.edu/ehost/detail?hid=106&sid=79e234ee-5220-489e-b5ec-5f733dd97ef2%40sessionmgr104&vid=9&bdata=JnNpdGU9ZWhvc3QtbGl2ZSZzY29wZT1zaXRl#db=aph&AN=1707576.

Bachelard, Gaston. *The Poetics of Space*. New York: Orion, 1964.

Bailey, Beth. *From Front Porch to Back Seat: Courtship in Twentieth-Century America*. Baltimore: Johns Hopkins UP, 1988.

Baker, Carlos. "Small Town Peep Show." *New York Times*, 23 Sept. 1956. Pro-Quest Historical Newspapers. http://o-proquest.umi.com.lib.rivier.edu/pqdweb ?index=0&did=958123 80&SrchMode=1&sid=10&Fmt=10&VInst=PROD &VType=PQD&RQT=309&VName=HNP&TS=1299692451&clientId =8921.

Bakhtin, Mikhail. *Rabelais and His World*. Trans. Helene Iswolsky. Bloomington: Indiana UP, 1984.

Bal, Mieke. "Visual Poetics: Reading with the Other Art." In *Theory between the Disciplines: Authority/Vision/Politics*, ed. Martin Kreiswirth and Mark A. Cheetham, 135–51. Ann Arbor: U of Michigan P, 1990.

Barnett, Louise. *Ungentlemanly Acts: The Army's Notorious Incest Trial*. New York: Hill and Wang, 2001.

Bederman, Gail. *Manliness and Civilization: A Cultural History of Gender and Race in the United States, 1880–1917*. Chicago: U of Chicago P, 1995.

Bender, Lauretta, and Abram Blau. "The Reaction of Children to Sexual Relations with Adults." *American Journal of Orthopsychiatry* 7, no. 4 (October 1937): 500–518. doi: 10.1111/j.1939-0025.1937.tb05293.x.

Bergen, Raquel Kennedy. "Marital Rape: New Research and Directions." *VAWnet: Applied Research Forum* (Feb. 2006): 1–13. http://new.vawnet.org/Assoc_Files _VAWnet/AR_MaritalRapeRevised.pdf.

Bergland, Renée L. *The National Uncanny: Indian Ghosts and American Subjects*. Hanover, NH: UP of New England, 2000.

Bhabha, Homi K. *The Location of Culture*. London: Routledge, 1994.

Bogle, Donald. *Toms, Coons, Mulattoes, Mammies, & Bucks: An Interpretive History of Blacks in American Films*. New York: Continuum, 1996.

Borstelmann, Thomas. *The Cold War and the Color Line: American Race Relations in the Global Arena*. Cambridge, MA: Harvard UP, 2001.

Boyle, Hal. "Grace Unfolds to Hal Boyle Hazard of Husband Losing Job: Hal Calls Peyton Place Tobacco Road with a Yankee Accent." *Laconia Evening Citizen*, 29 Aug. 1956. Metalious folder, Gale Public Library, Laconia, NH.

Breines, Wini. *Young, White, and Miserable: Growing Up Female in the Fifties*. Chicago: U of Chicago P, 1992.

Brier, Evan. "The Accidental Blockbuster: *Peyton Place* in Literary and Institutional Context." *Gender and Culture in the 1950s*. Special issue of *WSQ* 33 nos. 3–4 (2005): 48–65.

———. *A Novel Marketplace: Mass Culture, the Book Trade, and Postwar American Fiction*. Philadelphia: U of Pennsylvania P, 2009.

Brooks, David. "Cracking the Shells." Op-Ed. *New York Times*, 20 Aug. 2006. http://query.nytimes.com/gst/fullpage.html?res=9C06E3D9153EF933A1575 BC0A9609C8B63.

Brooks, Peter. *Body Work: Objects of Desire in Modern Narrative*. Cambridge, MA: Harvard UP, 1993.

Brown, Dona. *Inventing New England: Regional Tourism in the 19th Century*. Washington, D.C.: Smithsonian Institution Press, 1995.

Callahan, Michael. "*Peyton Place*'s Real Victim." *Vanity Fair*, Mar. 2006, 332+.

Cameron, Ardis. "Open Secrets: Rereading *Peyton Place*." Introduction to *Peyton Place*, by Grace Metalious, vii–xxx. Boston: Northeastern UP, 1999.

Carby, Hazel. *Cultures in Babylon: Black Britain and African America*. London: Verso, 1999.

———. *Reconstructing Womanhood: The Emergence of the Afro-American Woman Novelist*. New York: Oxford UP, 1987.

"Castle History." Kimball Castle Site. Kimball Castle Properties, 2007. http://www.kimballcastle.com/castle-history.html.

Chandler, Marilyn. *Dwelling in the Text: Houses in American Fiction*. Berkeley: U of California P, 1991.

Clark, Clifford E., Jr. "Ranch-House Suburbia: Ideals and Realities." In May, Lary, ed., 171–95.

Clines, Francis X. "The Testing of a President. The Scene; a Lawmaker Asks: Watergate or Peyton Place." *New York Times*, 6 Oct. 1998. http://query.nytimes.com/gst/fullpage.html?res=9405EFDB1F38F935A35753C1A96E958260.

Cohan, Steven. *Masked Men: Masculinity and the Movies in the Fifties*. Bloomington: Indiana UP, 1997.

Conforti, Joseph. *Imagining New England: Explorations of Regional Identity from the Pilgrims to the Mid-Twentieth Century*. Chapel Hill: U of North Carolina P, 2001.

Coontz, Stephanie. *The Way We Never Were: American Families and the Nostalgia Trap*. New York: Basic Books, 2000.

Cuordileone, K. A. "Politics in an Age of Anxiety: Cold War Political Culture and the Crisis in American Masculinity, 1949–1960." *Journal of American History* 87 (2000): 515–45. doi: 10.2307.2568762.

Davis, Angela Y. *Women, Race, & Class*. New York: Random House, 1981.

DeHart, Jane Sherron. "Containment at Home: Gender, Sexuality and National Identity in Cold War America." In Kuznick and Gilbert, eds., 125–55.

D'Emilio, John, and Esther Freedman. *Intimate Matters: A History of Sexuality in America*. New York: Harper & Row, 1988.

Dickstein, Morris. Introduction to *Main Street*, by Sinclair Lewis, vii–xxi. New York: Bantam, 1996.

Doane, Janice, and Devon Hodges. *Telling Incest: Narratives of Dangerous Remembering from Stein to Sapphire*. Ann Arbor: U of Michigan P, 2001.

Dodson, James. "Pandora in Blue Jeans." *Yankee* 54, no. 9 (1990): 92–137.

Doherty, Thomas. *Cold War, Cool Medium: Television, McCarthyism, and American Culture*. New York: Columbia UP, 2003.

Doolen, Andy. *Fugitive Empire: Locating Early American Imperialism*. Minneapolis: U of Minnesota P, 2005.

Douglas, Ann. Introduction to *Charlotte Temple, and Lucy Temple*, by Susanna Rowson, vii–xiii. New York: Penguin, 1991.

Douglas, Mary. *Purity and Danger: An Analysis of the Concept of Pollution and Taboo*. 1966. London: Routledge, 2006.

Dudziak, Mary L. *Cold War Civil Rights: Race and the Image of American Democracy*. Princeton, NJ: Princeton UP, 2000.

Dyer, Richard. *White*. London: Routledge, 1997.

Ehrenreich, Barbara, and Deirdre English. *For Her Own Good: Two Centuries of Experts' Advice to Women*. New York: Anchor, 2005.

Ellis, Kate Ferguson. *The Contested Castle: Gothic Novels and the Subversion of Domestic Ideology*. Urbana: U of Illinois P, 1989.

Faulkner, William. "A Rose for Emily." 1931. In *Collected Stories of William Faulkner*, 119–31. New York: Vintage, 1995.

Ferguson, Frances. "Rape and the Rise of the Novel." *Misogyny, Misandry, and Misanthropy*. Special issue of *Representations* 20 (1987): 88–112. JSTOR. http://www.jstor.org/stable/2928503.

Fialkoff, Francine. "University Presses Mix It Up: The Ridiculous—*Peyton Place*— and the Sublime—Prize-Winning Monographs Online." *Library Journal*, 15 Apr. 1999, 74. Academic Search Premier. http://o-web.ebscohost.com.lib.rivier.edu/ehost/detail?hid=106&sid=a5e11afo-df1f-4988-aa1f-bob65e8fee68%40session mgr110&vid=5&bdata=JnNpdGU9ZWhvc3QtbGl2ZSZzY29wZT1zaXRl#db=aph&AN=1752816.

Filene, Peter. "Cold War Doesn't Say It All." In Kuznick and Gilbert, eds., 156–74.

Filosa, Gwen. "NH 100: Metalious's *Peyton Place* Was Controversial, Popular." *Concord Monitor*, 27 Mar. 1999. http://www.fawi.net/Grace/GwenFilosa.html.

Fine, Michelle, Lois Weis, Linda C. Powell, and L. Mun Wong, eds. *Off White: Readings on Race, Power, and Society*. New York: Routledge, 1997.

Fine, Michelle, Lois Weis, Linda Powell Pruitt, and April Burns, eds. *Off White: Readings on Power, Privilege, and Resistance*. New York: Routledge, 2004.

Fischer, Nancy. "Oedipus Wrecked? The Moral Boundaries of Incest." *Gender and Society* 17 (2003): 92–110. JSTOR. http://www.jstor.org/stable/3081816.

Foreman, Joel, ed. *The Other Fifties: Interrogating Midcentury American Icons*. Urbana: U of Illinois P, 1997.

Frankenberg, Ruth, ed. *Displacing Whiteness: Essays in Social and Cultural Criticism*. Durham, NC: Duke UP, 1997.

———. "The Mirage of Unmarked Whiteness." In *The Making and Unmaking of Whiteness*, ed. Birgit Brander Rasmussen, Eric Klinenberg, Irene J. Nexica, and Matt Wray, 72–96. Durham, NC: Duke UP, 2001.

———. *White Women, Race Matters: The Social Construction of Whiteness*. Minneapolis: U of Minnesota P, 1993.

Fredrickson, George. *The Black Image in the White Mind: The Debate on Afro-American Character and Destiny, 1817–1914*. Hanover, CT: Wesleyan University Press, 1987.

Freeman, Mary E. Wilkins. *A New England Nun and Other Stories*. 1891. Introduction by Sandra Zagarell. New York: Penguin, 2000.

Freud, Sigmund. "The Uncanny." 1919. In *The Uncanny*. Translated by David McLintock, 123–61. New York: Penguin Books, 2003.

Friedan, Betty. *The Feminine Mystique*. 1963. Introduction by Anna Quindlen. New York: Norton, 1997.

Friedman, Andrea. "Sadists and Sissies: Anti-pornography Campaigns in Cold War America." *Gender and History* 15 (2003): 201–27. doi: 10.1111/1468-0424 .00299.

Fryer, Peter. *Staying Power: The History of Black People in Britain*. London: Pluto Press, 1984.

Gaddis, John Lewis. *The Cold War: A New History*. New York: Penguin, 2007.

Garner, Steve. *Whiteness: An Introduction*. London: Routledge, 2007.

Gault, Cinda. "Grace Metalious' *Peyton Place*: Sentimental Storm-Trooper or Popular Throw-Back?" *Journal of Popular Culture* 39 (2006): 985–1001. doi: 10.1111/j.1540-5931.2006.00330.x.

Gordon, Linda. *Heroes of Their Own Lives*. New York: Viking, 1988.

Gross, Barry. "'The Revolt That Wasn't': The Legacies of Critical Myopia." *CEA Critic* 39, no. 2 (1977): 4–8.

Gunning, Sandra. *Race, Rape and Lynching: The Red Record of American Literature, 1890–1912*. New York: Oxford UP, 1996.

Gwin, Minrose. *The Woman in the Red Dress: Gender, Space and Reading*. Urbana: U of Illinois P, 2002.

Hackett, Alice Payne. *70 Years of Best Sellers: 1895–1965*. New York: R. R. Bowker, 1967.

Halberstam, David. *The Fifties*. New York: Villard Books, 1993.

Hall, Kim F. *Things of Darkness: Economies of Race and Gender in Early Modern England*. Ithaca, NY: Cornell UP, 1995.

Hall, Meredith. *Without a Map*. Boston: Beacon Press, 2007.

Hareven, Tamara K. "The Home and the Family in Historical Perspective." *Social Research* 58, no. 1 (1991): 253–85.

Harrington, Michael. *The Other America: Poverty in the United States.* 1962. Introduction by Irving Howe. New York: Touchstone, 1997.

Hartigan, John, Jr. "Who Are These White People?: 'Rednecks,' 'Hillbillies,' and 'White Trash' as Marked Racial Subjects," 95–111. *White Out: The Continuing Significance of Racism.* New York: Routledge, 2003.

Haskell, Molly. *From Reverence to Rape: The Treatment of Women in the Movies.* Chicago: U of Chicago P, 1987.

Hawthorne, Nathaniel. *The House of the Seven Gables.* 1851. Ed. Mary Oliver. New York: Modern Library, 2001.

Hayden, Dolores. *Redesigning the American Dream: The Future of Housing, Work, and Family Life.* New York: W. W. Norton, 1984.

Hellman, Caroline. "The Other American Kitchen: Alternative Domesticity in 1950s Design, Politics, and Fiction." *Americana: The Journal of American Popular Culture, 1900 to Present* 3, no. 2 (2004). JSTOR. http://www.american popularculture.com/journal/articles/fall_2004/hellman.htm.

Hendler, Jane. *Best-Sellers and Their Film Adaptations in Postwar America: From Here to Eternity, Sayonara, Giant, Auntie Mame, Peyton Place.* New York: Peter Lang, 2001.

Henriksen, Margot. *Dr. Strangelove's America: Society and Culture in the Atomic Age.* Berkeley: U of California P, 1997.

Hepworth, Mike. "Privacy, Security and Respectability: The Ideal Victorian Home." In *Ideal Homes? Social Change and Domestic Life*, ed. Tony Chapman and Jenny Hockey, 17–29. London: Routledge, 1999.

Herman, Judith, with Lisa Hirschman. "Father-Daughter Incest." 1981. In *Violence against Women: The Bloody Footprints*, ed. Pauline B. Bart and Eileen Geil Moran, 47–56. Thousand Oaks, CA: Sage Publications, 1993.

Hilfer, Anthony Channell. *The Revolt from the Village: 1915–1930.* Chapel Hill: U of North Carolina P, 1969.

hooks, bell. *Black Looks: Race and Representation.* Boston: South End Press, 1992.

———. *Where We Stand: Class Matters.* New York: Routledge, 2000.

James, Mertice M., and Dorothy Brown, eds. *The Book Review Digest: Fifty-Second Annual Cumulation, March 1956–February 1957, Inclusive.* New York: H. W. Wilson, 1957.

Jones, David M. "Blacks, Greeks, and Freaks: Othering as Social Critique in *Peyton Place*." Paper presented at the Annual Meeting of the American Popular Culture Association, Philadelphia, April 2001. http://www.uwec.edu/jonesm/engl245/Peyton%20Place%20Paper.htm.

Jordan, Winthrop D. *White over Black: American Attitudes toward the Negro, 1550–1812.* Chapel Hill: U of North Carolina P, 1968.

Kaplan, Amy. *The Anarchy of Empire in the Making of U.S. Culture*. Cambridge, MA: Harvard UP, 2002.

———. "Manifest Domesticity." *No More Separate Spheres!* Special issue of *American Literature* 70 (1998): 581–606.

Kargon, Robert, and Arthur Molella. "The City as Communications Net: Norbert Weiner, the Atomic Bomb, and Urban Dispersal." *Technology and Culture* 45 (2004): 764–77. doi: 10.1353/tech.2004.0190.

Kimmel, Michael. *The Gender of Desire: Essays on Male Sexuality*. Albany: SU of New York P, 2005.

———. *Manhood in America: A Cultural History*. 2nd ed. New York: Oxford UP, 2006.

Kingston, Anne. "The Original Desperate Housewife: This Month Marks the 50th Anniversary of Grace Metalious's Blockbuster *Peyton Place*." *Maclean's*, 25 Sept. 2006, 88. Academic Search Premier. http://o-web.ebscohost.com.lib .rivier.edu/ehost/detail?hid=106&sid=a5e11afo-df1f-4988-aa1f-bob65e8fee 68%40sessionmgr110&vid=11&bdata=JnNpdGU9ZWhvc3QtbGl2ZSZzY29 wZT1zaXRl#db=aph&AN=22456050.

Korda, Michael. *Making the List: A Cultural History of the American Bestseller, 1900–1999*. New York: Barnes and Noble, 2001.

Kristeva, Julia. *Powers of Horror: An Essay on Abjection*. New York: Columbia UP, 1982.

Kuznick, Peter J., and James Gilbert. *Rethinking Cold War Culture*. Washington, DC: Smithsonian Institution Press, 2001.

Latrobe, Margaret. "Fairly Spoken." *Laconia Evening Citizen*, 10 Oct. 1956. Metalious folder, Gale Public Library, Laconia, NH.

Lekachman, Robert. *The Age of Keynes*. New York: Random House, 1966.

Levy, David. *Maternal Overprotection*. 1943. New York: W. W. Norton, 1966.

Lhamon, W. T. *Deliberate Speed: The Origins of a Cultural Style in the American 1950s*. Washington, DC: Smithsonian Institution Press, 1990.

Lloyd-Smith, Allan. "Nineteenth Century Gothic." In Punter, ed., 109–21.

Loeb, William. "The Filth They Live By." *Manchester Union-Leader*, Jan. 1957 (no day indicated). Metalious folder, Gale Public Library, Laconia, NH.

López, Ian F. Haney. *White by Law: The Legal Construction of Race*. New York: New York UP, 1996.

Lundberg, Ferdinand, and Marynia F. Farnham. *Modern Woman: The Lost Sex*. New York: Harper and Brothers, 1947.

Lutz, Tom. *Cosmopolitan Vistas: American Regionalism and Literary Value*. Ithaca, NY: Cornell UP, 2004.

"Lynchings by State and Race: 1882–1968." Famous American Trials: The Trial of Sheriff Joseph Shipp et al., 1907. Site developed and maintained by Douglas O.

Linder, University of Missouri–Kansas City School of Law. Statistics provided by the Archives at Tuskegee Institute. http://law2.umkc.edu/faculty/projects/ftrials/shipp/lynchingsstate.html.

MacMaster, Anne. "Wharton, Race, and *The Age of Innocence:* Three Historical Contexts." In *A Forward Glance: New Essays on Edith Wharton*, ed. Clare Colquitt, Susan Goodman, and Candace Waid, 188–205. Newark: U of Delaware P, 1999.

Mailer, Norman. "The White Negro: Superficial Reflections on the Hipster." 1957. *The Time of Our Time*, 211–30. New York: Modern Library, 1999.

Masters, Edgar Lee. *Spoon River Anthology.* 1915. Introduction by May Swenson. New York: Touchstone, 2004.

May, Elaine Tyler. *Homeward Bound: American Families in the Cold War Era.* New York: Basic Books, 1999.

May, Lary, ed. *Recasting America: Culture and Politics in the Age of the Cold War.* Chicago: U of Chicago P, 1989.

McClintock, Anne. *Imperial Leather: Race, Gender, and Sexuality in the Colonial Contest.* New York: Routledge, 1995.

McDermott, John A. "'Do You Love Mother, Norman?': Faulkner's 'A Rose for Emily' and Metalious's *Peyton Place* as Sources for Robert Bloch's *Psycho.*" *Journal of Popular Culture* 40 (2007), 454–67. doi: 10.1111/j.1540-5931.2007.00403.x.

McEnaney, Laura. *Civil Defense Begins at Home: Militarization Meets Everyday Life in the Fifties.* Princeton, NJ: Princeton UP, 2000.

McKeon, Michael. *The Origins of the English Novel: 1600–1740.* 1987. Baltimore: Johns Hopkins UP, 2002.

Mercer, Kobena. "Reading Racial Fetishism: The Photographs of Robert Mapplethorpe." In *Fetishism as Cultural Discourse*, ed. Emily Apter and William Pietz, 307–29. Ithaca, NY: Cornell UP, 1993.

Metalious, Grace. *Peyton Place.* 1956. Introduction by Ardis Cameron. Boston: Northeastern UP, 1999.

Mezei, Kathy, and Chiara Briganti. "Reading the House: A Literary Perspective." *Signs* 27 (2002): 837–46. JSTOR. http://www.jstor.org/stable/10.1086/337928.

Miller, Douglas T., and Marion Nowak. *The Fifties: The Way We Really Were.* Garden City, NJ: Doubleday, 1977.

Miller, Laura J. "Family Togetherness and the Suburban Ideal." *Sociological Forum* 10 (1995): 393–418. JSTOR. http://www.jstor.org/stable/684782.

Mills, Charles W. *The Racial Contract.* Ithaca, NY: Cornell UP, 1997.

Miner, Madonne. *Insatiable Appetites: Twentieth-Century American Women's Bestsellers.* Westport, CT: Greenwood, 1984.

Mitchell, Margaret. *Gone with the Wind.* 1936. London: Pan Books, 1988.

Monteyne, David. "Shelter from the Elements: Architecture and Civil Defense in the Early Cold War." *Philosophical Forum* 35 (2004): 179–99. Academic Search Premier. http://o-web.ebscohost.com.lib.rivier.edu/ehost/pdfviewer/pdfviewer?hid=106&sid=a5e11afo-df1f-4988-aa1f-bob65e8fee68%40sessionmgr110&vid=21.

Morrison, Toni. *Playing in the Dark: Whiteness and the Literary Imagination.* New York: Vintage, 1993.

Nixon, Richard. "Veto of the Economic Opportunity Amendment of 1971," 10 Dec. 1971. In *The American Presidency Project*, ed. John Woolley and Gerhard Peters. University of California, Santa Barbara. http://www.presidency.ucsb.edu/ws/?pid=3251#axzz1G8H5jaef.

Oakes, Guy. *The Imaginary War: Civil Defense and American Cold War Culture.* New York: Oxford University Press, 1994. Print.

OED Online. Oxford English Dictionary. http://o-www.oed.com.lib.rivier.edu.

Perloff, Richard. "The Press and Lynchings of African Americans." *Journal of Black Studies* 30, no. 3 (2000): 315–30. JSTOR. http://www.jstor.org/stable/2645940.

*Peyton Place.* Dir. Jerry Wald. Perf. Lana Turner, Lee Philips, Lloyd Nolan, Arthur Kennedy. Twentieth Century Fox, 1957. DVD.

"Peyton Place (from the *Franklin Journal-Transcript*)." Editorial. *Laconia Evening Citizen*, 18 Oct. 1956. Metalious folder, Gale Public Library, Laconia, NH.

Pleck, Elizabeth. *Domestic Tyranny: The Making of American Social Policy against Family Violence from Colonial Times to the Present.* Urbana: U of Illinois P, 2004.

Poe, Edgar Allan. "The Fall of the House of Usher." 1839. In *The Portable Poe.* New York: Penguin, 1977.

Punter, David. ed. *A Companion to the Gothic.* Oxford: Blackwell, 2000.

———. "Shape and Shadow: On Poetry and the Uncanny." In Punter, ed., 193–205.

Punter, David, and Glennis Byron. *The Gothic.* Malden, MA: Blackwell, 2004.

Reumann, Miriam. *American Sexual Character: Sex, Gender, and National Identity in the Kinsey Reports.* Berkeley: U of California P, 2005.

Richardson, Samuel. *Clarissa; or The History of a Young Lady.* 1747–48. Ed. and introd. Angus Ross. Harmondsworth, England: Penguin Books, 1985.

Roberts, Diane. *The Myth of Aunt Jemima: Representations of Race and Region.* London: Routledge, 1994.

Robinson, Edward Arlington. *Selected Poems.* Ed. and introd. Robert Faggen. New York: Penguin, 1997.

Roediger, David. *The Wages of Whiteness: Race and the Making of the American Working Class.* Rev. ed. London: Verso, 2007.

Rowe, Karen. "Feminism and Fairy Tales." In *Don't Bet on the Prince: Contemporary Feminist Fairy Tales in North America and England*, ed. Jack Zipes, 209–26. New York: Routledge, 1986.

Rowson, Susanna. *Charlotte Temple, and Lucy Temple*. 1794. Ed. and introd. Ann Douglas. New York: Penguin Books, 1991.

Royle, Nicholas. *The Uncanny: An Introduction*. London: Routledge, 2003.

Russell, Diana E. H. *Rape in Marriage*. Expanded and rev. ed. with new intro. Bloomington: Indiana UP, 1990.

Ryan, Rebecca. "The Sex Right: A Legal History of the Marital Rape Exemption." *Law and Social Inquiry* 20 (1995): 941–1001. JSTOR. http://www.jstor.org/stable/828736.

Rybczynski, Witold. *Home: A Short History of an Idea*. New York: Penguin, 1987.

Sammons, Mark J., and Valerie Cunningham. *Black Portsmouth: Three Centuries of African American Heritage*. Lebanon, NH: U of New Hampshire P, 2004.

Schlesinger, Arthur M., Jr. "The Crisis of American Masculinity." 1958. In *The Politics of Hope*, 237–46. Boston: Houghton Mifflin, 1962.

Schorer, Mark. Introduction. In *Sinclair Lewis: A Collection of Critical Essays*, ed. Mark Schorer, 2–9. Englewood Cliffs, NJ: Prentice Hall, 1962.

———. *Sinclair Lewis: An American Life*. New York: McGraw Hill, 1961.

Schweitzer, Sarah. "Finally, a Return to 'Peyton Place': Vilified during Life, Author Is Celebrated 50 Years after Book's Publication." *Boston Globe*, 8 Apr. 2007. doi: 1252815391.

Sielke, Sabine. *Reading Rape: The Rhetoric of Sexual Violence in American Literature and Culture, 1790–1990*. Princeton, NJ: Princeton UP, 2002.

Skolnick, Arlene. *Embattled Paradise: The American Family in an Age of Uncertainty*. [New York]: Basic Books, 1991.

Smith, Raymond. "Grace at C of C." *Laconia Evening Citizen*, 10 Oct. 1956. Metalious folder, Gale Public Library, Laconia, NH.

"Someone to Watch over Me." *Crossing Jordan*. Episode Guide. A&E Television Network Online. http://www.aetv.com/crossing_jordan/ cj_episode _guide.jsp ?episode=181030.

Stephens, Judith L. "Racial Violence and Representation: Performance Strategies in Lynching Dramas of the 1920s." *African American Review* 33 (1999): 655–71. JSTOR. http://www.jstor.org/stable/2901345.

Stokes, Mason. *The Color of Sex: Whiteness, Heterosexuality, and the Fictions of White Supremacy*. Durham, NC: Duke UP, 2001.

Strasser, Susan. *Never Done: A History of American Housework*. New York: Pantheon, 1992.

Sweeting, Adam. *Beneath the Second Sun: A Cultural History of Indian Summer*. Hanover, NH: UP of New England, 2003.

Swenson, May. Introduction to *Spoon River Anthology*, by Edgar Lee Masters. New York: Touchstone, 2004.

Tatar, Maria M. "The Houses of Fiction: Toward a Definition of the Uncanny." *Comparative Literature* 33 (1981): 167–82. JSTOR. http://www.jstor.org/stable/1770438.

Tilley, Abigail. "*Winesburg, Ohio*: Beyond the Revolt from the Village." *Midwestern Miscellany* 31 (2003): 44–52.

Timmins, Anne Marie. "Students File Suit against Haubrich: Three Female Athletes Want Images, Money." *Concord Monitor*, 8 Sept. 2007. Concord Monitor and New Hampshire Patriot. http://www.concordmonitor.com/article/students-file-suit-against-haubrich.

Tobin, Kathleen A. "The Reduction of Urban Vulnerability: Revisiting 1950s American Suburbanization as Civil Defense." *Cold War History* 2, no. 2 (2002): 1–32. Academic Search Premier. http://o-web.ebscohost.com.lib.rivier.edu/ehost/pdfviewer/pdfviewer?hid=13&sid=15c6f028-744a-482f-b640-3a5cd7c163c5%40sessionmgr11&vid=5.

"'To Have and to Hold': The Marital Rape Exemption and the Fourteenth Amendment." *Harvard Law Review* 99 (1986): 1255–73. JSTOR. http://links.jstor.org/sici?sici=0017-811X%28198604%2999%3A6%3C1255%3ATHATHT%3E2.0.CO%3B2-I.

Toth, Emily. "Fatherless and Dispossessed: Grace Metalious as a French Canadian Writer." *Journal of Popular Culture* 15 (1981): 28–38.

———. "How to Teach a Dirty Book." *Inside Higher Ed*, 22 Sept. 2006. Inside Higher Ed. http://www.insidehighered.com/views/2006/09/22/toth.

———. *Inside Peyton Place: The Life of Grace Metalious*. 1981. Jackson: UP of Mississippi, 2000.

Van Doren, Carl. "The Revolt from the Village: 1920." *Nation* 113 (October 1921): 407–12.

Vidler, Anthony. *The Architectural Uncanny: Essays in the Modern Unhomely*. Cambridge, MA: MIT Press, 1992.

———. "The Architecture of the Uncanny: The Unhomely Houses of the Romantic Sublime." *Assemblage* 3 (1987): 6–29. JSTOR. http://links.jstor.org/sici?sici=0889-3012%28198707%290%3A3%3C6%3ATAOTUT%3E2.0.CO%3B2-4.

Wald, Gayle. *Crossing the Line: Racial Passing in Twentieth-Century Literature and Culture*. Durham, NC: Duke UP, 2000.

Wald, Priscilla. "Terms of Assimilation: Legislating Subjectivity in the Emerging Nation." In *Cultures of United States Imperialism*, ed. Amy Kaplan and Donald Pease, 60–84. Durham, NC: Duke UP, 1993.

Wall, Cheryl A. "Introduction: Taking Positions and Changing Words." In *Changing Our Own Words: Essays on Criticism, Theory and Writing by Black Women*, ed. Cheryl A. Wall, 1–15. New Brunswick, NJ: Rutgers UP, 1989.

Ware, Vron. *Beyond the Pale: White Women, Racism and History*. London: Verso, 1992.

Watt, Ian. *The Rise of the Novel: Studies in Defoe, Richardson, and Fielding*. 1957. Berkeley: U of California P, 2001.

Watters, David. "*Peyton Place*'s New Hampshire." 2004. Unpublished manuscript. Typescript.

Weiss, Jessica. *To Have and to Hold: Marriage, the Baby Boom, and Social Change*. Chicago: U of Chicago P, 2000.

Wharton, Edith. *The Age of Innocence*. 1920. Ed. and introd. Candace Waid. New York: Norton, 2003.

Wiese, Otis. "Live the Life of *McCall's*." *McCall's*, May 1954, 27.

Willner, Dorothy. "Definition and Violation: Incest and the Incest Taboo." *Man* 18 (1983): 134–59. JSTOR. http://www.jstor.org/stable/2801768.

Wilson, Elizabeth. "Not in This House: Incest, Denial and Doubt in the White Middle Class Family." *Yale Journal of Criticism* 8 (1995): 35–58.

Wood, Ruth Pirsig. *Lolita in Peyton Place: Highbrow, Middlebrow, and Lowbrow Novels of the 1950s*. New York: Garland, 1995.

Wylie, Philip. *Generation of Vipers*. New York: Rinehart, 1942.

Zarlengo, Kristina. "Civilian Threat, the Suburban Citadel, and Atomic Age American Women." *Institutions, Regulation and Social Control*. Special issue of *Signs: Journal of Women in Culture and Society* 24 (1999): 925–58. JSTOR. http://www.jstor.org/stable/3175598.

# Index

generosity toward, 67–68, 72, 122, 190n15; Lucas Cross's "ownership" of body of, 68, 72; physical maturity of, 41, 65; raped by her stepfather, 34, 40–41, 42, 59, 66–67, 69, 93–94; relationship with Peter Drake, 122, 165; relationship with Ted Carter, 65–66, 70, 79, 120, 121–22, 163, 165; remains silent about her abuse, 58, 70–71; renovates the shack, 69–70, 162, 163–64, 195n18; town's pity for, 56; trial of, 4, 5, 15, 32, 49, 70–71, 121, 123, 127–29, 162, 164–65

Cross family: as abject, 57–58; as dysfunctional, 48–49, 54; family structure, 55; home of, 56–61, 80, 162, 163–64

*Crossing Jordan* (television program), 178

Cunningham, Valerie, 179n2

Cuordileone, K. A., 103, 113, 114, 188n2, 189n10

Davis, Angela, 105

DeHart, Jane Sherron, 183n5

Delaney, 123, 128, 167

Derleth, August, 10

*Desperate Housewives* (television program), 16

Dickstein, Morris, 10

Doane, Janice, 64

Doherty, Thomas, 183n3

domesticity: as Cold War battle front, 138–40; domestic ideal of 1950s, 49–54; imperial, 136; race and, 137; in "separate spheres" ideology, 136–37; single-family bourgeois house and emergence of ideal of, 135; suburban, 139

domestic violence, 55–56, 65

domestic work, 59–60

Doolen, Andy, 40

Douglas, Mary, 60

Douglass, Frederick, 105

Drake, Peter, 122, 165

Du Bois, W. E. B., 180n6

Dudziak, Mary L., 25, 26

Dyer, Richard, 36, 46, 56–57, 69, 116, 127, 189n11

Ehrenreich, Barbara, 75

Eisenhower, Dwight, 50

Ellsworth, Kathy, 54, 132–33, 165, 167

English, Deirdre, 75

Ennis, Stephen, 11

fallout shelters, 140, 142, 145, 191n3

families: American domestic ideal of 1950s, 49–54; in *Peyton Place*, 15, 17, 47, 48, 54–61; television depictions of, 182n3; typical postwar family, 55. *See also* domesticity

Farnham, Marynia, 186n6

Farrow, Mia, 28

"Fatherless and Dispossessed" (Toth), 30, 181n10

*Fear of Flying* (Jong), 16

Federal Civil Defense Administration (FCDA), 134, 139

Federal Housing Administration (FHA), 143, 144

femininity. *See* women

feminism: anti-rape discourse of, 187n10; and Cameron's reading of *Peyton Place*, 30; Carby on addressing of race by, 37; and Hendler's reading of *Peyton Place*, 32; on incest, 64, 71; *Peyton Place* as not feminist text, 16; *Peyton Place* treats issues of second-wave, 14; on rape as violence not sex, 81; and Toth's reading of *Peyton Place*, 29

Ferguson, Frances, 82–85, 87–88, 89, 98, 187n10

Filene, Peter, 183n5

Fine, Michelle, 36–37

Fitzgerald, Francis, 61, 94

Foreman, Joel, 24, 27, 180n4

Frankenberg, Ruth, 36, 37, 44

Frankenheimer, John, 190n13

*Franklin Journal-Transcript* (newspaper), 173

Frazier, Clayton, 148, 153

Fredrickson, George, 106, 107

Freud, Sigmund, 63, 134, 150

Friedman, Andrea, 112

*From Here to Eternity* (Jones), 28

Fryer, Peter, 106

fun house, 132–33

Gaddis, John Lewis, 192n7
Garner, Steve, 35, 181n11
Gault, Cinda, 81
gender: in colonial ideologies, 21–23; and race and class as interacting, 38, 182n14; racial difference as sexual difference, 16–17, 104–7; retrenchment of roles in 1950s, 52, 184n7; "separate spheres" ideology, 136–37. *See also* masculinity; women
*Generation of Vipers* (Wylie), 186n5
Gilmanton (New Hampshire), 1, 176
*Gone with the Wind* (Mitchell): Ashley Wilkes's lightness, 16–17, 110–11, 115; competing masculinities in, 107–12; as female-authored text, 99; *Peyton Place* dethrones from top of bestseller list, 99, 172; rape scene in, 16–17, 99–100, 109–10; Rhett Butler as dark-skinned, 109, 110; robbery of Scarlett by black man, 108–9, 189n7
Goodale, Hester: Allison MacKenzie attempts to write story of, 160; Allison MacKenzie on house of, 159, 166, 194n15; Norman Page kills cat of, 118, 119; single life of, 54; spies on the Cards, 118–19; whiteness of, 46, 190n12
Gordon, Linda, 63
gothic literature, 17, 148–49, 192n9
Graham, Lindsey, 196n5
Greenberg, Clement, 26
Griffith, D. W., 107–8, 189n11
Gross, Barry, 10
Guarino, Donald, 176
Gunning, Sandra, 126
Gwin, Minrose, 59, 185n14

Hale, Lord Matthew, 84
Hale, Sarah Josepha, 8
Hardy, Thomas, 167
Harrington, Elizabeth Fuller, 115, 190n12
Harrington, Leslie, 115–16; drives his wife to early death, 54, 115; end of bloodline of, 54, 55, 115, 129; fear about his own masculinity, 116; power and corruption of, 115; shell behind which he hides, 94; threatens Betty Anderson with solicitation

charge, 31; Tom Makris contrasted with, 102; town stands by him at death of his son, 120; whiteness of, 46, 116
Harrington, Michael, 57
Harrington, Rodney: death of, 115, 116, 120; gets Betty Anderson pregnant, 31, 101; kisses Allison MacKenzie at her birthday party, 96; lessons from his father, 115; Norman Page bullied by, 117; as only child, 54; Tom Makris contrasted with, 102
Hartigan, John, Jr., 35, 67
Haskell, Molly, 110
haunting: Allison MacKenzie on Peyton's castle as haunted, 148, 158–60; Peyton's castle haunts the town, 154
Hawthorne, Nathaniel, 155
Hayden, Dolores, 135
Hellman, Caroline, 61, 184n10
Hendler, Jane, 26, 28, 32
Hepworth, Mike, 195n18
Herman, Judith, 63–64
Hewlett, Sylvia Ann, 15
high art, middlebrow culture contrasted with, 26–27
Hilfer, Anthony Channell, 9, 10, 11, 12, 13, 179n1
Hirschman, Lisa, 63–64
Hitchcock, Alfred, 190n13
Hodges, Devon, 64
Holmes, Bradley, 194n16, 195n20
home, 131–71; affective significance of word, 134–35; as Cold War battle front, 138–40; of Constance MacKenzie, 154–56, 161, 164; of Cross family, 56–61, 80, 162, 163–64; domestic work, 59–60; of Hester Goodale, 159, 166, 194n15; versus houses, 134–38; postwar suburban, 140–44; the uncanny as the "unhomely," 150. *See also* domesticity; houses
homosexuality, 24, 49, 76, 114, 116, 120
hooks, bell, 189n11
*House of the Seven Gables, The* (Hawthorne), 155
houses: in American fiction, 135–36, 149–50, 191n2; Cape Cod–style, 7,

17, 33, 34–35, 39, 40, 45, 47–48, 56,
131, 133–34, 136, 147–49, 152–54,
158–61, 166–67, 179n2; deferral of
his tale in *Peyton Place*, 5, 159, 164,
166–67; excluded from Boston society, 5, 40, 47, 131, 153, 154; failed
family of, 47, 48; as founder of Peyton Place, 3, 5, 8, 14–15, 23, 34–35,
40, 48, 148, 166; origins of character,
179n2; said to have aided Confeder-
acy, 5, 35, 148; as slave, 5, 40, 147,
153; white wife of, 5, 34, 35, 147,
154, 160, 166
Peyton Place: Allison MacKenzie as no
longer afraid of, 161–62, 169; Allison MacKenzie looks down on from
hill top, 7, 147, 170–71; black man
as founder of, 3, 5, 8, 14–15, 23,
34–35, 48, 148, 166; castle in, 5, 17,
33, 34–35, 39, 40, 45, 47–48, 56,
131, 133–34, 136, 147–49, 152–54,
158–61, 166–67, 179n2; class divisions in, 6–7; Gilmanton, New
Hampshire, as basis for, 1; as model
New England town, 6, 40; origin of
name, 179n2; population of, 184n12;
postwar suburban developments
compared with, 147; racial homogeneity of, 147; represses story of its
origins, 23, 35, 40, 47–48, 133, 136,
148, 166–67; Selena Cross incorporated into town's future, 44, 72, 132,
165, 167–68; shack district, 6–7, 54,
57, 58, 65; three sources of scandal
in, 62, 164; Tom Makris incorporated into town's future, 44, 132,
168–69; as uncanny civic space, 133–
34; World War II's effect on, 169–70
*Peyton Place* (Metalious): as about race,
14, 43, 45–46, 177–78; academic
views of, 29–35; approaching through
whiteness studies, 23, 35–40; ban-
ning of, 27; as best-seller, 27, 47,
172; book reviewers on, 173–75; as
byword for scandal, 1–2; characters
continue to live with their secrets, 12;
Cold War creeps into text in surprising ways, 170; construction of whiteness critiqued in, 43–44; as contro-

versial, 14, 16, 19, 27–28, 174, 176;
as critique of power and privilege,
2–3; cynicism about, 1; as "dirty
book," 3, 28; effect of environment
emphasized in, 13; evolution from
sensation to novel, 20, 175; families
and households in, 15, 17, 47, 48,
54–61; as female *bildungsroman*, 3;
female sexuality as central to, 14,
28–29, 74–75; fiftieth anniversary of,
176, 177; film and television adaptations, 28, 31, 32, 177, 181n8, 196n2;
gothic and supernatural undergird
narrative, 17, 33, 148; happy endings
of, 9, 169; hauntings in, 18, 148, 154,
158–60; home in, 131–71; Joyce's
*Ulysses* compared with, 174–75; Kinsey reports compared with, 14; list of
unpleasantness, bad behavior, and
broken taboos in, 5; millennial reconsiderations of, 177–78; moral guardians' reaction to, 172–73, 176; as
more than just a dirty book, 3–5;
narrative moves toward model of
integration, 132; as "New Hampshire" novel, 3, 40; as novel of 1950s,
23–29; opening lines, 15, 20–21; as
opening salvo in sexual revolution,
81; pale males of, 114–30; rape rhetoric of, 87, 97–98; reviews of, 19,
172–75; and "revolt from the village"
tradition, 8–14; sales of, 19, 27, 172,
176; as sensitive subject, 1–2; sex in,
14, 16, 28, 31, 34, 43; simultaneous
subversion and complicity in dominant ideologies in, 22–23, 100;
sources of scandal in, 20–46; as synonym for rampant impropriety, 3, 6;
title as epithet of derision, 175–76
Pleck, Elizabeth, 184n11
Poe, Edgar Allan, 159, 194n15
popular culture, high culture disdain for,
26–27
porno-tropic tradition, 21–22
Potter, Richard, 179n2
poverty: American attitude toward,
57; incest and, 62, 64–65, 72; shack
district of Peyton Place, 6–7, 54, 57,
58, 65

*Preparing for Marriage* (1938), 75–76
*Psycho* (film), 190n13
psychoanalysis, 62–63, 186n6
Punter, David, 149, 154, 192n9

race: American racism as postwar public relations problem, 25, 180n5; anti-Asian sentiment in containment thesis, 180n3; black male sexuality, 91, 98, 104–5, 112–13; black man as founder of Peyton Place, 3, 5, 8, 14–15, 23, 34–35, 48, 148, 166; black rapist myth, 105, 106–8, 190n16; in Breines's reading of *Peyton Place,* 34; civil rights movement, 24, 25, 146; constructedness of, 44, 182n15; dark immigrants from southern and eastern Europe, 8; darkness associated with prurience, 42; Doc Swain's racist jokes, 124; in domestic ideal of 1950s, 50; and domesticity, 137; and gender and class as interacting, 38, 182n14; homogeneity of Peyton Place, 147; incest in African American families, 64–65; in Jones's reading of *Peyton Place,* 35; literary blackness, 37; lynching, 67, 69, 105, 107, 122, 125–27; in Miner's reading of *Peyton Place,* 33–34; miscegenation, 26, 49, 148, 154; *Peyton Place* as about, 14, 43, 45–46, 177–78; raced space, 39–40; "racial contract," 39, 40; racial difference as sexual difference, 16–17, 104–7; racialization of sex, 14, 20–21; racial "purity," 38; racism in American national identity, 40; scholarly work on *Peyton Place* neglects, 29; sexual depravity attributed to blacks, 105–6; in Toth's reading of Peyton Place, 181n10; white anxiety about racial identity, 178; whiteness as unmarked marker of, 35–36. *See also* whiteness
ranch-style houses, 141–42, 145
rape, 74–98; black rapist myth, 105, 106–8, 190n16; of Constance MacKenzie by Tom Makris, 16, 31, 32, 34, 44–45, 74, 80–82, 90–98, 99, 102–3, 109, 158, 196n7; flashback

used for Tom Makris's rape of Constance MacKenzie, 82, 92–93, 97, 103; literary representations of, 85–87; lynching associated with, 125; marital, 84–85, 98, 186n6; in Mitchell's *Gone with the Wind,* 16–17, 99–100, 109–10; and Norman Page's kiss of Allison MacKenzie, 96; "rape, silence, refiguration," 86, 92, 97; rhetoric of, 74, 82–87; in Richardson's *Clarissa,* 87–88, 91, 93; in Rowson's *Charlotte Temple,* 88–90, 91, 93; of Selena Cross by stepfather Lucas, 34, 40–41, 42, 59, 66–67, 69, 93–94; as violence not sex, 81
"Rape and the Rise of the Novel" (Ferguson), 82
Reumann, Miriam, 14
"revolt from the village" tradition, 8–14
Richardson, Samuel, 87–88, 91, 93, 167
Roberts, Diane, 42
Roediger, David, 35
Roosevelt, Theodore, 113–14, 129
Rowson, Susanna, 88–90, 91, 93, 167
Royle, Nicholas, 151, 156, 193n12
Russell, Diana, 64, 184n13
Rybczynski, Witold, 134–35

Sammons, Mark, 179n2
Schlesinger, Arthur, Jr., 103
Schnore, Leo F., 192n5
Schorer, Mark, 12
*Seduction of the Innocent* (Wertham), 112
"separate spheres" ideology, 136–37
sex: birth control, 52, 184n6; black male sexuality, 91, 98, 104–5, 112–13; chastity, 65, 75, 76, 79, 185n2; consent, 82–85, 92, 98, 99; depravity attributed to blacks, 105–6; in domestic ideal of 1950s, 51–52; female sexuality in 1950s, 75–80; homosexuality, 24, 49, 76, 114, 116, 120; illegitimacy, 62, 78, 183n4; Kinsey reports, 14, 28, 78; in marriage, 75–76, 138; national security related to sexual behavior, 76–77; orgasms, 77, 92; in *Peyton Place,* 14, 16, 28,